C. F. Moritz, Adele Kahn

The Twentieth Century Cook Book

C. F. Moritz, Adele Kahn
The Twentieth Century Cook Book
ISBN/EAN: 9783744795746

Printed in Europe, USA, Canada, Australia, Japan
Cover: Foto ©Lupo / pixelio.de

More available books at **www.hansebooks.com**

THE TWENTIETH CENTURY COOK BOOK.

BY

MRS. C. F. MORITZ AND MISS ADÈLE KAHN.

NEW YORK:
G. W. Dillingham Co., *Publishers.*
MDCCCXCVIII.

PREFACE.

ONLY so much of preface seems necessary, as may justify the publication of this volume.

Influenced by the repeated requests of friends, and convinced of the merits of the recipes herein contained, we feel fully warranted in adding another volume to the many that have recently appeared on the subject.

Of late years cooking has come to be regarded as a science no less than as an art, and in the preparation of the recipes that we herewith submit, the most scientific methods have been employed. In addition every recipe has been subjected to many careful tests, and if directions be accurately followed, success in the preparation is assured. We have also endeavored to bring our recipes within the scope of the most moderate income, and in many cases where elaborateness is called for, we have given another simpler and less expensive recipe for the same dish. Not only has the quantity of ingredients been given, but also explicit directions as to mixing and baking.

Realizing the annoyance to which housekeepers are subjected in selecting a menu for supper and luncheons, we have prepared a special chapter on "Supper and Luncheon Dishes." We have also added a chapter on "Diet for Invalids," which has been prepared under

Medical Direction, and which must prove a boon to those hitherto inexperienced in the preparation of such dishes. Our "Obesity List," will also be found of use to many.

Though particular attention has been given to the subjects of "Entrées and Desserts," each department will be found complete, presenting in its entirety a book that will, we trust, commend itself to every housekeeper.

CONTENTS.

	Page
APPETIZERS.	
Oyster Cocktail	35
" on half shell	35
" à la Tartare	36
Eggs " "	36
Stuffed Eggs with Sardellen	36
" " " Chicken	36
" " " Sardines	37
" " " Anchovies	37
" " " Sardellen. No. 2	37
" " " Mayonnaise	37
" " " Appetit Sils	37
Anchovy Sandwiches. No. 1	38
" " No. 2	38
" Butter	38
Sardellen Sandwiches. No. 1	38
" " No. 2	38
Sardine "	38
Sardellen Butter	39
Caviare Sandwiches. No. 1	39
" " No. 2	39
Broiled Sardines	39
Club House Sandwiches	39
Paté de foie gras "	40
Anchovy Salad	40
Herring "	40
Luncheon Toast	41
Marron Sandwiches	41
Peanut "	41

APPETIZERS — *Continued*.

	Page
Italian Sandwiches	41
Filled Dates	42
Musk Melons	42
Sugared Nuts	42
Limes or Grape Fruit	42
Grape Fruit Liqueur	42
Salted Almonds	43
Strawberries au Naturel	43

SOUPS.

	Page
Soup Stock	44
Bouillon	44
Consommé	45
Beef Tea	45
Julienne	45
Chicken Broth	45
Mutton "	46
Noodle	46
Barley	46
Green Kern	46
Vegetable Soup	47
Puree of Potato	47
" " Pea	47
Dried "	47
Split "	48
Gumbo	48
Chicken Gumbo	48
Crab "	48
Tomato	49
Brown Flour	49
Cream	49
Cream of Chicken	50
" " Pea	50
" " Potato	50
" " Celery. No. 1	50
" " " No. 2	51
" " " No. 3	51
" " Asparagus	51
" " Tomato	51
" " Oyster	52

SOUPS—*Continued.*

	Page
Oyster Soup. No. 1	52
" " No. 2	52
Ox Tail "	53
Green Turtle Soup	53
Mock " " No. 1	54
" " " No. 2	54
Bisque of Clams	54
" " Lobster	55
Clam Soup	55
" Chowder	55
Wine Soup	56
Red Wine Soup	56
Cream " "	56

BALLS AND DUMPLINGS FOR SOUPS.

Potato Dumplings	57
Drop "	57
Farina "	57
Boiled Cracker Balls	58
" Flour "	58
Fried Cracker Drops	58
Macaroons	58
Bread or Matzo Balls. No. 1	58
" " No. 2	59
Marrow Balls	59
Grated Irish Potato	59
" Egg	60
Noodles	60
Bread Croutons	60
Batter "	60
Egg Custards	60

FISH, CRABS, SHRIMPS & OYSTERS.

How to Clean Lobsters	61
" " " Soft Shell Crabs	61
" " " Hard " "	61
Fried Oysters. No. 1.	61
" " No. 2.	62
Creamed " on Toast	62
Oysters à la Poulette	62
Broiled Oysters	63

FISH, CRABS, ETC.—*Continued.*

	Page
Escalloped Oysters	63
Oysters and Sweetbreads	63
Oyster Pie	64
Boiled Crabs	64
Fricasseed Crabs	64
Fried "	65
Soft Shell "	65
Boiled Lobster	65
Broiled "	65
Lobster Cutlets	66
Steamed Mussels or Cockles	66
" Clams	66
Fricasseed Shrimps	66
Terrapin Stew	67
Sweet Sour Fish	67
" " " with Wine	67
Stewed or Sharp Fish	68
Coube on Fish	68
Fried Smelts	69
" Scallops	69
Boiled Fish	69
Tenderloin Trout, Wine Sauce	69
Fish Piquant	70
Cream Lemon Fish	70
Fish with Lemon Sauce	71
Baked Fish, Lemon Sauce	71
Sole au Gratin	71
Baked Fish with Tomatoes	71
" Red Snapper	72
" Trout or Sole, Mushroom Sauce	72
Fried " " " " "	73
Broiled Pompano or Shad	73
Tenderloin Trout, Tartare Sauce	73
Fried Pompano " "	73
" Red Snapper " "	73
Codfish Balls	74
Frog Legs	74
" " with Cream	74
Fish Roe	74

FISH, CRABS, ETC.—*Continued.*

	Page
Fish Chowder	75
Boiled Salmon with Sauce Verte	75

ENTRÉES.

	Page
Oyster Patties	76
Chicken "	76
Sweetbread Patties	77
Sardellen Soufflé	77
Chicken Croquettes. No. 1	77
" " No. 2	78
Crab "	78
Salmon "	78
Sweetbread "	79
Shrimp "	79
Lobster "	79
" Farcé	80
" à la Newburg	80
Shrimps " "	80
Lobster Timbales	80
Shrimp "	81
Jellied Asparagus Timbales	81
Chicken, Fish, or Liver Timbales	81
Cream Sauce for "	82
Chicken "	82
Sauce for Chicken "	82
Fish "	82
Sauce for Fish "	82
Salmon "	83
Chicken with Cheese in Shells	83
Coquille of Fish	83
Deviled Brains	84
" Sweetbreads	84
" Crabs	84
Chicken with Mushrooms. No. 1	84
" " " No. 2	85
" " Green Peas	85
Sweetbreads with Mushrooms	85
Crab à la Creole	86
Baked Tomatoes Stuffed with Crabs	86
" " " " Shrimps	86

ENTRÉES—*Continued.*

	Page
Green Peppers Stuffed with Shrimps	87
Wined Sweetbreads	87
Creamed "	87
Sweetbreads and Peas	88
Smoked Tongue	88
Cheese Straws	89

POULTRY AND GAME.

	Page
Crumb Dressing	90
Bread Dressing	90
Pecan or Chestnut Dressing	91
Oyster " No. 1.	91
" " No. 2.	91
Plain Fried Chicken	91
Fried Chicken à la Maryland	91
Fried Chicken with Mushroom Sauce	92
Fricasseed " with Dumplings	92
" " " Puffs	92
Smothered "	93
Chicken with Cauliflower	93
Broiled Chicken. No. 1	93
" " with Mushrooms	94
" " No. 2	94
Baked "	94
Roast "	95
Chicken with Rice	95
" Pot Pie	95
Broiled Squabs on Toast.	96
" Birds " "	96
Potted Ducks	96
Potted Squabs	97
" Quails or Birds	97
Stuffed " Anchovy Dressing	97
" " Oyster "	97
Roast Turkey	97
" Goose	98
" Duck	98
" Wild Duck	98
Stewed Goose	99
Goose Livers	99

CONTENTS.

POULTRY AND GAME—*Continued.*   Page
- Pickled Goose Breast . . . 99
- Stuffed   "   Neck . . . 100
- Goose Cracklings . . . 100
- Chicken Tamales . . . 100
- Fricassee of Squirrel . . . 101
- "   Rabbit . . . 101
- Fried   " . . . 101
- "   Squirrel . . . 101

FISH, MEAT AND VEGETABLE SAUCES.
- Hollandaise 102
- Béarnaise 102
- Mushroom. No. 1 . . . 102
- "   No. 2 . . . 103
- Brown 103
- Tomato 103
- Caper 103
- Mint 103
- Maître d'Hotel Butter . . . 104
- Egg Sauce 104
- Apple Sauce 104
- Cranberry Sauce. No. 1 . . 104
- "   "   No. 2 . . 105
- Drawn Butter Sauce . . 105
- Cream Sauce for Asparagus or Cauliflower   105
- Whipped-Cream Sauce for Asparagus . 105
- Lemon Sauce for Asparagus . . 106
- White Sauce for Asparagus . . 106
- Cream Mayonnaise. No. 1 . . 106
- "   "   No. 2 . . 106
- French Mayonnaise . . . 107
- Mayonnaise Sauce. No. 1 . . 107
- "   "   No. 2 . . 107
- Tartare   "   No. 1 . . 107
- "   "   No. 2 . . 108
- "   "   No. 3 . . 108

MEATS.
- Beef Drippings 109
- Roast Beef 109

MEATS—*Continued.*

	Page
Roast Beef with Potatoes	109
Rolled Ribs of Beef	110
Beef à la Mode	110
Wiener Braten	111
Brisket of Beef—Horseradish Sauce.	111
Filet de Boeuf à la Jardinière.	112
Filet or Broiled Tenderloin of Beef. No. 1	112
Filet or Broiled Tenderloin of Beef. No. 2	113
Filet de Boeuf au Champignons	113
" " " à la Béarnaise	113
Broiled Beefsteak	113
" " Mushroom Sauce	114
" " Tomato or Oyster Sauce	114
Fried Steak with Onions	114
Baked Hamburg Steak	114
" " "	115
Filled Calf Shoulder	115
Stuffed Breast of Veal	115
Spring Lamb, Mint Sauce	116
" " Tomato "	116
Barbecued Lamb	116
Roast "	117
" Mutton	117
Spring Lamb, Green Peas	117
" " Stewed, Piquant	117
Boiled Leg of Mutton, Caper Sauce	118
Pork Roast, Apple Sauce	118
Veal Roast	118
Brown Hash	118
Irish Stew	119
Camp "	119
Casserole of Rice and Meat	119
Boiled Ham	120
Broiled "	120
" Lamb Chops	120
Pork Chops	120

CONTENTS.

MEATS—*Continued*.

	Page
Spare Ribs. No. 1	120
" " No. 2	121
Breaded Veal Cutlets	121
Veal Cutlets, with Tomato or White Sauce	121
Fried Brains	121
Sweet, Sour Brains	122
Fried Sweetbreads	122
" Calf Liver	122
" Tripe	122
Stewed "	122
" Kidneys	123
Sausage Meat	123
Liver Sausage	123
Vienna "	123
Smoked "	124
Pork "	124
KITCHEN TIME TABLE	125
TABLE OF WEIGHTS AND MEASURES	126

VEGETABLES.

	Page
Boiled Potatoes in jackets	127
" " without "	127
Mashed "	127
Potato Vermicelli	127
" Cakes	128
" Croquettes	128
" Soufflé	128
" with Cream	128
Baked Potatoes	129
Stuffed "	129
" " with Meat	129
New "	129
Imitation New Potatoes	130
French Fried "	130
Lyonnaise "	130
Potatoes Browned Whole	130
Saratoga Chips	130
Julienne Potatoes	131
Stewed "	131

VEGETABLES—*Continued.*

	Page
Hash Brown "	131
Escalloped "	131
Potato Balls	132
Potatoes au Parmesan	132
Baked Sweet Potatoes	132
Boiled " "	132
Sweet Potato Croquettes	133
Fried Sweet Potatoes	133
Candied Yams	133
Sugared "	133
Sweet Potato Purée	133
Farina Dumplings	134
Yorkshire Pudding	134
Rice, plain Boiled	134
Sweet Rice	135
Rice Croquettes	135
Pilaff	135
Apples with Rice	135
Green Corn, Boiled. No. 1	136
" " " No. 2	136
Fried "	136
Stewed "	136
Succotash	137
Fresh Corn Fritters	137
Canned " "	137
Corn Pudding	137
Cream String Beans	137
Stewed " "	138
Sweet, Sour String Beans	138
Lima Beans	138
Boston Baked Beans	139
Baked Yankee "	139
Spinach	139
Stuffed Egg Plant	140
Baked " "	140
Fried " "	141
Egg Plant Fritters	141
Stewed Squash	141
Stuffed Squash	142

CONTENTS.

VEGETABLES—_Continued._ Page

- Oyster Plant Fritters . . . 142
- Fried Oyster Plant . . . 142
- Parsnips . . . . , 142
- Steamboat Cabbage . . . 142
- Stuffed Cabbage with Meat . . 143
- " " " Bread . . 143
- " " " Chestnut Dressing 144
- Red " 144
- Kohlraben. No. 1. . . . 144
- " No. 2. . . . 145
- Sauerkraut. No. 1. . . . 145
- " No. 2. . . . 145
- Turnips 146
- Creamed Turnips 146
- Stewed Tomatoes . . . 146
- Baked " 146
- Deviled " 147
- Stuffed " 148
- " " with Meat . . 148
- Escalloped Tomatoes . . . 148
- Stuffed Peppers 148
- " " with Meat . . 148
- Canned Green Peas . . . 149
- Green Peas 149
- Carrots, Sweet and Sour . . . 149
- " and Peas . . . 149
- Baked Onions 149
- Boiled " 150
- " Okra 150
- Chestnuts and Raisins . . . 150
- Purée of Chestnuts . . . 150
- Chestnuts and Prunes . . . 151
- Fresh Asparagus with Sauce . . 151
- " " on Toast . . 151
- " " 151
- Canned " 152
- " " on Toast . . . 152
- Stewed Celery 152
- Stuffed Mushrooms . . . 152

VEGETABLES—*Continued*.

	Page
Artichokes with Sauce	153
" " Tartare Sauce	153
Cauliflower with Sauce	153
Baked Cauliflower	154
Creamed Cucumbers	154
Macaroni with Tomatoes	154
" au Gratin	155
Noodles with Mushrooms	155
Purée of Chestnuts	156

SALADS.

	Page
Sauce for Asparagus Salad	157
Mayonnaise for Salad No. 1	157
" " " No. 2	157
French Mayonnaise	157
Tartare Sauce	158
French Dressing	158
Chicken Salad. No. 1	158
" " No. 2	159
" " No. 3	159
Veal "	160
Beets Stuffed with Salad	160
Tomatoes Stuffed with Chicken Salad	160
" " " Shrimps	160
Whole Tomatoes with Mayonnaise	161
Tomato Salad—French Dressing	161
" " Mustard "	161
Baldwin Salad	162
Celery "	162
Waldorf "	162
Fruit " No. 1	162
" " No. 2	163
Potato "	163
Potato and Oyster Salad	163
Cucumber Salad	164
Lettuce " No. 1	164
" " No. 2	164
Chicory	164
Cold Slaw	165

CONTENTS.

SALADS—*Continued.*   Page
   Cold Slaw with Mustard Sauce . 165
    "   "   " Cream "   . . 165
   String Bean Salad . . . 166
   Okra   " . . . 166
   Beet   " . . . 166
   Asparagus " No. 1 . . 166
    "   " No. 2 . . 166
   Fresh Asparagus with Mayonnaise . 167
   Brazilian Salad . . . 167
   Lobster   " . . . 167
   Herring " . . . 168
   Salmon   " . . . 168
   Mackeral " . . . 168
   Shrimp Salad No. 1 . . 169
    "   " No. 2 . . 169
   Fish Salad . . . 169
   Crab   " . . . 169
   Tomatoes with Crab Salad . . 169
   Brain Salad . . . 170
   Sweet Bread Salad . . . 170
   Oyster   " . . . 170

COMPOTES.
   Baked Apples . . . 171
   Filled   " . . . 171
   Jellied   " . . . 171
   Stewed   " . . . 172
   Apple Float . . . 172
   Baked Pears . . . 172
   Compote of Fresh Pears . . 172
    "   "   " Peaches . . 173
    "   " Canned Peaches . . 173
    "   "   " Pears . . 173
    "   "   " White Cherries . 173
    "   "   " Green Gages . 173
    "   "   " Pine Apple . 174
   Stewed Plums . . . 174
    " Blackberries . . 174
    " Strawberries. No. 1 . 174
    "   " No. 2 . 174

COMPOTES—*Continued*.

	Page
Stewed Prunes	174
Filled "	175
Stewed Rhubarb	175

BAKED PUDDINGS.

Farina	176
Farina, Chocolate	176
Ante Farian	176
Dandy	177
Kiss	177
Delightful	177
Peach	178
Fruit Custard	178
Rice "	178
Cream Rice	179
Indian Meal	179
Sago	179
Tapioca	180
Queen	180
Caramel	180
Grated Pineapple	180
Sliced "	180
Orange	181
Cocoanut	181
Cream and Banana	181
Orange	181
Pineapple	182
Sweet Potato	182
Bird Nest	182
Grated Apple. No. 1.	182
" " No. 2.	183
Apple	183
Apple, Chocolate	183
Baked Chocolate. No. 1	183
" " No. 2	184
Lemon. No. 1	184
" No. 2	184
Orange	184
Cottage	185
Macaroon	185

BAKED PUDDINGS—*Continued.*

	Page
Macaroon, Apple	185
Almond Custard	185
Tipsy Pudding	185
Kugle	186

BOILED PUDDINGS.

How to Boil	187
Almond	187
Chocolate. No. 1	188
" No. 2	188
Individual Chocolate	188
Chocolate. No. 3	188
Rye Bread	189
Prince Albert	189
Prune	189
Potato	189
Cherry. No. 1	190
" No. 2	190
Napkin	190
Cabinet	191
Old Fashioned Plum	191
English "	192
Suet	192
Noodle	192
Pineapple	193
Peach	193
Apricot	193
Apple	193

PUDDING SAUCES.

Chaud' Eau	194
Lemon	194
Caramel. No. 1	194
" No. 2	195
Wine. No. 1	195
" No. 2	195
" No. 3	195
Hard Sauce	196
Cream or Vanilla	196
Sherry. No. 1	196
" No. 2	196

PUDDING SAUCES—*Continued.*

	Page
Roman	196
Fruit	197
Orange	197
Foam	197
Chocolate	197
Jelly	198
Custard	198

PASTRY, PIES, CUSTARD, ETC.

	Page
Puff Paste	199
Paste for Pies. No. 1	200
" " " No. 2	200
" " Tartlets	201
Charlotte Dough	201
Fruit Risolettes	201
Apple Charlotte. No. 1	202
" " No. 2	203
Apple Strudel	203
Noodle Charlotte. No. 1	203
" " No. 2	204
Strawberry Shortcake. No. 1	204
" " No. 2	204
Roly Poly	205
Fruit Tartlets	205
Cheese "	206
Cocoanut "	206
Cream "	206
Almond "	206
Orange Pie	207
Lemon Pie. No. 1	207
" " No. 2	207
Lemon Custard	208
Cocoanut, Lemon	208
Lemon Tart	208
Cocoanut	208
Transparent	209
Custard	209
Cream	209
Apple. No. 1	210
" No. 2	210

PASTRY, PIES, ETC.—*Continued.*

	Page
Grated Apple	210
Grated Pineapple	211
Fresh Strawberry. No. 1	211
" " No. 2	211
Canned "	211
Huckleberry. No. 1	212
" No. 2	212
Canned Peach	212
Fresh " No. 1	213
" " No. 2	213
Blackberry	213
Pumpkin	213
Sweet Potato	214
Mince	214
Mock Mince	214
Cranberry	215
Cheese	215
Chocolate	215

MISCELLANEOUS DESSERTS.

Cream Puffs. No. 1	216
Chocolate Eclairs. No. 1	216
Cream Puffs. No. 2	217
Chocolate Eclairs. No. 2	217
Orange Baskets	218
Maraschino Punch	218
Queen of Trifles	218
Macaroon Island	219
Syllabub	219
Whipped Cream	219
Neapolitan "	220
Eiderdown "	220
Boiled Custard	220
French Float	220
Baked Custard	220
Cup "	221
Floating Island	221
Marshmallow Custard	221
St. Honoré Torte	222
Ambrosia	222

MISCELLANEOUS DESSERTS—*Continued.*

	Page
Fruit Salad	222
Banana "	223
Strawberry Salad	223
Iced Watermelon	223
Tipsy "	223
Charlotte Russe. No. 1	224
" " No. 2	224
White Charlotte Russe	224
Chocolate " "	225
Charlotte Polonaise	225
Fruits à la Crême	225
Bavarian Cream	226
Strawberry Bavarian Cream	226
Blanc Mange	226
Chocolate Blanc Mange	227
Neapolitan " "	227
Italian Cream	228
Spanish "	228
Lemon Cream Pudding	228
Lemon Gelatine "	228
Cold Cream "	229
Jaune Mange	229
Snow Pudding	229
Chocolate Gelatine Pudding	230
Coffee " "	230
Macaroon, Wine "	230
" Custard	231
Wine Jelly	231
Ribbon Jelly	231
Lemon "	231
Orange "	232
Strawberry Jelly	232
Pineapple Charlotte	232
Lemon Puffs	232

ICE CREAM, FROZEN FRUITS AND SHERBETS.

	Page
Vanilla Ice Cream. No. 1.	234
" " " No. 2.	234
Custard " "	234

CONTENTS.

ICE CREAM, ETC.—*Continued.*   Page

   Neapolitan Ice Cream. No. 1. . . 235
      "   "   " No. 2. . . 235
   Chocolate "   " No. 1. . . 235
      "   "   " No. 2. . . 236
   Pineapple, Apricot, Peach, Strawberry,
      Banana Ice Cream. No. 1. . . 236
   Pineapple, Apricot, Peach, Strawberry,
      Banana Ice Cream. No. 2. . . 236
   Banana Ice Cream. No. 3. . . 236
   Caramel "   " . . . 237
   Bisque Glacé 237
   Tutti Frutti Ice Cream . . . 237
   Burnt Almond " " . . . 237
   Almond   " " . . . 237
   Orange or Lemon Ice Cream No. 1. . 238
     " " " " " No. 2. . 238
   Nougat   "   " . . 238
   Italian   "   " . . 238
   Maraschino Ice Cream . . 239
   Nessselrode "   " . . . 239
   Frozen Peaches. No. 1 . . . 239
     "   Fruits. No. 1 . . . 239
     "   Peaches. No. 2 . . . 239
     "   Fruits. No. 2 . . . 239
     "   Apple Float . . . 240
   Coffee Mousse . . . 240
   Frozen Egg-Nog . . . 240
     "   Milk Punch . . . 240
   Roman Punch . . . 240
   Meringue Glacés . . . 241
     "   en Surprise . . . 241
   Strawberry Sherbet . . . 241
   Lemon Water Ice . . . 241
     "   Sherbet No. 1 . . 242
     "   " No. 2 . . 242
   Orange " . . . 242
   Orange Water Ice . . . 242
   Pine Apple Sherbet . . . 242
   Tutti Frutti " . . . **243**

ICE CREAM, ETC.—*Continued.*

	Page
Claret Sherbet	243
Apple "	243
Milk "	243
Mint "	244
Frozen Cream Cheese	244
Moonshine	244

FROZEN PUDDINGS.

How to Pack	245
Bisquit Tortoni	245
Coffee Pudding	246
Pudding Imperatrice	246
Hazel Nut Cream	246
Chocolate Cream	246
Delightful	247
Maraschino Cream	247
Pudding Glacé	247
Crême de la Crême	248
Rum	248
Nesselrode	248
Diplomat	249
Strawberry Glacé au Crême	249
Orange Glacés	250
Strawberry Mousse	250

ICING FOR CAKES.

Meringue	251
Raw Icing	251
Boiled "	251
Pistache Icing	251
Cream "	252
Transparent Icing	252
Chocolate " No. 1	252
" " No. 2	253
" Glazing	253
" Caramel Icing	253
White " "	253
Marshmallow "	254
Golden "	254

LARGE CAKES.

Cake Making	255

LARGE CAKES—*Continued.*

	Page
Fruit Cake. No. 1	256
" " No. 2	256
White Fruit Cake. No. 1	256
" " " No. 2	257
Cheap White Fruit Cake	257
Angel Food. No. 1	257
" " No. 2	258
Gold Cake. No. 1	258
" Wedding Cake	258
" Cake No. 2	259
Silver " No. 1	259
" " No. 2	259
Lady "	259
Silver Marble Cake	259
Delicate Cake	260
Marble "	260
Cup " No. 1	260
" " No. 2	260
1-2-3-4 "	260
Large Cream Cake	261
One Minute "	261
Lemon "	261
Sand Tart	261
" Torte	261
Pound	262
Imperial	262
Sunshine	262
Brown Coffee	263
Sponge. No. 1	263
" No. 2	263
Hot Water Sponge	263
Chocolate "	263
Matzo "	264
Nut " Tart	264
Bisquit Torte	264
Spice. No. 1	264
" No. 2	264
Almond Tart. No. 1	265
Mandle, or Almond Tart. No. 2	265

LARGE CAKES—*Continued.*

	Page
Brod Tart	265
Chocolate Brod Torte	265
Hazel Nut Tart	266
German Hazel Nut Tart	266
Walnut Tart	266
Reginten Torte	267
Macaroon Tart	267
Chocolate Cake	267
Rum Tart	267
Chocolate Tart	268
Cherry Cake	268
Date "	268

LAYER CAKES.

Marshmallow	269
Cream	269
Banana Cream	270
Delicate	270
Lemon Jelly	270
Orange "	271
Mocha Torte	271
" Tart	271
White Mountain	272
Ice Cream	272
Pine Apple	272
Jelly	273
Grand Duke	273
Walnut Filled	273
Ribbon	274
Neapolitan	274
Orange	274
Custard Tart	274
Cocoanut Meringue	275
Chocolate Cream	275
Filled Chocolate	276
Brown Stone Front	276
Chocolate	277
" Nougat	277
" Ice Cream	278
Linzer Torte	278

LAYER CAKES—*Continued.*

	Page
Macaroon Tart	278
Brod Torte	279
Almond Tart	279
Cracker "	279
Nut "	279
Strawberry Short Cake	280
" Matzo Short Cake	280
Coffee Cake	281
Railroad Cake	281
Soft Ginger Bread. No. 1	281
" " " No. 2	281
Brown Cake	282
Ribbon "	282
Caramel "	282
Nut "	283

SMALL CAKES.

Butter Cakes	284
Sugar Kringel	284
Short or Mürba	284
Small Sugar	285
Sugar	285
Tea	285
Cookies	285
Chocolate Cookies	286
Ginger Snaps. No. 1	286
" " No. 2	286
Small Lemon Snaps	286
Anise Seed	286
" " Matzo	287
Leb Kuchen. No. 1	287
" " No. 2	287
Old Fashioned Leb Kuchen	288
Small Spice	288
Chocolate Cakes	288
Cocoanut "	289
" Drops	289
Almond "	289
" Slices or Mandel Snitten	289
Chocolate, Almond Sticks	290

SMALL CAKES—*Continued.*

	Page
Macaroons	290
Kisses or Meringues	290
Pecan Kisses	291
Little Indians	291
Minute Cakes	291
Small Pineapple	292
" Sponge	292
" Ice Cream	292
Jelly Roll. No. 1	292
" " No. 2	293
Lady Fingers	293

COFFEE CAKES AND KUCHEN

Coffee Cake or Kuchen	294
Cinnamon "	294
Cheese Pie	295
Apple Pie. No. 1	295
" " No. 2	296
Fresh Strawberry Pie. No. 1	296
" " " No. 2	296
Canned " "	297
Huckleberry Pie. No. 1	297
" " No. 2	297
Canned Peach Pie	298
Fresh " "	298
Onion Pie	298
Fresh Prune Cake	299
Pocketbooks	299
Dampfundeln	299
Buntkuchen	300

YEAST, BREAD, BISCUITS, MUFFINS, WAFFLES, HOT CAKES, ROLLS, DOUGH NUTS, ETC.

Bread Making	301
Rendered Butter	301
Butter Milk Yeast	302
Potato Yeast	302
Vienna Bread	302
White Mountain Bread	303
Rye Bread	303

YEAST, BREAD, ETC.—*Continued.*

	Page
Water Bread	304
Boston Brown Bread	304
Graham Bread	304
Corn Bread	305
Excelsior Egg Bread	305
Egg Bread with Sweet Milk	305
Sally Lunn	306
Auflauf	306
Yeast Powder Biscuits	306
Soda Biscuits	307
Beat " No. 1	307
" " No. 2	307
Muffins with Soda	307
" Plain	308
Sweet Muffins. No. 1	308
" " No. 2	308
Corn Meal Muffins	308
Graham Muffins. No. 1	309
" " No. 2	309
Pop Overs	309
Waffles	309
Butter Waffles	310
German "	310
French "	310
Cornmeal Cakes. No. 1.	310
" " No. 2.	311
Flour Cakes	311
Flour Buttermilk Cakes.	311
Flannel Cakes	311
" " with Yeast	312
White Mountain Flannel Cakes	312
Old Fashioned Buckwheat "	312
Buckwheat Cakes with Buttermilk	312
Self Raising Buckwheat Cakes	313
Snip Noodles	313
" " Boiled	313
Capital City Rolls	314
Vienna Rolls	314
Parker House Rolls	314

YEAST, BREAD, ETC.—*Continued.*

	Page
Plain Rolls	315
Turnovers or Rolls	315
Doughnuts	315
Filled Doughnuts	316
Puffs (Purim)	316
Doughnuts	316

TOAST, PANCAKES, FRITTERS, WAFERS, DUMPLINGS, ETC.

Buttered Toast	318
Milk or Cream Toast	318
French Toast	318
Egg Pancakes	318
German " No. 1	319
" " No. 2	319
Bread "	319
Potato " No. 1	320
" " No. 2	320
Plain Wafers	320
Sweet "	320
Crullers	321
Queen Fritters	321
Matrimonies	321
Bell Fritters	322
Banana Fritters	322
Apple "	322
Lemon "	322
Delmonico Fritters	322
Chrimsel	323
Fried Apples	323
" Bananas	323
French Puffs, Windbeutel	323
Baked Apple Dumplings	324
" " Roll	324
Boiled Apple Dumplings	324
" " Roll	325

EGGS.

Boiled	326
Fried	326
" with Ham	326

CONTENTS.

	Page
EGGS—*Continued.*	
Fried with Sausage	326
Shirred	326
Poached	327
Scrambled. No. 1	327
" No. 2	327
" with Brains	327
Deviled	327
Fried Eggs and Oysters	328
Eggs à la Champignon	328
Egg Vermicelli	328
Escalloped Eggs. No. 1	329
" " No. 2	329
Plain Omelet	329
Ham "	329
Cheese "	329
Oyster "	330
Sweet "	330
Rum "	330
Omelette au Rum	330
Banana Omelet	330
Omelette Soufflé	331
Crab Omelet	331
BREAKFAST DISHES.	
Farina	332
" Fried	332
Oatmeal Pap	332
Rice "	332
Flour "	333
Cornstarch Pap	333
Arrowroot	333
Boiled Hominy	333
Fried "	334
Flake Oatmeal	334
Big Hominy	334
SUPPER OR LUNCHEON DISHES.	
Salmon Cakes. No. 1	335
Fish "	335
Salmon " No. 2	335
Pressed Chicken	335

SUPPER, ETC.—*Continued.*

	Page
Chicken Aspic	336
Meat "	336
" Soufflé	337
Cold Meat Croquettes	337
Brain Croquettes	337
Cold Meat Stew	338
Veal Croquettes	338
Chicken Soufflé	339
Individual Oyster Loaves	339
Broiled Sardines on Toast	339
Mock Duck	339
Smoked Tongue	340
Pickled "	340
" Meat	340
Cheese Soufflé	341
Cheese Cream Pudding	341
Pressed Cheese	341
Cottage "	342
Eggs à la Hausman	342
" au Parmesan	342
Sweet Breads à la Creole	342
Veal Salad	343
Liver with Tomato Sauce	343
Welsh Rarebit	343
Cheese Fondu	344
Leaf Puffs	344
Snowballs	344
Noodle Puffs	345

BEVERAGES.

	Page
Coffee, How to Roast	346
" " " Make	346
" Iced	346
Chocolate	347
Cocoa	347
Tea	347
" Iced	347
" Russian	347
Lemonade	348
" Apollinaris	348

BEVERAGES.—*Continued.*

Page
- Champagne Punch . . . 348
- Claret Punch 348
- Milk " . . . 349
- Glee Wine or Hot Claret Punch . 349
- Claret Cup 349
- Sauterne Cup 349
- Mint Julep 350
- Egg-nog 350
- Egg Flip. No. 1. . . . 350
- " " No. 2. . . . 350
- Tom and Jerry 350
- Geranium Cordial . . . 351
- Blackberry " . . . 351
- Cherry Bounce. No. 1. . . . 351
- " " No. 2. . . . 352
- Raspberry Vinegar . . . 352
- Raspberry Syrup 352
- Maraschino Glacé . . . 352
- Strawberry " . . . 353
- Champagne Punch . . . 353
- Claret " . . . 353

CANDIES.

- Molasses Candy 354
- Cream " . . . 354
- Peanut Nougat 354
- Plarines 355
- Fondant or French Cream . . 355
- Walnut Creams 355
- Coffee " . . . 356
- Pistache " . . . 356
- Date " . . . 356
- Fruit Roll 356
- Strawberry Creams . . . 356
- Cherry Creams 357
- Chocolate Creams . . . 357
- Peppermint " . . . 357
- French Cream Candy (Uncooked) . 357
- Walnut Creams " . . 358
- Coffee Walnut Creams " . 358

CANDIES—*Continued.*

	Page
Chocolate Caramels	358
Cream "	358
Taffy Buttercups	358
Glacé for Candies	359

PRESERVES.

	Page
Strawberry Preserves. No. 1	360
" " No. 2	360
Blackberry "	360
Seedless Blackberry Jam	361
Blackberry Jam	361
Plum Preserves. No. 1	361
" " No. 2	362
Fig "	362
Peach "	362
" Butter	363
Pear Preserves	363
Crab Apple Preserves	363
Citron or Watermelon Rind Preserves	364
Canteloupe Preserves	364
Quince "	365
Ripe Tomato "	365

JELLIES.

	Page
Apple Jelly	366
Crab Apple Jelly	367
Strawberry Jelly. No. 1	367
" " No. 2	367
Peach Jelly	367
Wild Plum Jelly	367
Plum Jelly	368
Grape "	368
Currant Jelly	368
Currant and Raspberry Jelly	368
Calf's Foot Jelly	368

CANNING.

	Page
Canning Peaches.	370
" Pears	370
" Pineapple	370
" Huckleberries.	370

CONTENTS.

CANNING.—*Continued.*

	Page
Canning Strawberries	371
" Green Gages	371
" Blue Plums	371

PICKLES AND CATSUPS.

Pickles	372
Sweet Pickles	372
Sweet Pickle Peaches	372
Pickled Figs	373
" Pears	373
" Watermelon Rind	373
Piccalilli	374
Chowchow	374
Mustard Pickles. No. 1	374
" " No. 2	375
Cucumber Salad	375
Pepper Mangoes	376
Mangoes	376
Pepper Hash	377
Tomato Catsup	377
Cucumber "	377
Chili Sauce	378
Salt Water or Dill Pickle	378
Okra, how to keep	378

BRANDIED FRUITS.

Melange. No. 1	379
" No. 2	379
Brandied Peaches	380
" Figs	380
" Pears	380

FOODS FOR INVALIDS.

Barley Water	381
Oatmeal "	381
Lime "	381
Raw Beef Juice	381
Beef Broth	382
Chicken Broth	382
Veal "	382
Mutton "	382
Barley Jelly	382

FOODS FOR INVALIDS—*Continued.*

Page
- Flour Ball 383
- Whey 383
- Junket 383
- Rice Milk Pudding . . . 383
- Prunes with Senna . . . 383

OBESITY LIST 385
FACTS WORTH KNOWING . . 386

APPETIZERS.

In these days of extreme luxury, one would imagine that diners-out required only faith in the resources of a hostess and her cook to whet the edges of their appetites. Nevertheless, most fashionable dinners and luncheons are preceded by these important vanguards to the feast.

Appetizers should always be daintily served and garnished, as they help to decorate the table, and should be what their name implies, an incentive to the appetite.

Oyster Cocktail.

Have as many punch glasses as there are guests at table. Put in each glass 4 small oysters, season them with salt, pepper, tomato catsup, Worcestershire sauce, a few drops of lemon juice, a drop of Tobasco sauce and a little grated horse-radish. Serve very cold.

Oysters on Half Shell.

Serve 4 oysters in the half shells, laid on a plate filled with finely crushed ice. Lay a quarter of a lemon sliced lengthwise, in the centre of the plate. Celery, salt, pepper, Worcestershire sauce, and tomato catsup, and crackers should be served with the oysters. 1 plate for each guest.

Little Neck clams are served the same way, only serving each guest with 6 clams.

Oysters à la Tartare.

Scald as many oysters in their own liquor, as needed, until firm and plump. Put on ice until very cold. Take a lettuce leaf from the heart of the bunch, line an oyster shell with it. Cut each oyster in half, lay 4 halves in a pyramid over each leaf, and cover just before serving with "Tartare Sauce." Allow 2 shells for each plate.

Eggs à la Tartare.

Boil hard as many eggs as required, allowing 1 for each person. When cold, slice in half lengthwise with a sharp knife. Remove the yolk from each half, mash smooth with some deviled ham, allowing 1 small box to 8 eggs. Make a "mayonnaise" dressing from any of the mayonnaise recipes; mix enough of the dressing with the yolks and ham to flavor it. Fill each half of egg with the filling; lay 2 halves on lettuce leaves for each person, divide the balance of the mayonnaise over the tops of the eggs and serve very cold.

Stuffed Eggs with Sardellen.

Boil hard as many eggs as required, allowing 1 for each guest. When cold slice in half lengthwise with a sharp knife, and place 2 sardellen, with the bones removed, between each egg.

Tie each egg together with baby ribbon to match other table decorations and serve in small fancy plates.

Stuffed Eggs with Chicken.

Chop some cold veal or chicken very fine, season with salt and white pepper, parsley and thyme. Add gravy made of 1 teaspoonful butter, 1 teaspoonful flour and a little cream dissolved together on the stove. Add yolks of the hard-boiled eggs and a few bread crumbs. Put the whole on to boil, stirring hard. Remove from fire and fill the hard-boiled whites. Can be served either hot or cold. Serve on a lettuce leaf.

Stuffed Eggs with Sardines.

Boil hard 12 eggs; mash the yolks fine, mash contents of 1 can sardines fine and mix with the yolks. Fill the halves with this mixture and put together to look like whole eggs. Serve on lettuce leaves.

Stuffed Eggs with Anchovies.

Boil as many eggs hard as needed. When cold cut in half; remove yolks and mash them fine; mash some anchovies and mix with yolks. Season with white pepper, 1 teaspoonful melted butter and juice of ½ lemon. Fill the eggs, and coil around each half where they were cut, 1 anchovy. Serve on lettuce leaves.

No. 2 Stuffed Eggs with Sardellen.

Prepare same as "stuffed eggs with anchovies," using sardellen instead of anchovies.

Eggs with Mayonnaise.

Prepare same as for "stuffed eggs with sardellen." Put on a platter lined with lettuce leaves and pour mayonnaise over.

Eggs with Appetit Sils.

Prepare same as eggs with mayonnaise, using appetit sils instead of sardellen.

Anchovy Sandwiches. No. 1.

Toast squares of bread, shorn of crust, to a nice even brown. Place 2 anchovies on each piece of toast. Over the whole, sprinkle the yolks of hard-boiled egg crumbled up fine, chop the whites in cubes, and lay them around the yolks; or squeeze the whole egg through a potato-masher and sprinkle over the fish. Sprinkle salt and pepper over the whole.

Anchovy Sandwiches. No. 2.

Cut circles of stale bread ¼ inch thick and fry in butter until light brown. When cold, spread over each slice a thin layer of anchovy butter, and around the edge coil 1 small well-cleaned anchovy. Sprinkle finely-chopped olives on top.

ANCHOVY BUTTER.

Cream two parts of butter to one of anchovy until mixture is stiff.

Sardellen Sandwiches. No. 1.

Get the very thin biscuit cracker, or butter wafer. Put a slice of hard-boiled egg in the center, and coil 1 well-cleaned sardelle around the edges.

Sardellen Sandwiches. No. 2.

Cream 1 large kitchen spoon of butter. Clean, bone and mash smooth ½ lb. sardellen, mix with the butter, add juice of ½ lemon, a bit of prepared mustard and white pepper. Spread on slices of round toast or round crackers.

Sardine Sandwiches.

Prepare same as Sardellen Sandwiches, No. 2., only using 1 can French sardines instead of sardellen.

Sardellen Butter.

Take ½ lb. sardellen, wash first in warm water, then in cold; remove the bones and as much of the skin as possible. Now mash them thoroughly to a paste.

Take a small lump of fresh butter, rub together with the yolks of three hard-boiled eggs until perfectly smooth, then add to the sardellen paste. Mix well and spread thickly on pieces of round, square, or triangular toast which have had the crust removed.

Caviare Sandwiches. No. 1.

Cut 2 circles of bread for each person, toast brown; put lemon juice over the caviare, spread thickly one piece of toast, and cover with the dry piece.

Caviare Sandwiches. No. 2.

Toast some squares of bread without crust. Spread in the center with caviare, on one side place hard-boiled yolks of egg, and on the other side hard-boiled whites, all cut in very small pieces.

Broiled Sardines.

Broil 1 can French sardines on a broiler, lay 2 sardines on each piece of toast, which has been shorn of crust. Decorate with small pieces of olives and a thin slice of lemon.

Club House Sandwiches.

Have ready some nice cold white breast of turkey or chicken sliced thin, also some crisp leaves of lettuce. Just before they are to be served, toast 2 slices of bread without crust for each sandwich. Broil some nice slices of ham.

Now put a lettuce leaf on a small fancy plate, lay a piece of toast on the leaf. In the centre of the toast, put a piece of the turkey or chicken, on each side of the fowl put a small piece of broiled ham, cover with another piece of toast, and then lay another lettuce leaf on top. The toast and ham should be hot. The fowl and lettuce cold.

Patè de foi gras Sandwiches.

Patè de foi gras can be bought in small cans, and is then spread on thin pieces of toast without the crust.

Or is made from the livers of geese, ducks or turkeys if the livers are in good condition. If the latter, make as follows:

Put ½ cup goose grease in a fryer on stove, when hot, lay in ½ lb. of the livers, and baste with a spoon until done (not hard). Remove the livers from the pan, and chop *very* fine, add ¼ onion fried brown, and mix in some of the grease in which livers were fried, season with salt and pepper. The mixture must resemble paste. Spread on nice pieces of toast shorn of crust, or on thin crackers.

Anchovy Salad.

Chop the yolks and whites of 3 hard-boiled eggs separately. Chop anchovies fine and season with salt and pepper. Arrange anchovies in the center of dish and put yolks of eggs in a ring around it, the whites around the yellow, then put finely-chopped lettuce in a ring around the whites. Put in cold place until ready to serve. Have ready some vinegar mixed with the oil from the bottle of anchovies, and only when ready to serve at table, pour the vinegar and oil over the salad in dish, mix all together thoroughly with a fork and serve.

Herring Salad.

Soak 3 nice fat herring in cold water 3 hours. Then remove the head and tail and bones. With a scissors cut in pieces as small as dice, add a handful English walnuts cut fine, 1 tablespoonful boiled beets cut fine, 2 tablespoonfuls capers, 1 large apple cut in small pieces and 1 dill pickle cut up. Then take the soft egg (milchiner) and mix with 2 cups white vinegar until soft, add 1 teaspoonful sugar, 3 cloves and allspice and pour the sauce over the ingredients. The sauce should not be too thick. Mix all well together, and serve a spoonful on a lettuce leaf for each person.

This salad will keep for weeks.

Luncheon Toast.

Brown slices of toast in hot butter. Take 2 tablespoonfuls chopped ham, 2 of grated cheese, 2 eggs beaten with 4 tablespoonfuls thick sweet cream, add salt and pepper to taste, stir until creamy and spread on toast. Serve on *very hot* dish. If there are many slices of toast take double quantity of ingredients.

Marron Sandwiches.

Take a slice of sandwich bread cut round with the crust removed. Put a marron *glacé* in the center, and around it lay whipped cream which has been sweetened and flavored. Nice for afternoon luncheons. The bread can be cut with a biscuit cutter.

Peanut Sandwiches.

With a biscuit cutter, cut slices of bread round, cover with whipped cream, not sweetened, mash some peanuts fine and sprinkle thickly over the cream. Nice for afternoon luncheons.

Italian Sandwiches.

Cut 2 round slices of bread with a biscuit cutter for each person. Take 2 dried figs for each person, fill

the figs with English walnuts, roll the figs in sugar and put 2 between slices of bread.
Nice for afternoon luncheons.

Filled Dates.

Get 1 lb. best dates and remove the stone from each one. Blanch ¼ lb. almonds. Put an almond inside of each date. Roll the date in sugar and serve.
Nice for afternoon luncheons.
The dates can also be filled with pecans, English or American walnuts, and are very nice.

Musk Melons.

Get the very small firm green kind (nutmeg melons). Cut in half, seed and put on ice 1 hour before serving. When ready to serve, fill with crushed ice and sprinkle with powdered sugar. Allow half a melon for each person. Very refreshing for summer luncheons or dinners. For dinner, serve before the soup.

Sugared Butternuts, Pecans or Walnuts.

Shell, and skin if butternuts are used, if not the skins cannot be removed.
Boil 1 cup sugar with ½ cup cold water until it ropes. Drop in the nuts, stir briskly until it sugars, shaking the pan all the while. Remove from fire and serve cold. This quanty is for ½ lb. nuts.
Nice for luncheons.

Limes or Grape Fruit.

Cut in half, loosen pulp, pour in white wine or sherry to moisten, and sprinkle with powdered sugar.

Grape Fruit Liqueur.

Secure as many grape fruit as desired, allowing half a one for each guest. Cut each one in half with a sharp knife. The knife should be wiped after each cutting, so that the bitter juice of the rind may be avoided. The various compartments are then scooped out with a narrow spoon, and the seeds removed. The empty shell should be dusted with powdered sugar, the pulp replaced in the compartments, and over the whole should be poured as much kirschwasser as will fill nicely without spilling over.

More powdered sugar is sprinkled over the top, and if procurable, Marachino cherries form a charming addition. A curved orange-spoon and also two straws tied together with ribbon, should be placed on the plate when served. Nice for luncheon.

Salted Almonds.

Put ½ lb. shelled almonds in boiling water, drain and remove the skins.

In a long baking-pan on top of stove, melt 1 tablespoonful butter, when hot, pour in the blanched almonds, put the pan inside a hot stove, and brown a nice even brown. The pan must be shaken constantly. When done, sprinkle thickly with fine table salt, rub together, and set aside until cold.

Strawberries au Naturel.

Wash the berries in a colander, being careful to drain well, and leave the stems on.

Wash some leaves of rose geranium, dry, and lay four on each plate. Pile the strawberries on the leaves; and on one side of the plate, put a tablespoonful powdered sugar.

To be eaten with beaten biscuits or hot rolls.

Can be served as a first course **either at luncheon, breakfast or afternoon tea.**

SOUPS.

Soup Stock.

All meat soups should be boiled in a closely-covered kettle used for no other purpose. Boil slowly and steadily. Skim soup as soon as it begins to boil, and keep skimming until no more scum rises. Then add seasonings and vegetables, such as celery, tomatoes, onions and potatoes, salt, pepper, parsley.

For a medium-size family, put on 4 quarts of cold water and 1 good size shin bone, and about 1½ to 2 lbs. of brisket of beef. Mutton should not be used for beef soups. After the soup begins to boil, skim, season with salt and pepper, add 1 or 2 spoonfuls tomatoes, 1 small potato cut up, a small piece of onion cut up, and some cut celery. Carrots may also be added if desired. Boil slowly 4 or 5 hours, then strain and skim off fat, and add any ingredient desired.

Bouillon.

Put on 1 chicken to boil in 3 quarts water, as for soup. Take 1½ or 2 lbs. rump of beef, and the same quantity thick part of veal, put in a baking-pan, set in the stove, and brown quickly with just enough water to keep from burning. When brown, cut the meat in pieces, add this with all the juice it has drawn, to the chicken soup. Set on the back of the stove, and cook slowly all day. Set in a cold place, or on ice over night, and next morning after it is congealed, skim off every particle of fat.

Melt and season to taste when ready to serve. Excellent for the sick. When used for the table, cut up carrots, and French peas already cooked can be added while heating.

Consommé.

Put in a soup pot one large shin bone, about 5 lbs, also 3 or 4 lbs of fresh lean beef, add 1 carrot cut up, 1 small onion, 1 small Irish potato cut up, a spoonful of cut up celery, 3 cloves, 1 bay leaf and a little red or black pepper (any cold chicken or chicken bones added is an improvement). Cover the whole with 1 gallon of cold water, mix well, then put on the stove and boil steadily (not too fast) 4 or 5 hours. Remove from the fire, strain and mash through a fine sieve, and put on ice until it forms a jelly. Then skim off every bit of fat, and heat just before ready to serve.

Beef Tea.

Take 1 lb of lean thick round steak, remove every bit of fat and skin, cut in small pieces, put in a crock and pour 1 scant pint of cold water over it. Let stand 1 hour then put on in agate boiler, not tin, and let *boil* 15 minutes. Remove from fire and strain through a piece of thin cloth into a bowl, put in cool place and when it settles can be strained again. Very strengthening for invalids.

Julienne Soup.

Have soup stock ready. Boil in water until tender 1 cup green peas, 3 carrots cut up in small pieces and some cabbage chopped fine. Brown 2 tablespoonfuls flour in a skillet in hot fat or butter, then stir in the vegetables. Fry some livers and gizzards of fowls if handy and add, then stir in the strained soup stock.

Chicken Broth.

Take an old fat hen, after cleaning and singeing, lay in fresh water ½ hour. Cut each joint apart, crack the bones. Put all on in about 2 quarts of cold water and boil steadily and slowly for about 3 hours. Season with salt and pepper to taste and add a little parsley. Nice for invalids. Rice, barley, noodles or dumplings can be boiled in this soup. If rice or barley are used, put on with the chicken. If dumplings are to be used, drop in soup 10 minutes before serving. Skim every particle of fat off of soup before serving.

Mutton Broth.

Cut 3 lbs. of lean lamb or mutton into small pieces, cover closely with 3 quarts cold water, and boil slowly and steadily for 2 hours, then add 2 tablespoonfuls well-washed rice, boil one hour longer, stirring occasionally. Strain, and if not thick enough, add a little flour that has been mixed smoothly with a little milk, also add a small lump of butter. Just before serving stir in 1 cupful of thin sweet cream. Can be made without adding the cream. Nice for invalids.

Noodle Soup.

Make soup stock, and strain clear. Make noodles of 1 egg, cut and dry, drop in hot soup 10 minutes before serving. Boil constantly, and when 10 minutes have elapsed, pour into tureen.

Barley Soup.

Cook ½ cup barley in 2 cups water until very tender. If water cooks out before barley is done, add some soup stock, and continue to boil; stir occasionally, to keep from burning. Add to strained soup stock and thicken with a little flour.

Green Kern Soup.

Cook the same as barley soup, only do not thicken. Beat up the yolks of 1 or 2 eggs in soup tureen, and stir the soup into it. Drop in some bread croutons before serving.

TWENTIETH CENTURY COOK BOOK. 47

Vegetable Soup.

Make a soup stock as usual, when skimmed and clear, add 2 large potatoes cut in dice, 2 small carrots cut up, a small piece white cabbage cut, 1 small onion, 1 pint tomatoes cut up, a little thyme, and 1 tablespoonful rice, season well with salt and pepper, and cook down until all vegetables are tender, and stock is strong. A little freshly-cut corn can be added if desired.

Purèe of Potato.

Boil 12 peeled Irish potatoes in a good deal of water, when done, drain off the water, save it, and mash the potatoes smooth. Heat in a skillet 1 tablespoonful butter, brown in this ½ onion cut up, and 1 tablespoonful flour; then stir in the water in which the potatoes were boiled. Now stir in the potatoes and mash until smooth. Add sufficient soup stock to make desired consistency.

Dried Pea Soup.

Soak 1 cup dried green peas over night, put on next morning with 1 quart cold water, put in a good size piece of smoked meat, or smoked tongue or sausage, let cook some hours until thoroughly done, season with salt and pepper and 1 scant tablespoonful butter. Mash through strainer and if not thick enough put back on stove and thicken with a little flour. If more than 1 quart soup is required, use 2 cups peas and 2 quarts water.

Purèe of Peas.

Have soup stock ready and strained and 1 hour before serving add 1 can green peas to stock, let cook until done, mash through strainer, put back on stove, and thicken with flour that has been mixed with ½ cup milk, add 1 tablespoonful butter, season with salt and pepper. Serve with bread croutons in dish.

Split Pea Soup.

Boil in saucepan scant ½ cup split peas, 1 large slice sausage or bacon, and sufficient water to boil for 2 hours. Season with salt. When peas are tender, mash through a sieve. Have ready 1 qt. soup stock, mix strained peas, and serve immediately. Sausage or bacon cut up in small pieces can be added to the soup, but many do not care for it.

Gumbo Soup.

Put on to boil 1 pint okra, 1 pint tomatoes, corn cut from 2 ears and ½ cup rice. Cut up and fry 1 young chicken, remove chicken from fryer, and in the grease that remains brown a little flour and then add the okra mixture. Now add the strained soup stock, flavor with salt, pepper, cayenne pepper and 1 fresh bell pepper. Must be very thick.

Chicken Gumbo.

Heat some fat in fryer, wash and cut up in small pieces 1 pint okra, put in fat and fry light brown, also add 1 onion cut in small pieces, let it brown, and also brown 1 tablespoonful flour. Now add 1 quart tomatoes cut fine or 1 can tomatoes, and 1 ear of green corn grated, let boil together for a few minutes and add to soup stock that has been previously strained, season highly with salt and cayenne pepper. Cut up 1 chicken in small pieces, fry in boiling fat and add to soup.

Serve with or without boiled rice.

Gumbo Soup With Crabs, Shrimps or Oysters.

Chop fine 1 onion and 2 eyes of garlic, roll in flour, brown in hot butter; then cut fine 1 quart tomatoes and add to frying pan. Cut the heads off 1 quart okra, split each piece 3 or 4 times and cut into dice, add this to the fryer, add small pieces of raw ham, also a few small pieces of bacon, season with salt, pepper, finely-chopped parsley or celery, brown all together. Add to soup stock which has previously been strained, also add 1 chicken which has been cut up and fried, also some cut up crabs, shrimps or oysters. Let soup cook down to desired quantity with all the ingredients in it. Must be thick. Serve with rice.

Tomato Soup.

Add 1½ or 1 can tomatoes to soup stock as soon as it is first skimmed, the quantity of tomatoes to be added depends on quantity of soup required. Add 1 small onion cut up, also 1 Irish potato, cut up, a handful of celery and some salt and pepper. Cook three or four hours, strain, and mash tomatoes through strainer with potato masher. Put back on stove, thicken with a little flour, add 1 teaspoonful tomato catsup, 1 teaspoonful Worcestershire sauce and a tiny bit of cayenne pepper.

Brown Flour Soup.

Heat two tablespoonfuls fresh butter in a spider, add 4 tablespoonfuls flour to it and brown to light golden brown, then add 1 quart water, stirring constantly. Season with salt and pepper and a little nutmeg. Add 1 pint milk, let boil up once or twice and serve at once.

Cream Soup.

Let 1 quart sweet cream or rich milk come to a boil. If milk is used add 1 spoonful fresh butter; thicken with 1 tablespoonful flour or cornstarch that has been dissolved with a little cold milk. Season with salt and pepper and pour over some bread croutons or oyster crackers. Nice for invalids.

Cream of Chicken Soup.

Put on 1 old fat hen as for plain chicken soup. After having cooked down until very strong, strain through a fine seive and skim off every particle of grease. Put back on stove and stir in 1 cupful sweet milk in which 1 tablespoonful flour has been dissolved, add a lump of butter and just before ready to be served, stir in 1 cup sweet cream. Season with salt and pepper to taste. Nice for invalids.

Cream of Pea Soup.

Cook 1 pint shelled peas until tender, then remove from fire and put half of them aside. Mash the other half through a colander, add the water in which they were cooked. Scald 3 cups milk; rub 1 tablespoonful milk and 2 tablespoonfuls flour together until smooth and add to the boiling milk, then add the mashed peas; stir until thick, and just before removing stir in the whole peas and 1 cup sweet cream. Season with salt and pepper. Serve at once.

Cream Potato Soup.

Boil 12 peeled potatoes until tender, drain and mash. Melt 1 tablespoonful butter in porcelain kettle, stir in 1 pint sweet cream, let boil, then stir in the mashed potatoes. Season with salt and pepper. Thin to proper consistency with the water in which the potatoes were boiled.

Cream of Celery Soup. No. 1.

Two stalks of celery cut up in pieces and boiled tender. Mash through a colander, adding a little cold water. Mix with strained soup stock. Then add ½ pt. milk and ½ pt. cream. If not sufficiently thick add a little flour dissolved in milk. Season with salt and white pepper. Drop in croutons just before serving.

Cream of Celery Soup. No. 2.

Cut 2 stalks of celery into ½ inch lengths and cover with 1 pint cold water, add ½ teaspoonful salt, ½ teaspoonful white pepper, boil until tender, then mash fine in water in which it has been cooked.

Have ready 1 pint sweet milk in which 3 slices of onion have been boiled for five minutes, strain and thicken with 1 tablespoonful flour that has been dissolved in a little cold milk.

Pour contents of both boilers together, let come to a boil and serve with batter croutons in dish.

Cream of Celery. No. 3.

Boil 1 small cup rice in 3 pints of milk until it will pass through a sieve. Grate the white part of 3 heads of celery and add to the milk *after* it has been strained. Put to it 1 quart of strong soup stock, boil until celery is perfectly tender, season with salt and cayenne pepper and serve with batter crouton in the dish. If procurable, ½ milk and ½ sweet cream instead of all milk is better.

Cream of Asparagus.

Boil until tender in some soup stock 2 bunches of asparagus. Remove from fire. Cut tips off 1 bunch and set aside. Pass remainder through colander. Add to the other soup stock and thicken with 2 tablespoonfuls flour. Heat 1 pint sweet cream in double boiler and pour while boiling into the soup tureen, then stir in the prepared stock. Put in the asparagus tips, season with salt and pepper and drop in the small egg custards for soup.

Cream of Tomato Soup.

Cook 1 quart tomatoes (fresh or canned) with 1 pint water until done, and strain through a sieve. Boil 1 pint cream or ½ cream and ½ milk; drop in some finely-chopped celery and parsley and season with salt and pepper.

Just before ready to serve, stir the strained tomatoes in the milk or cream, stirring constantly. Add a pinch of soda to the tomatoes before adding to the cream. Serve at once.

If soup stock is convenient, use instead of water.

Cream of Oyster Soup.

Put on 1 pint oyster liquor in one boiler, and 1 pint of sweet cream or ½ milk and ½ cream in a double boiler. When liquor boils skim and season with salt, pepper, butter the size of an egg and parsley. Just before ready to be served drop oysters in the liquor and boil just long enough to get plump. Thicken the cream with 1 spoonful flour or cornstarch that has been wet with a little milk.

Beat up the yolks of 3 eggs in the soup tureen, pour the boiling cream over them stirring all the time, then stir in the oysters and liquor, and serve at once.

Oyster Soup. No. 1.

Strain oysters well. Put liquor on in porcelain-lined kettle, season with salt and pepper and finely-chopped parsley and celery and a good lump of butter. When boiling drop in oysters and remove as soon as oysters are plump. Put a few oyster crackers in tureen, pour boiling soup over them and serve at once.

Oyster Soup. No. 2.

Put on 1 pint of oyster liquor in one boiler, and 1 quart of rich sweet milk in another boiler. When liquor boils, skim and season with salt, pepper, a lump of butter size of an egg and a little parsley. Just before ready to serve drop the oysters in the liquor and let boil only long enough to get plump. Pour in soup tureen, then pour in the milk stirring all the time. Have ready some toasted oyster crackers and drop in the soup.

Ox-tail Soup.

Take 2 ox-tails, and break at the joints. Brown a tablespoonful of floor, and 2 onions cut up, in 1 tablespoonful fat or butter, then add ox-tails, and 1 cup water. Simmer for a few minutes, and put whole on to boil with 1 gallon of water, and 2 lbs. of extra soup meat, 2 carrots, 2 sprays of parsley and celery stalk. Cook 4 hours, then strain, and add meat cut from tails, and chopped, carrots cut in dice, salt, white pepper, and some celery which has been boiled and cut up in 1 inch pieces. Green peas (½ cupful) can also be added. Boil up once, then serve.

Green Turtle Soup.

Cut head off turtle, let bleed over night. Next morning open shell, take out entrails, then clean the liver, heart, and meat part. Skin feet, and put whole in boiling water for two minutes. Boil feet in hot water until tender. Make a soup stock the day previous, and reserve 3 pts. Brown 1½ tablespoonfuls of butter, then add 1 onion chopped fine, 3 oz. chopped ham, a tiny bit of garlic, until all is brown, then 1 tablespoonful of flour. When smooth add soup stock, 1 cupful canned tomatoes, a tiny pinch of red pepper, nutmeg, salt, and 1 teaspoonful green thyme chopped fine. Cook fifteen minutes. Strain into another saucepan, add turtle meat cut up in pieces and let cook until meat is tender. Then add 1 glassful Madeira or sherry wine, juice of 1 lemon. Skim grease off top, slice lemon in bits, put in soup tureen. Let soup cook ten minutes more, pour into tureen, and serve hot.

TWENTIETH CENTURY COOK BOOK.

Mock Turtle Soup. No. 1.

Make a regular soup stock, strain and skim, and remove meat. Brown 1 cup flour, dissolve it in a little soup stock until smooth and even, and mix with rest of soup stock. Season with salt and pepper. Cook with the soup, before meat is removed, a teaspoonful of whole spice tied in a muslin bag. Cut up in soup tureen 1 whole lemon cut in pieces, 3 slices hard-boiled eggs, and part of the soup meat cut in dice. Just before serving pour a cup of white wine (sherry is best) in the tureen, then pour in soup stock. Serve immediately.

Mock Turtle Soup. No. 2.

Wash well a calf's head, remove brains, and put on to boil in 1 gallon of water. Season with salt, pepper, 8 whole cloves, teaspoonful whole spice, and boil until meat leaves bones. Strain, chop meat and return to soup pot. Grate rind of lemon, add tiny pinch cayenne pepper, 1 teaspoonful of mace, one cup browned flour, ½ cup tomato catsup (can be omitted if desired). Let boil up, then drop in mock eggs. Cut up one lemon in slices, then quarter the slices, and put in soup tureen. Just before serving pour in 1 cup white wine in tureen, then pour in boiling soup and serve.

MOCK TURTLE EGGS.

Mash 3 hard-boiled yolks well with one teaspoonful butter, add 1 raw yolk, and a teaspoonful of sifted flour. Roll into eggs, shape and size of turtle eggs, drop in boiling water 2 minutes before putting in soup.

Bisquè of Clams.

Scald 24 large clams in their own juice and drain off the liquor. Then chop them very fine and put back in same liquor. Add 1 quart of soup stock that has been well seasoned, add also 1 cup rice and boil ¾ of an hour. Strain through a fine sieve and add 1 cupful sweet cream that has been scalded in double boiler. Serve with bread croutons in dish.

Bisque of Lobster.

Made same as bisque of clams. Use the meat of 2 or 3 boiled lobsters.

Clam Soup.

Put on the liquor from 3 doz. clams with 3 quarts of water, let come to boil quickly, then add the 3 dozen clams chopped finely, boil quickly, for 3 minutes, then add 3 tablespoonfuls fresh butter, and four of flour which has previously been dissolved in 1 pint milk, add salt and pepper to taste, boil up once stirring all the time, and pour over the well-beaten yolks of 3 eggs. Serve at once.

Clam Chowder.

Peel and wash six medium sized Irish potatoes, cut them in dice shaped pieces, put in a large stew pan, add some white celery cut in very small pieces, cut 2 carrots in small pieces, also 1 small onion and 1 turnip, and add to the potatoes, season with a small pinch of salt and pepper, add two quarts of water, place on the stove and boil slowly until the potatoes are nearly done. Stew 1 can of tomatoes in a saucepan for 10 minutes, then mash through a sieve and add to the vegetables, add also 1 tablespoonful fresh butter. Cut a nice slice of bacon in small pieces and fry crisp, drain it from the grease and add it to the broth. Brown 1 tablespoonful flour in the bacon grease, and add also to the broth. Cut 3 dozen clams in quarters, add to the broth, also add the liquor of the clams. Boil about 5 minutes. Add a few broken crackers if desired, season with salt and pepper, also a little Worcestershire sauce if desired, but do not boil after the crackers are added.

Serve at once.

Wine Soup.

Boil 1 pint white wine with 1 teaspoonful sugar. Beat in a bowl the yolks of 2 eggs until light, then stir in the boiling wine. Add croutons and serve at once. Nice for invalids.

Red Wine Soup.

Put on to boil 1 cup good red wine and ½ cup water, sweeten to taste, add 3 whole cloves and 3 small pieces of cinnamon bark, let boil 10 minutes, and pour while boiling over the well-beaten yolk of 1 egg. Eat hot or cold. This quantity serves 1 person.

Cream Wine Soup.

Put 1 cupful of white wine and ½ cupful cold water on to boil, add a few pieces of stick cinnamon and 7 lumps of cut loaf sugar ; while boiling scald 1 cupful of sweet cream in double boiler. Have ready the well-beaten yolks of two eggs, pour over this the hot cream, stirring all the time, then pour in the boiling wine, being careful to stir well or it will curdle.

Very nice for invalids. Can be eaten hot or cold.

BALLS, DUMPLINGS, ETC., FOR SOUPS.

Potato Dumplings.

Boil 3 Irish potatoes until done. Peel and run through a potato masher very light, add salt to taste and a little sugar, cinnamon and nutmeg. Also add 2 eggs, beat all together very light, then add flour enough to make them hold together. Try by dropping a little into the soup. If not stiff enough add more flour. Drop in soup by tablespoonfuls 10 minutes before serving and let boil.

Drop Dumplings.

Break into a cup the whites of 3 eggs; fill the cup with milk, put it with a tablespoonful of fresh butter and 1 cupful sifted flour in a spider and stir as it boils until it leaves the spider clean. Set aside until cool and stir in the yolks of the 3 eggs. Season with salt, pepper and nutmeg, mix thoroughly and drop by teaspoonfuls in the boiling soup 10 minntes before ready to be served.

Farina Dumplings,

Put in double boiler 1 kitchen spoonful fresh butter, stir in 1 cupful milk. When it begins to boil stir in enough farina to thicken. Take off the stove and when cold add the yolks of 2 eggs and the stiffly-beaten whites, and a little salt and nutmeg and ½ cup grated almonds if desired. Let cool, then make into little balls and 10 minutes before soup is to be served, drop in boiler and let boil up once or twice.

Boiled Cracker Balls.

Three tablespoonfuls cold, hard goose grease or butter, rubbed to a cream, add 2 eggs, some finely-chopped parsley, salt, ginger and nutmeg. Add 5 rolled soda crackers. Roll into balls and drop in boiling soup 5 minutes before serving.

Boiled Flour Balls.

Two yolks of eggs beaten very light, add a pinch of salt, pepper and finely-chopped parsley. Add 6 blanched almonds grated, enough sifted flour to make stiff batter, then add the stiffly-beaten whites of eggs and ½ teaspoonful baking powder. Drop by teaspoonfuls in soup 10 minutes before serving.

Fried Cracker Drops.

Cream 1 scant tablespoonful goose grease with 3 eggs, then stir in ½ cupful grated almonds, ½ teaspoonful sugar, a pinch of salt and ¼ of a nutmeg grated, and just enough cracker meal to thicken, not very thick. Drop by teaspoonfuls in boiling fat, fry light brown, and put in soup just when sending to table.

Maccaroons.

Three tablespoonfuls cracker meal, scalded with 3 spoonfuls hot soup, then add yolks of 3 eggs, a pinch of salt and sugar, a little grated nutmeg and the stiffly-beaten whites of the eggs. Stir well and fry by ½ teaspoonfuls in hot fat. Drop in soup just when ready to serve. Put them in the stove a few minutes to get warm before putting in the soup tureen.

Bread or Matzo Balls. No. 1.

Soak ¼ of a five-cent loaf of bread or about 2 matzos in cold water; when thoroughly soaked, squeeze out every particle of water.

Heat some fat or goose grease in a spider, and fry ¼ of an onion cut very fine in it, now put the soaked bread in and fry, stirring occasionally, until it will not stick to the pan. Pour into a bowl, break in 3 or 4 eggs, some finely-chopped parsley, and season with salt, pepper and ginger, add one tablespoonful matzos or cracker meal, make into small balls, and drop into boiling soup 15 minutes before serving.

Matzo Balls. No. 2.

Beat yolks of two eggs very light with one spoonful of chicken grease or goose grease. Butter can also be used. Stir in sufficient matzos meal (sifted) until a smooth batter is obtained, then stir in beaten whites, add pinch salt. Take a portion of soup stock, and boil balls for soup ¾ hour before ready for serving. Then pour in with rest of soup. If not boiled sufficiently, will be hard and tasteless.

Marrow Balls.

Split the bones and remove the marrow. Put on ice till cold, then cream until smooth and soft, stir in 1 egg and enough cracker meal to make them stick together. Try one by dropping in soup, being careful not to get too stiff. Season with salt, pepper, and nutmeg. Drop in the boiling soup 15 minutes before serving.

Grated Irish Potato.

Peel, wash and grate 1 large Irish potato, or 2 medium sized ones. Put it in a sieve and let hot water run over it until it is perfectly white. Have the white of 1 egg beaten to a very stiff froth, then stir in the potatoes and 20 minutes before serving add it to the boiling soup. Beat the yolk of an egg up in the soup tureen, and pour the hot soup over it, stirring carefully at first.

Grated Egg for Soup.

Into the yolk of 1 egg stir enough flower until it is too stiff to work. Grate on coarse grater, and spread on board to dry. After soup is strained, put in and boil 10 minutes before serving.

Noodles.

Take 1 handful flour, make hole in the center, break in 1 egg, and work enough of the flour in the dough to make a stiff dough. Now make into 2 balls, and roll each out with a rolling-pin as thin as a wafer. Lay on a cloth until dry, not too dry, then fold together in long narrow strips, and cut with noodle-cutter or a sharp knife, in very fine strips. Drop in soup 10 minutes before serving, and boil.

Bread Croutons.

Cut up 2 slices of bread into small dice, drop them into very hot fat, and fry a light brown. Pour soup in tureen, drop in croutons, and serve immediately.

Batter Croutons.

Make a batter of 1 egg, 1 cup of milk, and enough flour to make as stiff as paste. Pour this in a flannel bag, or drop through a colander, drop by drop, into a kettle of boiling fat or lard, fry a light brown, and throw in soup just when ready to serve.

Egg Custard.

Break 2 eggs in a cup, and fill up with milk, stir until whole is smooth. Pour into a small earthenware or china bowl, add a pinch of salt, and set in a pan of boiling water on stove, until it becomes thick. Turn out, cut in pieces, and put in tureen, just before serving. Do not remove from stove until custard is set.

FISH, CRABS, SHRIMPS AND OYSTERS.

How to clean Lobsters.

Plunge them into boiling water, seasoned with salt and pepper, boil 25 minutes. When done, take off the claws and remove the meat, which is very good, split the body in half, from the head down, with a sharp knife, and remove a thin thread like entrail, that runs on one side; that is the intestine.

The soft green part, if any, is the egg, and is good to eat; stir into the lobster before serving, unless the lobster is to be served in the shell, then leave it where it lies.

How to c'ean Soft-Shell Crabs.

Always get the crabs alive. Place on ice until ready to prepare them. Take off the part under the stomach, lift up the soft shell on each side, and take out the "dead men;" they have a greyish look, and look something like fish gills.

How to clean Hard-Shell Crabs.

Always get live crabs. Plunge them into boiling water that has been well seasoned with salt and red pepper, and ½ cup vinegar. When done wash in cold water, take hold of a small straight piece underneath, and with your two hands pull, and the shell will separate from the crab. Then with a knife, scrape off all the soft substance in the center, and remove the "dead men." They look like fish gills.

Fried Oysters. No. I.

Secure large, plump oysters. Drain in colander, then dry on clean towels. Dip in cracker meal that has been seasoned with salt and pepper, then dip in some well-beaten eggs, then in cracker meal again, and fry in a kettle of boiling lard or butter. Serve with slices of lemon.

Fried Oysters. No. 2.

Secure large, plump oysters. Drain in colander, then dry on clean towels, and season with salt and pepper.

Make a stiff batter of flour, milk and eggs. Dip each oyster in separately, and drop them in a skillet of boiling hot lard or butter.

Serve with slices of lemon.

Creamed Oysters on Toast.

Drain 1 pint oysters from their liquor. Then heat the liquor to boiling point, add pepper and salt, let boil, skim and then add the oysters. Cook them until plump then remove from the liquor.

While oysters are cooking make a cream sauce by rubbing togetherful 1 tablespoonful fresh butter and 2 tablespoonfuls flour; rub until smooth, put on stove and stir in 1 pint sweet cream or milk. Stir until it thickens and is perfectly smooth. Add salt, pepper and parsley.

Dip small slices of well-browned toast in the oyster liquor after oysters have been taken out. Add oysters to cream sauce, heat through and pour oysters and sauce over the toast, which has been put on a hot dish.

Oysters a la Poulette.

Scald 2 dozen oysters in their own liquor for 3 minutes on stove. Remove from fire, drain, and save liquor. Put in saucepan 2 tablespoonfuls butter with 1 tablespoonful of flour. Mix until smooth, then add liquor of oysters and liquor of mushrooms. Let boil 2 minutes and add ½ cupful cream, 1 teaspoonful lemon-juice, pinch salt and pepper, then last the beaten yolks of 3 eggs. Stir a moment, but do not boil as it will curdle. Mix oysters with a few chopped mushrooms and 1 teaspoonful chopped parsley, add to sauce and serve immediately.

Broiled Oysters on Toast.

Put in wire boiler, over coals, or on top grating of stove and baste with fresh butter. Toast light bread, butter the slices, and arrange broiled oysters, allowing five oysters to each slice. Put a bit of melted butter over whole. A slice of lemon on top of each piece, and a spray of parsley, garnish nicely.

Escalloped Oysters.

Sprinkle bottom of pudding dish, or granite baking-pan, with cracker meal. Put over this a layer of oysters. Sprinkle salt, pepper, butter, chopped parsley and another layer of cracker meal. Then add another layer of oysters, and so on until pan has been almost filled, but leaving a margin. Then beat yolks of two eggs light, mix with one cup of milk and pour in pan over whole. Sprinkle top with cracker-meal, and bake in oven from 30 to 45 minutes.

Oysters and Sweetbreads.

Boil sweetbreads until tender, remove from fire, skim, clean, and press between two plates to flatten. Put in saucepan on stove 2 tablespoonfuls butter, and 1 tablespoonful of flour, rubbing until smooth; then add liquor of oysters and mushrooms, pinch salt, pepper, nutmeg, and juice of ½ lemon. Let sweetbreads and mushrooms cook in this 20 minutes, then add oysters. When oysters begin to swell, add beaten yolk of 1 egg, and wineglass of cream. Serve immediately.

Oyster Pie.

Make a rich pie dough, line bottom and sides of a pudding dish with crust and bake in hot oven. Remove before it is brown. Put on to boil a little oyster liquor with 1 tablespoonful of butter, teaspoonful of salt, pinch of pepper, and when boiling add oysters. Let boil up once, and remove immediately. Put a layer of cracker meal on bottom of crust, then oysters and bits of butter, another layer of cracker meal, oysters, and butter, and so on until pan is filled. Pour liquor oysters were cooked in over whole, and cover with a top crust of raw dough. Bake in a very hot oven until crust is brown, and serve immediately in same pan it was baked. Requires from 24 to 48 oysters, according to size of pan.

Boiled Crabs.

Secure live crabs. Put on a large boiler half full of water, throw in a handful of salt and 1 teaspoonful cayenne pepper; when it comes to a boil, throw in the crabs and boil 15 minutes when the shells will be red. Set aside to get cold. Before serving, remove the red shell from each crab, remove the spongy part and the "dead men," lay in the centre of a platter, put slices of lemon around the dish and stick crisp sprigs of parsley on top of crabs.

Fricasseed Crab.

Boil crabs in salt water well seasoned with salt and red pepper until red, remove from water, clean and break apart. Set a sauce-pan on stove, pour in 1 can tomatoes, 1 pt water. Let boil, and thicken with 1 tablespoonful flour dissolved in water. Season with pinch salt, pepper, cayenne, teaspoonful tomato catsup, and one red pepper chopped fine, and chopped parsley. Crack the claws, and drop broken crabs and claws into this, boil for 15 minutes and serve. Many prefer picking the crab meat from the claws and shells before adding to the sauce.

Fried Crabs.

Boil crabs in boiling water seasoned with salt and red pepper. Clean them and separate claws from the body, crack on the backs to make tender and remove meat from claws. Dip first in beaten eggs, then in cracker-meal and fry in boiling hot lard or butter. Serve with slices of lemon and sprigs of parsley.

Soft-Shell Crabs.

Secure live crabs, remove the sand bags and spongy part from the sides, wash thoroughly, then dry on clean towel. Dip each crab in cracker meal that has been seasoned with salt and pepper, then dip into some well-beaten eggs, and put back in the cracker meal again. Fry in a skillet half full of boiling hot butter or lard. Serve hot with slices of lemon and sprigs of crisp parsley on platter.

Boiled Lobster.

Procure nice live lobsters, as many as required. Plunge them in boiling water well seasoned with salt and red pepper. Boil 25 minutes. then wash and place on ice. When ready to serve, cut each one in half lengthwise, remove the intestine and serve cold. Garnish with parsley.

Broiled Lobster.

Procure as many live lobsters as required. Split them in half while alive with a sharp knife or hatchet, take out the intestines, rub slightly with butter, season with salt and pepper, then broil them on a hot broiler for seven minutes on each side. Pour over them some freshly-melted butter, and garnish with parsley and slices of lemon. Serve hot.

Lobster Cutlet.

One pint lobster meat chopped fine, season with saltspoonful of salt and 1 of dry mustard, and a little cayenne pepper. Moisten with 1 cupful cream sauce before the wine is added. Roll in crumbs, eggs and crumbs again, and fry by spoonfuls in boiling grease, flatten each one to look like a cutlet, using a claw of the lobster to decorate each piece when served.

Cream Sauce.

Melt 2 tablespoonfuls fresh butter in fryer on stove, add 4 tablespoonfuls flour or 2 tablespoonfuls corn starch, and stir until mixed, season with salt and pepper, add 1 pint sweet cream, stir until it thickens, take out 1 cupful for chops, and to the other add 1 wine glass of sherry or Madeira wine, and remove from fire. Serve over lobster cutlets.

Steamed Mussels or Cockles.

Put on to boil water seasoned with salt, pepper and a lump of butter, add also a tiny bit of garlic. When boiling drop in shell-fish, and as soon as they open, remove from water and place in a dish. Serve with melted butter.

Steamed Clams.

Put on to boil water seasoned with salt and pepper. When boiling drop in clams, and as soon as opened remove from water with perforated skimmer, place on dish, and serve at once with melted butter, salt and pepper, and slices of lemon.

Fricasseed Shrimps.

Put 1 tablespoonful butter in saucepan, when hot brown in it ½ of a small onion and 2 tablespoonfuls flour. Pour in 1 can tomatoes, season with salt and pepper, cook 15 minutes, then add 1 quart shelled shrimps, cook 10 minutes, and stir in the yolk of 1 egg to thicken. Eat at once. Can be eaten with rice.

Terrapin Stew.

Drop the live terrapins in hot water. Boil a few minutes. Separate the shells and remove the meat, retaining everything except the head, outer skin, gall and sand bags. Keep small bones to cook in stew, for they are the proofs of the real terrapin. Twenty minutes before dinner place terrapin in a porcelain-lined pan, and set on stove, allowing it to stew in its own juice for 15 minutes. For each terrapin, add 2 tablespoonfuls melted butter, 2 tablespoonfuls rich cream, pepper and salt to taste. Stir gently, and cook 5 minutes more. For each terrapin add 2 tablespoonfuls of Madeira wine. Serve immediately in individual dishes.

Sweet Sour Fish.

First cut up and salt the fish. Shad or trout is best.

Put on fish kettle with 1½ cupfuls water and 1 cupful vinegar, add 1 onion cut in round slices, 1 dozen raisins, 1 lemon cut in round slices, 2 bay leaves, 6 cloves. When this mixture begins to boil, lay in your fish and cook thoroughly. When done remove fish to platter.

Put liquor back on stove, add 3 tablespoonfuls granulated sugar (which has been melted and browned in a pie plate without water), then add 2 tablespoonfuls flour which has been rubbed smooth with a little water Let boil well and pour over fish. If not sweet enough add more sugar.

Serve cold.

Sweet Sour Fish With Wine.

Put on to boil in fish kettle 1 glass water, ½ glass vinegar, 2 tablespoonfuls brown sugar, ½ dozen cloves,

½ teaspoonful ground cinnamon, 1 onion cut in round slices. Boil thoroughly, then strain and add to it 1 lemon cut in round slices, 1 goblet red wine, 1 dozen raisins, 1 tablespoonful pounded almonds; put on stove again, and when it comes to a boil, add fish that has been cut up and salted. Cook until done, remove fish to a platter, and to the liquor add a small piece Leb-kuchen or ginger cake, and stir in the well-beaten yolks of 4 eggs; stir carefully or it will curdle. If not sweet enough add more sugar.

Pour over fish. Shad or trout is the best fish to use.

Stewed or Sharp Fish.

Put in fish kettle on stove 1 tablespoonful fresh butter, when melted add ½ onion cut fine, a tiny piece of garlic, cut fine; let brown, then add 1 tablespoonful flour, brown light, and add enough water to cook fish. To this liquor add some cut up celery or celery seed, some finely-chopped parsley, 2 cloves, 1 bay leaf, a tiny pinch of mace, small pinch cayenne pepper, some black pepper, a little ginger, and 1 tablespoonful fresh butter. When this mixture begins to boil, add fish which has been cut up and salted. Cook until done. Remove fish to platter and to the liquor add 1 cupful sweet milk, stirring constantly; boil 1 minute, then pour over the beaten yolks of 2 eggs, stirring all the time. Slice a lemon over the fish, then pour the liquor over. Eat hot or cold.

Coube on Fish.

Slice the fish in pieces (red fish is best), season with salt and pepper, boil till done. Put 2 tablespoonfuls butter in a skillet, when hot slice in one large onion and brown it, add ½ can tomatoes, season with 1 teaspoonful pepper, ½ teaspoonful allspice, some finely-chopped parsley, and ½ cupful tomato catsup. Just before it begins to boil add 1 goblet good claret.

Cut some bread in small cubes, fry in butter to garnish the dish.

Place fish in center of platter, pour the gravy over and garnish with the bread cubes.

Fried Smelts.

Clean, wipe dry, salt and set aside until ready to cook. Dip them in beaten egg and cracker meal and fry in very hot butter or fat. Can be served with " Tartare Sauce " if desired.

Fried Scallops.

Drain the scallops, wipe dry, season with salt and pepper. Season some cracker or bread crumbs with salt and pepper. Roll the scallops first in crumbs, then dip them one by one in beaten egg, then roll in crumbs again. Have a deep skillet half full of boiling hot butter or lard, drop in scallops, not too many at a time, and fry quickly until a nice even brown.

Serve at once with Tomato Catsup or Tartare Sauce.

Boiled Fish.

Clean the fish well, and put on whole, in water that has had salt and pepper added, also a piece of onion. Use only enough water to cover well. Boil gently until done, then drain off all the water, and decorate with parsley and slices of hard-boiled eggs.

Serve with mayonnaise or Hollandaise Sauce.

Tenderloin Trout with Wine Sauce.

Cut a large salt-water trout in pieces, lay on a dish, cover over it 1 large onion sliced, and 1 can mushrooms. Put in cool place 1 hour. Then take 1 cup flour and 1 cup fresh butter, stir well together, add to this the water that has drained from the fish, stirring constantly, so that it will not lump, put on to boil, add some finely-chopped parsley, continue to stir, add 1 cup Madeira wine, boil a few minutes, take off to cool. When cool, stir in 3 whole eggs.

Take the onions off the fish (they are only to flavor), cut mushrooms in halves. Put fish in baking-pan or dish, sprinkle well with bread crumbs, lay the mushrooms on top, then put a layer of oysters, then a layer of shrimps, then pour the gravy over all and bake. Serve in same dish in which it is baked.

Fish Piquant.

Boil the fish whole in water seasoned well with onion, celery, salt, red pepper, and a tiny bit of garlic. When tender, drain and lay on a platter.

Stir a lump of butter the size of an egg with 3 tablespoonfuls flour, then add the juice of 1 or 2 lemons (according to size). Stir into this 3 cups of the water in which the fish was boiled; put back on the stove, and stir until thickened. Remove from the fire, pour over the well-beaten yolks of 2 eggs, add some cut up pickles and olives, pour over the fish, and garnish the dish with parsley or celery tops.

Cream Lemon Fish.

Boil the trout, which has been cut in slices, until tender, in enough water to cover it, to which a lump of butter, ½ cup vinegar, and salt and pepper have been added.

Beat until light, yolks of 2 eggs and 2 teaspoonfuls sugar, and add the juice of 1 lemon.

Take fish out of water, lay on platter in which it is to be served. Thicken the gravy with flour that has first been dissolved in a little water. When thick pour 2 cupfuls of the gravy over the eggs and lemon, stirring all the time. When cold add ½ cup cream whipped until stiff, and pour over the fish.

Fish with Lemon Sauce.

Put on to boil in wide open porcelain-lined skillet sufficient water to boil fish. Add ½ cupful vinegar, ½ cupful wine. Add heaping tablespoonful of butter, and when melted put slices of fish, which have already been seasoned. Let boil until fish is tender. In the meantime, beat yolks of four eggs until light with ½ cupful sugar, and juice of two lemons. Remove 1 cupful fish stock from stove, pour it into egg mixture, and put back whole in skillet with fish. Let boil up until thoroughly mixed, shaking pan all the while to prevent curdling. Put in dish, and garnish with slices of lemon and parsley.

Baked Fish with Lemon Sauce.

Bake fish in pan, with water and butter, taking care to add water when all in pan has been absorbed. When fish is done, drain off all gravy which is in pan, and put on stove to boil with 1 cupful white wine. Beat yolks of 4 eggs with ½ cupful sugar, stir wine in, add juice of 2 lemons, put back on stove to thicken, and just before serving, pour sauce over fish in dish. Half the quantity of sauce can be used for a small family.

Sole au Gratin.

Butter pan, put in a layer of bread crumbs, and a layer of finely-chopped parsley, some chopped onion and bits of butter. Season fish with salt, pepper and ginger, and stuff with oysters, shrimps and mushrooms. Put in pan and cover with another layer of bread crumbs, parsley and butter. Bake 15 minutes and when nearly done add ½ glass white wine and bake until done. Pompano or shad are best prepared this way.

Baked Fish with Tomatoes.

Butter a baking pan, put in a layer of bread crumbs, some finely-chopped parsley, some finely-chopped onion, and bits of butter. Season fish with salt, pepper, and ginger. Stuff fish with oysters, shrimps and mushrooms, or plain bread dressing. Put in pan, and pour over the fish 1 small can of tomatoes (which has been seasoned with salt, pepper, a bit of sugar and a teaspoonful of vinegar and then strained). Bake until almost done, then lay some oysters in and cook a few minutes longer. Red snapper, shad or pompano are best prepared this way.

Baked Red Snapper.

Clean and season fish an hour before cooking. Pour 1 tablespoonful vinegar over fish to make firm. Lay in baking pan with a little water, some parsley and bits of butter. Bake in hot stove until done. Lay in platter and pour tomato sauce over.

TOMATO SAUCE.

Brown 1 tablespoonful butter in a skillet, stir in 1 spoonful flour, then add 1 pint tomatoes, mash well and season with salt, pepper, a pinch of cayenne pepper, 1 teaspoonful vinegar and a bit of sugar. Boil up and pour over fish.

Fish can be first stuffed with bread dressing if desired.

Baked Trout or Sole with Mushroom Sauce.

Line a baking pan with bread crumbs, lay the whole fish (that has been seasoned some) on top, cover with bread crumbs and bits of butter, and moisten with a little vinegar and cold water. Bake quickly. Lay fish on platter and pour over it the following mushroom sauce: Melt 1 tablespoonful butter in a skillet, then brown in it 1 tablespoonful flour, stir in 1 wine glass Madeira wine, liquor of 1 can mushrooms, some oyster liquor, and let all boil. After boiling a few minutes add ½ pint shrimps and ½ pint oysters and 1 can mushrooms. Season with salt and pepper and boil thick. Serve hot.

Fried Trout or Sole with Mushroom Sauce.

Take slices of raw fish cut lengthwise 1 inch thick and 4 inches long, season, dip in eggs, then in cracker meal, fry in boiling butter or lard. Serve hot with above "Mushroom Sauce" hot.

Broiled Pompano or Shad.

Split fish open down the back, remove back bone, season well with salt and pepper and put in baking pan open with flesh side up. Put bits of butter on top and put in hot stove 15 to 20 minutes. Garnish with slices of lemon and sprigs of parsley. If desired can be served with Mayonnaise Sauce.

Tenderloin Trout with Tartare Sauce.

Cut slices of raw trout lengthwise about 1 inch thick, having first removed the bone; press hard with the hand to shape like croquettes. Season well, dip first in egg, then in bread crumbs or cracker meal and fry in boiling lard or fat.
Serve with "Tartare Sauce."

Fried Pompano with Tartare Sauce.

Cut raw pompano in small slices and fry same as Tenderloin trout. Serve with "Tartare Sauce."

Fried Red Snapper with Tartare Sauce.

First clean a good sized red snapper. Remove the large centre bone, also cut off the skin. Now with a sharp knife slice the raw fish in *thin* slices downward from head to tail. Roll these slices up to look like a long croquette—if too long make 2 out of one piece of fish. Dip in egg, then in cracker meal. Fry in boiling hot lard or fat. Serve hot with cold Tartare Sauce.

Cod Fish Balls.

Put the salt fish to soak overnight in luke-warm water. Remove all the skin and bones. Pull it into shreds, and put on the fire in cold water. When it begins to boil, change the water and let come to a boil a second time. Boil some Irish potatoes until tender. Use half as much potato as you have fish. Mix together while both are hot, until smooth, add a lump of butter, some pepper and 2 eggs beaten light. If necessary, add a little milk. Work until smooth. Form into balls and fry in boiling fat or lard. Garnish with parsley.

Frogs' Legs.

The hind legs only are used. Boil them 3 minutes in boiling salted water. Remove them from the water, wipe dry, dip them in cracker or bread crumbs, then in egg, then in crumbs again. Fry them in boiling butter or lard. Garnish with sprigs of parsley. Or serve with green peas in the center of the platter and frogs' legs in a circle around them.

Frogs' Legs with Cream Sauce.

Secure medium-sized frogs' legs, or, if large, cut them in half, separating them at the joint; season with salt and pepper, wet them with a little milk, roll each one in a little flour and fry in boiling fat until a nice brown. Serve them on a dish with crisp, green parsley. Serve a cream sauce in a separate sauce boat.

Fish Roe.

Wash and dry the roes nicely, season with salt and pepper, roll in corn meal and fry in hot butter or lard until a nice even brown. Garnish with slices of lemon and parsley. Serve hot.

Or, cover the roes with cold water and parboil until just tender (no longer). Lay them aside until cold, then season with salt and pepper, dip them in beaten egg, then roll in cracker meal, and fry a nice even brown in boiling butter or lard. Serve hot. Garnish with slices of lemon and parsley.

Fish Chowder.

Cut 3 pounds of bass or cod into strips 3 inches long and 1 inch thick. Clean and skin. Fry six or seven slices of bacon; then slice two onions thin, and brown with bacon. Put bacon and onions in bottom of pot, then put a layer of fish, then a layer of raw Irish potatoes, cut in thin slices, then soda wafer crackers, soaked first in milk, then 1 tablespoonful of butter broken in bits, teaspoonful of chopped parsley, a bit of salt, pepper, a tiny pinch of cayenne, and 1 tablespoonful of tomato catsup. Then add another layer of fish, potatoes, crackers, and seasoning, until all ingredients are used. Put a quart of water over whole and let boil from 20 to 30 minutes, until fish and potatoes are thoroughly done. Taste, and if not quite hot enough add a few drops of tobasco sauce and more tomato catsup. Pour out in a dish and garnish with slices of lemon. If desired a pint of oysters with their liquor can be added to whole. Cayenne pepper may be omitted if a highly seasoned chowder is not desired.

Boiled Salmon with Sauce Vert.

Boil salmon until tender in salt water, but leave the fish firm. Remove and put on platter, saving the water it was cooked in. Melt in a saucepan ½ cup butter, stir in 2 tablespoonfuls of flour, and cook 3 minutes, stirring constantly. Then add 1 cup strained fish stock. If too thick add more stock until the required consistency. Chop very fine 2 sprigs of parsley, and two tablespoonfuls of capers. Add to sauce and strain whole through a fine cloth. Add juice of one lemon, mix well, then one tablespoonful of fresh butter, *just before serving.* Pour sauce over fish in platter, and serve immediately.

ENTREES.

Oyster Patties.

Have ready as many patties as required. To 1 dozen patties take 36 select oysters; put in colander and drain thoroughly. Put on 1½ cupfuls sweet milk. When it comes to a boil, stir in 2 heaping tablespoonfuls flour that have been rubbed smooth with a little cold milk, stir into milk, add 1 tablespoonful fresh butter, season highly with salt and pepper and some finely-chopped parsley. When *very* thick add the well drained oysters. Stir constantly to keep from burning, and when oysters are *plump* remove from fire. Fifteen minutes before serving fill the patties with this mixture, put inside of stove to heat thoroughly and serve at once with green peas.

A pretty way to serve patties is to place a patty on a fancy plate, lay a clean crisp lettuce leaf next to it, and fill the leaf with the green peas.

Chicken Patties.

Prepare a 4 lb. chicken as for stew and let boil until very tender. Take the white meat only and cut in small pieces.

Wash 1 pair sweetbreads, cover with boiling water and boil until tender. When done pick into small pieces and add to chicken. Add also ½ can of mushrooms cut into pieces, and 2 truffles cut fine.

Melt 2 tablespoonfuls butter without browning, add 2 tablespoonfuls flour and stir until smooth, then add 2 cupfuls sweet cream, and then the chicken and other ingredients. Stir continually until it thickens. Take from fire, add the yolks of 2 eggs, season highly with salt, pepper and finely-chopped parsley before removing from the fire. Fill the heated patty shells and serve at once with green peas. The mushrooms and truffles can be omitted if desired.

Sweetbread Patties.

Have 1 dozen patties ready. Boil 2½ sets of sweetbreads until very tender, then take out of water, and chop fine.

Put in double boiler 1 cupful sweet cream, and when it begins to boil, stir in 1 tablespoonful butter that has been rubbed together with 1 tablespoonful flour until smooth, season highly with salt, pepper and some finely-chopped parsley. Add the chopped sweetbreads, and cook 10 minutes. Fifteen minutes before serving fill the patties with the mixture, set back in stove to heat thoroughly, and serve at once. Serve with green peas.

Sardellen Souflè.

Beat yolks 6 eggs with 2 tablespoonfuls of butter, stir in 1 cupful sifted flour, 1 pint cream whipped stiff, and beaten whites 6 eggs, pinch salt. Take small muffin rings, butter, and drop in a spoonful of batter. Bake in oven 20 minutes. Just before serving put a dab of sardellen butter on top. Half the quantity is sufficient for a small family. Make only when ready to use; they cannot stand.

Sardellen Butter.

Mash fine ½ lb. cleaned sardellen, cream 1 large tablespoonful butter, mix with sardellen, flavor with lemon juice. The sardellen butter can be rolled in round balls like butter, and laid on top of the Souflès.

Chicken Croquettes. No. 1.

Boil a fat hen until tender, remove the skin and bones, and cut the meat into dice.

Put 1 tablespoonful butter in a saucepan, when melted, not brown, stir in 2 tablespoonfuls flour, stir until it is smooth and begins to cook, then stir in 1 cupful sweet cream, stir until it begins to thicken, then add the cut up chicken, season with salt and pepper, stir until thick, then remove from fire, and add the beaten yolks of 2 eggs. When cold, form into croquettes, dip in beaten egg, then cracker meal, and fry in boiling hot lard or fat.

Chicken Croquettes. No. 2.

Boil 1 large chicken until very tender, remove skin, bones and fat, and chop the chicken up fine, season with salt, pepper, a little cayenne pepper, some finely-chopped parsley, a small lump butter, 2 eggs beaten separately, and enough sweet cream or rich milk to make them stick together. Make into croquettes by rolling a large spoonful lengthwise between the palms of both hands. Dip in cracker meal, then in some beaten egg, then in cracker meal again. Fry in a skillet half full of boiling hot fat or lard. Serve with green peas.

Crab Croquettes.

Make same as "chicken croquettes," using either canned crabs or the meat of fresh crabs that have been boiled in salt water. Serve with green peas.

Salmon Croquettes.

Flake 1 lb. fish and set aside. Put on stove in saucepan 1 cupful milk or cream, 2 tablespoonfuls flour, yolks 2 eggs, pinch salt, pepper, and teapoonful chopped parsley. When sauce has thickened stir in with the salmon, and lastly add beaten whites 2 eggs. Make in croquettes, dip in bread crumbs, fry in hot fat, and serve with tomato catsup heated.

Sweetbread Croquettes.

Take cleaned and boiled sweetbreads, and cut in small pieces. Cut ½ can mushrooms in pieces, and add to sweetbreads. Make a cream sauce of 1 tablespoonful melted butter, stir in 1 tablespoonful flour, then ½ cupful cream, pinch salt and pepper. Add sweetbreads and mushrooms, and mix well. Beat yolks of two eggs light, add to sweetbreads. Shape into croquettes, dip first in cracker meal, then in egg, then in cracker meal. Fry in hot fat. Can be served either with a sauce made of the remainder of the mushrooms and the liquor, or with green peas. Serve hot.

Shrimp Croquettes.

Buy 1 quart of shrimps, shell, then chop up fine. This generally makes from 1 to 1¼ pints unshelled. Make a cream sauce of 1 tablespoonful of butter, 1 tablespoonful of flour, and ¾ cupful milk. Mix with shrimps, stir in 3 whole beaten eggs, a pinch of pepper. When cool, shape in croquettes, dip in bread crumbs, and fry a golden brown in hot fat. Serve with Hollandaise sauce or Sherry sauce.

Lobster Croquettes.

Put 2 tablespoonfuls butter in saucepan on fire, let it melt (not brown), stir in 2 heaping tablespoonfuls flour until smooth. Beat until light yolks of 3 eggs, add 1 pint sweet cream or milk, mix thoroughly and stir into the saucepan with butter and flour, season with salt and pepper and some finely-chopped parsley. Stir well, and when the mixture begins to boil stir in 1 can of lobster (that has been cut into small bits) and cook until thick, stirring all the time. Remove from fire, put in a platter and squeeze the juice of 1 lemon over it. Set in cool place until perfectly cold and stiff.

Make into croquettes, dip in beaten eggs, then in cracker meal, and fry in boiling hot fat.

Lobster Farcé.

Boil 2 lobsters for 25 minutes; pick meat from shells and cut in pieces. Melt 2 tablespoonfuls butter in saucepan, stir in 3 tablespoonfuls flour until yellow (not brown), then add 1 pint sweet cream, salt and pepper to taste, boil until thick, stirring all the time.

Remove from fire, add lobster meat and put on ice 2 or 3 hours. Fill lobster shells, sprinkle bread crumbs and lumps of butter over them and bake until brown and serve hot.

Lobster a la Newburg.

Boil 1 large lobster; when done pick meat from shells, cut in 1-inch pieces, and season with salt and a pinch of cayenne pepper. Add butter size of an egg. Let all simmer for 5 minutes, then add 1 glass Madeira or sherry wine, with 1 teaspoonful sugar in it, and let boil 3 minutes. Beat the yolks of 3 eggs with 1 cupful sweet cream, add to mixture and boil 5 minutes longer. Serve very hot, in shells or chafing dish.

Shrimps a la Newburg.

Prepare as above.

Lobster Timbales.

Make a soup the day before of a knuckle of veal and an old hen. Put on in cold water, and cook seven hours, being careful not to let stock get too low. If it does, add a little water. Set aside on ice over night, and let jell. In the morning, skim fat, put on stove to heat, and season with salt and pepper. Cook together, in a little salt water, 1 cupful green peas, 1 cupful carrots cut in small squares, and 1 cupful asparagus tips. When tender remove from fire, and drain off water. Have ready small timbale molds, or one large pudding mold will do. Boil lobster, and remove meat from shell and claws. Put a large piece of lobster in each mold, surround with asparagus, carrots, and peas, and pour over all the stock until mold is full. Put on ice, and let jelly again, then remove from mold. Serve with Tartare Sauce. To be served either before soup, or as an entreè.

Shrimp Timbales.

Prepared same way as lobster timbales, using shrimps instead. Canned shrimps can be used where fresh are not obtainable.

Jellied Asparagus.

Prepare jelly same as for lobster timbales. Heat 1 can of asparagus tips, or 2 bunches freshly cooked asparagus tips, in a little of the melted jelly. Season strongly as it loses flavor in the cooling. Put asparagus in mold (melon shape preferable), pour melted jelly over and set on ice to harden. Let stand 5 or 6 hours before serving. Serve with Tartare Sauce.

Chicken, Fish, or Liver Timbales.—No. 1.

Grate or grind very fine raw chicken, fish or liver, pass through colander to make smooth and fine. If chicken or fish is used, must be boned, skinned, and all gristle removed from chicken. Grate in onion, and add pinch salt and pepper. Soak ⅛ loaf of stale bread in cold water, squeeze dry and mash through colander. Mix with meat, then add first beaten yolks 3 eggs, then beaten whites. Butter timbale forms (or one large tin pudding form), put a mushroom in bottom of each mold, and add ½ cupful chopped mushrooms to meat. Fill molds, place in a pan of boiling water, cover with another pan and bake inside stove. When done remove pan, and if top is not sufficiently brown, let bake a little longer until it browns. For large chicken or liver molds bake 2 hours, small ones 30 minutes. For large fish mold bake ¾ hour, for small ones 15 minutes. If stove is not sufficiently hot, will take longer. Serve with cream sauce.

Cream Sauce for Timbales.

Put in a saucepan on stove ½ pint cream and heaping tablespoonful butter, and a little flour dissolved in milk. Cook until thick. If too thick thin with more milk. Add last, wineglass of sherry wine. Season with salt.

Chicken Timbale.

Boil a chicken until tender, skin, bone and chop fine. Stir 4 yolks of eggs with tablespoonful of butter to a cream, add ½ cupful chopped mushrooms, pinch salt and pepper and ½ pint cream. Then mix well with chicken and add beaten whites 4 eggs. Bake in forms same as above recipe. This takes only ¾ hour to bake. Serve with sauce.

SAUCE.

Mushroom liquor thickened with a bit of dissolved flour (dissolved in milk), 1 tablespoonful of cream, pinch salt and pepper.

Fish Timbale.

Take cooked fish, bone, and chop fine. Soak ⅛ loaf white bread, squeeze dry, mash through colander and add to fish. Melt a tablespoonful of butter on stove, stir in a little flour, then onion, and mix fish in last. Remove from fire, and pass through colander. Add finely-chopped truffles, mushrooms, and yolks 6 eggs. Put in forms, and bake same as in recipe No. 1. Serve with the following sauce:

SAUCE.

1 cupful strained tomatoes put in saucepan on stove, wineglass sherry, ½ cupful cream, shrimps, small oysters, and lastly beaten yolks 2 eggs. Season with salt and pepper.

Salmon Timbales.

Shred 1 pound of salmon. Rub smooth, add pinch salt, white pepper, a little grated onion, a tablespoonful chopped almonds, and unbeaten whites of 3 eggs. Then stir in 1 cupful cream whipped stiff. Put in timbale molds (the little individual tin pudding molds are the same), put in a biscuit pan filled with boiling water, and cook in oven for 20 minutes. Serve with Hollandaise sauce.

Chicken with Cheese in Shells.

Boil chicken, cut meat fine, mix with poulette sauce, then add asparagus tips, which have been cooked a little. Put in shells. Sprinkle each shell with Parmesan cheese and bake.

POULETTE SAUCE.

Mix 1 oz. butter with ½ tablespoonful of flour, stir over fire until dissolved. Beat yolks of 2 eggs in ½ cupful cream or milk, then stir into butter. Then add ½ cupful more milk. Stir until thick. Add pinch salt and pepper.

Coquille of Fish.

One lb. of any fish which has been boiled and shredded carefully.

Put on a saucepan with 2 tablespoonfuls fresh butter, let melt, smooth in 1 tablespoonful flour, add a pinch cayenne pepper, stir in 1 cupful milk and 1 tablespoonful sweet cream, and add 1 teaspoonful Anchovy sauce or Worcestershire, and pinch of salt. Let thicken, remove from fire, and mix sauce with fish.

Line individual shells or 1 large pudding-dish with fried bread crumbs, first greasing dish or shells. Fill with mixture, sprinkle fried crumbs on top, and bake in hot oven until brown. This can also be made of canned salmon.

Deviled Brains.

Put 1 tablespoonful butter in skillet, and when hot add 2 tablespoonfuls flour, rub until smooth, and brown lightly, then add ½ can tomatoes, season with salt, pepper, finely-chopped parsley, and a dash of cayenne pepper, and the brains, which have previously been cleaned, scalded with boiling water, and cut in small pieces. Cook a few minutes, and then fill the shells with the mixture. Over each shell sprinkle cracker crumbs and bits of butter. Put shells in pan, and brown nicely. Serve with green peas.

Deviled Sweetbreads.

Prepare the same as "Deviled Brains," only substituting sweetbreads for brains, and cooking until tender instead of scalding. Put in shells, sprinkle with cracker crumbs and bits of butter, and brown in oven. Serve with green peas.

Deviled Crabs.

Rub yolks of 2 hard-boiled eggs until smooth, add 1½ tablespoonfuls fresh butter melted, 2 tablespoonfuls vinegar, salt, pepper, and cayenne pepper to taste; then stir in the yolks of 3 raw eggs, then the stiff beaten whites, and the chopped whites of the 2 hard-boiled eggs. Mix all with the meat of 1 can of crabs, or fresh crab meat that has been taken from the boiled shells. Put lightly in individual shells, pour over each a little melted butter, and brown nicely in oven.
Serve with grean peas.

Chicken with Mushrooms. No. 1.

Boil 1 large young hen until tender, then remove the skin and bones, cut the meat up in dice-shaped pieces, and put aside.

Melt 1 kitchenspoonful fresh butter in a spider, lay

in a tiny piece finely-chopped onion or onion juice, add 1 heaping kitchenspoonful flour, and stir until smooth, not brown. Stir in 1 cupful milk, then add a little finely-chopped parsley, and ½ can mushrooms cut in small pieces, then add the cut-up chicken, and season with salt and pepper (a few drops of Worcestershire sauce can be added if desired). When the mixture begins to cook, stir in 1 cupful sweet cream, and continue stirring until it is thick and creamy; then remove from fire, pour in a bowl, and set aside to cool. When cold, fill individual shells with the mixture, sprinkle cracker crumbs and bits of butter on top, and brown nicely. Serve hot with green peas.

Chicken with Mushrooms. No 2.

Cold chicken or turkey left over can be used for this recipe. If you have none, steam a chicken until tender, remove skin and bones, cut meat in pieces size of dice.

Brown in saucepan on stove 1 small onion in 1 tablespoonful butter, add 1 tablespoonful flour, liquor of 1 can mushrooms, and the mushrooms and parsley chopped fine, boil a few minutes, then add the chicken. Boil up once, season with salt and pepper, and fill individual shells with the mixture. Sprinkle cracker meal and bits of butter on top, and brown quickly in oven.

This same mixture can be baked in pudding-dish, adding the cracker meal and bits of butter on top.

Chicken with Green Peas.

Prepared same as chicken with mushrooms, only substitute green peas for mushrooms.

Sweetbreads and Mushrooms.

Boil sweetbreads until tender, skin and clean, and season with salt, pepper and ginger.

Brown 1 tablespoonful fresh butter in saucepan, thicken with 1 teaspoonful flour, add some soup stock if convenient, if not, liquor from the mushrooms will serve. Add 1 bay leaf and boil sweetbreads in this liquor 1 hour. Add mushrooms 10 minutes before removing from fire.
Serve in individual dishes.

Crab a la Creole.

Boil live crabs in boiling salt water until red. Remove from fire and pick out the meat carefully from claws and body, and set aside.

Brown in saucepan on stove 1 small onion in 1 tablespoonful fresh butter, stir in 1 tablespoonful flour, add 1 cupful hot water and 1 can tomatoes, season with salt, pepper, cayenne pepper, and 1 saltspoonful sugar, add 1 tablespoonful tomato catsup. Boil until thick, add crab meat and let cook a few minntes. Line a platter with slices of toast bread, cover entirely with the mixture, and serve at once. Allow 1 slice of bread for each person.

Tomatoes Stuffed With Crabs.

Take 6 large tomatoes, cut off tops, scoop out insides, and put tops and insides on stove in saucepan to stew until done. Season with salt and pepper. Boil and clean 8 hard-shell crabs. Pick meat from claws and shells, add to cooked tomatoes. Flavor with chopped parsley, a little fresh butter, a tiny pinch of cayenne, and 1 teaspoonful of tomato catsup. Let whole cook up thick and strong, fill tomatoes, put in flat baking-pan inside stove, and add a very little water. Bake until done, and serve hot.

Tomatoes Stuffed With Shrimps.

Take 6 large tomatoes, slice off tops, and scoop out insides. Brown 1 tablespoonful of butter in skillet, add the tomato tops and scooped out part, and cook until smooth and thick. Season with salt, pepper, a little chopped parsley, and a very few drops of onion juice. Set part of this aside. Soak a small slice of bread in water, squeeze dry, and add to tomatoes. Chop 1 small can of shrimps very fine (or ½ pint of fresh shrimps), add to dressing and mix well. Fill tomatoes with this, sprinkle bread crumbs on top, put a small lump of fresh butter on top of each tomato, put tomatoes in a flat baking-pan, add a very little water, and bake until brown. Serve with the remainder of cooked tomato as sauce. Also is served with rice.

Green Peppers Stuffed With Shrimps.

Get large green peppers. Cut off tops and remove insides carefully. Soak in cold water with salt at least three hours. Make a dressing of shrimps and tomatoes same as for tomatoes stuffed with shrimps. Fill peppers with this dressing, put bread crumbs on top, and a small piece of butter. Put in a flat baking-pan with a very little water. Bake until tender, basting often.

Wined Sweetbreads.

Melt 2 tablespoonfuls butter in saucepan, then stir in 2 tablespoonfuls flour, then stir in 1 cup soup stock and some of the water in which the sweetbreads have been boiled, season with salt, pepper and ground ginger, add ½ teaspoonful mustard and juice of ½ lemon, some finely-chopped parsley and 1 glass sherry or white wine. Add sweetbreads which have been boiled very tender. Boil a few minutes, then serve in individual shells or dishes.

Creamed Sweetbreads.

Clean and boil 2 sets of sweetbreads, and cut them in pieces 2 inches long. Drain 1 can of mushrooms from the liquor and cut them in half. Put in a double boiler 1 cupful sweet cream, add 1 tablespoonful butter a pinch of salt and pepper; when the mixture begins to boil add 1 tablespoonful celery cut in very small pieces, 2 tablespoonfuls chopped almonds, ½ teaspoonful Worcestershire sauce, ½ teaspoonful French mustard, 4 drops Tobasco sauce, and 1 tablespoonful lemon juice. Boil well, stirring constantly, then add the sweetbreads and mushrooms; let them cook up once or twice and serve immediately. If desired the almonds can be omitted. If desired, put in individual shells, sprinkle cracker crumbs and bits of butter over and brown nicely. Serve with a border of green peas.

Creamed Chicken.

Boil a fat hen until tender, then prepare same as sweetbreads.

Sweetbreads and Peas.

Boil sweetbreads until tender and save the water.

Make a sauce of 1 cupful cream or milk and when boiling stir in 1 teaspoonful cornstarch which has been dissolved in a litttle cold milk, stir in the water from the sweetbreads, season with salt, pepper and 1 tablespoonful butter. Then add sweetbreads and 1 can or ½ can green peas according to quantity of sweetbreads. Boil 20 minutes then serve in individual dishes or one large dish.

Smoked Tongue.

Get a fat, fresh smoked tongue, put in a boiler and cover well with cold water. Boil steadily until done, two or three hours. Test by piercing with a fork. When done, drain from the water, peel off the outer skin while hot, cut off the root, and serve hot with **green peas.**

Cheese Straws.

Measure 6 heaping teaspoonfuls of flour, and sift on the board. Add 6 tablespoonfuls of grated Parmesan, American, or Swiss cheese, 2 tablespoonfuls of butter pinch salt, black pepper, nutmeg, and a very few grains of cayenne. Then add 2 tablespoonfuls of milk or cream. Mix well, roll out on board very thin, and cut 6 inches long, and ¼ inch wide. Put in flat, buttered tin pan, and bake a very light brown in oven. If desired the strip can be twisted, before baking, like a cork-screw, and looks very pretty when baked. To be served with any salad.

POULTRY AND GAME.

All fowls are best if seasoned from 12 to 24 hours before cooking.

Pick, singe, draw and clean them well. Season with salt, pepper, and ginger. Some like a tiny bit of garlic rubbed on the outside of the fowl, but this can be left out.

Crumb Dressing.

Melt one tablespoonful of butter, mix in 2 cupfuls of bread crumbs, pinch salt and pepper, a few drops of onion juice, 1 tablespoonful chopped parsley, and lastly one well-beaten egg. Mix all on stove in skillet, remove from fire, and stuff fowl.

Bread Dressing for Fowls or Game.

In a fryer on the stove heat 2 tablespoonfuls drippings or fat, drop in ½ onion cut fine, brown lightly and add ¼ loaf stale baker's bread (which has previously been soaked in cold water and then thoroughly squeezed out). Cook until it leaves the sides of the fryer, stirring occasionally. If too dry add a little soup stock.

Remove from the fire, put in a bowl, season with salt, pepper, ginger, and finely chopped parsley, add a small lump butter, break in 2 whole eggs, mix well and fill the fowls with it.

Pecan or Chestnut Dressing.

Prepare same as "Bread Dressing," but before taking from the fire add 1 cupful chopped pecans or chestnuts. If chestnuts are used they must first be peeled, then boiled until tender before they are chopped.

Oyster Dressing. No. 1.

Prepare same as bread dressing, adding 2 dozen oysters cut in half to it just before stuffing the fowl, and if too dry add a little of the oyster liquor.

Oyster Dressing. No. 2.

Take 1½ cupfuls grated bread crumbs, add some bits of butter, salt and pepper; add 2 dozen oysters and their own liquor, mix in 2 whole eggs. Mix well and stuff the fowl with it.

Plain Fried Chicken.

After cleaning, disjointing and seasoning the chicken for a few hours, wipe dry, dip in some beaten egg, then roll in flour. Have your frying pan half full of boiling lard or fat, lay the pieces of chicken in, fry on one side before turning, then on the other. Serve on platter decorated with sprigs of crisp parsley.

Cracker crumbs can be substituted for flour if preferred. And if the chickens are not very tender, it would be well to cover them while frying.

Fried Chicken à la Maryland.

After the ckicken has been cleaned, disjointed, and seasoned some hours wipe dry, then dip in a thin batter made of flour, milk, and eggs. Have your fryer half full of boiling lard or fat. Lay the chicken in, and fry until golden brown, turning occasionally. Serve following sauce over them ;

SAUCE.

Heat 1 tablespoonful butter in saucepan, stir in 2 tablespoonfuls flour until smooth, then stir in 1 pint milk, season with salt, pepper and finely-chopped parsley. Stir until thick and serve over chicken.

Fried Chicken with Mushroom Sauce.

Cut chicken, if young into four pieces, larger chicken into six. Put in salt water about 15 minutes before frying. Dredge with flour and fry in boiling fat. Drain out of pan all fat, put a tablespoonful of butter in pan, stir in liquor of 1 can mushrooms, ½ cupful cream, pinch salt. Pour over chicken and add mushrooms. Steam 20 minutes.

Fricassee Chicken with Dumplings.

Disjoint the chicken as for frying, only using fat hen instead of young chickens. Put the chicken in a deep saucepan, add salt, pepper, ginger, some celery, some parsley, 1 whole small onion, and 1 whole sound apple (not peeled), lay in all the fat that came from the chicken, cover with water and stew slowly and steadily. 20 minutes before it is done, thicken with 1 tablespoonful flour wet with water, and add dumplings. Cover and boil.

DUMPLINGS.

Make a pastry as for pies, cut in squares and drop in the boiling chicken 20 minutes before serving.

Fricassee Chicken with Puffs.

Disjoint chicken same as for frying, only using a fat hen instead of young chickens. Put the chicken in a deep saucepan or boiler, season with salt, pepper and ginger, cut in pieces ½ onion and lay in, put in some pieces of celery and parsley, lay in all the pieces of fat that came from the chicken, add a few tomatoes cut up, cover with water, and stew, slowly and steadily.

Just before serving rub 1 tablespoonful flour with cold water and add. Let boil up once or twice. Serve on platter with puffs around the edge of dish.

PUFFS.

Make a short pastry as for pies. Cut in squares and drop them in boiling butter or fat, fry until light brown.

Smothered Chicken.

Singe, clean and draw the chickens, split open down the back. Season well with salt, pepper and ginger, put in a baking-pan, sprinkle a little flour over them, and add bits of butter. Put about 2 cups of water in the pan, and set in a hot oven; baste often, and brown nicely on both sides. Dissolve a little flour in the pan after chickens have been removed, also add a little parsley. Pour gravy over chickens before sending to the table.

Chicken with Cauliflower.

Prepare chicken same way as in above recipe for smothered chicken. Break off outer leaves of cauliflower, and break whole bunch apart. Wash and soak in cold water ½ hour. Put in boiling salted water, with a teaspoonful corn meal (to whiten it), and boil until stalks are tender. When done remove from water. Put in a sauce-pan ½ tablespoonful butter, add 1½ tablespoonfuls flour, pinch salt and white pepper, 1 cupful hot milk, and 1 cupful of water in which cauliflower was boiled. Stir smooth until it thickens. Put cauliflower in sauce. Place chicken on hot platter, arrange cauliflower around, and pour sauce over whole. Serve immediately.

Broiled Chicken. No. 1.

Clean, singe, and draw young spring chickens, split down the backs, and season with salt and pepper. Melt 2 tablespoonfuls butter in a hot fryer, lay in the chickens, cover and press down with weights, brown on one side, then on the other; if not very young, add a spoonful or two of water. When done lay them on a hot platter; to the butter in the fryer add 1 teaspoonful flour, brown it, and add a little water, pour over the chickens, then decorate with sprigs of parsley. Or lay pieces of nicely toasted bread on the platter, put chickens on top, pour the sauce over, and decorate with thin slices of lemon.

Broiled Chickens, Mushroom Sauce.

Prepare the chickens the same as for plain "broiled chickens" No. 1. When done lay on a hot platter, and pour over them the following

MUSHROOM SAUCE.

Put 1 tablespoonful butter in saucepan on stove, when hot stir in 2 tablespoonfuls flour; when smooth and light brown, add liquor from 1 can of mushrooms, season with salt, 2 teaspoonfuls tomato catsup, 2 teaspoonfuls Worcestershire Sauce, add the mushrooms cut in half, cover, and boil fifteen minutes, stirring often.

Broiled Spring Chicken. No. 2.

Clean chicken well, and split down the middle. Season, and let stand at least two hours before cooking. Have a clear fire, butter the broiler, place chicken on, and broil on one side, then turn over on other. Butter side already broiled, as soon as turned. Have ready pieces of buttered toast, place chicken on each piece of toast, garnish with parsley, and serve.

Baked Chicken.

Singe, sponge and wipe well a 1 year old chicken. Stuff with crumb dressing, sew and draw it. Fill space from which you took the crop, sew up slit, and fold over on the back with a skewer. Put remainder of stuffing in other opening, and then sew it up. Skewer and tie the legs and wings of the chicken. Put in a roasting pan. Sear with melted fat. Place slices of salt pork in the pan, and put chicken on them. Place layers of pork on the breast of chicken. Baste often. Dredge with flour about 15 minutes before chicken is done, and let brown nicely on breast. Remove strings and skewers, place on a hot platter, and garnish with parsley.

Roast Chicken.

Prepare chicken same way as you would turkey or any other fowl, leaving whole, and season. Stuff either with chestnut, pecan, or bread dressing. Put a large spoonful of fat in double baking-pan, sufficient water to cook with, and bake until tender. Baste frequently, and when almost done, sprinkle flour over, and let brown.

Chicken with Rice.

Clean and season well an old hen. Put on stove in pot with plenty of water, first cutting chicken in pieces. ½ hour before chicken is done wash 1 cupful rice well, pour in same pot with chicken, and cook whole until it is tender. Serve on same platter. Taste before dishing, and add extra salt and pepper if necessary.

Chicken Pot Pie.

Clean, singe and draw a fat hen or large chicken. Cut in pieces as for fricassee, put on with water to cover it, season with salt and pepper, and if not very fat a piece of butter. Let cook until tender and thicken with some flour. Make a rich pastry as for pies, line a pudding pan with some of the dough, put in all of the cooked chicken, 3 hard-boiled eggs cut in slices, some small pieces of butter, a little more salt and pepper. If necessary pour in some of the gravy in which the chicken was cooked. Put a crust of the pastry on top, stick with a fork, make a hole in the center of the top crust and from time to time add more of the gravy if any was left out. The hole in the top lets the steam escape and keeps the pie from becoming soggy.

Broiled Squabs on Toast.

Singe, draw and split down the backs as many young squabs as desired, season with salt and pepper. Have a fryer on stove, heat in it some fresh butter, lay in the squabs, meat side down, put a pie plate or cover on top, press down with a smoothing iron or heavy weight. When browned on one side turn the squabs, add a little more butter, and if the birds are not young a spoonful or two of water. Cover and weigh down again until brown on other side. Lay as many pieces of nicely-browned toast on a platter as there are squabs, put one squab on each piece of toast, and to the butter in the fryer add 1 teaspoonful flour, brown it and add a little water, cook a few minutes and pour over squabs and toast; put a thin slice of lemon on each squab. Serve at once on hot dish.

Broiled Birds on Toast.

Prepare the same as Broiled Squabs on toast, but they seldom require water to be added.

They can also be broiled on a broiler over a coal fire after they are first seasoned with salt, pepper and rubbed with a little fresh butter or olive oil. Serve on toast with slices of lemon and sprigs of parsley over.

Potted Ducks.

Clean, singe and draw, tender fat ducks. Put on a closely covered iron skillet, heat 1 cup goose grease or drippings in it, then lay in the well-seasoned ducks and 1 whole white onion, cover closely and let brown nicely, turning over when brown on one side. Stuff with a bread or pecan dressing, and when almost done, skim off the grease, stir in 1 spoonful flour, add a little water for gravy and continue to cook until done.

Potted Squabs.

Clean, singe and draw the squabs, stuff with bread dressing and prepare same as "Potted Ducks." They take about 1 hour to prepare this way.

Potted Quails or Birds.

Prepare same as "Potted Ducks," only stuffing them before they are first put on.

Stuffed Quail with Anchovy Dressing.

Mix some anchovy paste or some anchovies mashed fine with bread crumbs, season with salt, pepper and 1 tablespoonful melted butter. Stuff quails with this mixture. Make several incisions in the birds with a sharp knife, and put butter in the gashes. Bake the birds in a hot oven 15 to 20 minutes.

Stuffed Quail with Oyster Dressing.

Allow 3 oysters and ½ cracker to each quail. Roll crackers fine, season oysters with salt, pepper and Worcester Sauce, dip then in the rolled crackers, and put 3 in each quail. Scar and fill the cuts with butter same as above, and bake 15 or 20 minutes in hot oven.

Roast Turkey.

Singe, clean, and draw the turkey. Season well with salt, pepper, ginger, and a little garlic if desired. Put aside from twelve to twenty-four hours. When ready to cook, stuff with either bread or oyster dressing, lay it in a patent roasting pan or baking pan that has another to fit over it, sprinkle flour over it, also add bits of butter, unless turkey is fat. Pour some water in the pan (quantity depends on the size of the turkey), set in a hot oven, and baste often. Requires from 3 to 4 hours to bake.

Roast Goose.

Clean, singe and draw, and prepare same as "Baked Turkey," using the bread dressing.

Roast Duck.

Singe, clean, and draw the ducks. Season well with salt, pepper, ginger and a little garlic if desired. Stuff with bread dressing. Lay them in a patent roasting pan. Do not add any water. Put two spoonfuls of fat or drippings in bottom of pan. Set in a hot oven, cover closely. When brown on one side turn and brown on the other, keeping covered all the time. When brown on both sides, skim off most of the grease, stir 2 tablespoonfuls flour in the gravy, add 1 cupful water to gravy, and then set the covered pan on top of the stove in the back, and let simmer slowly for a while. Ducks can only be prepared this way when young and fat, otherwise prepare like "Roast Turkey."

Roast Wild Duck.

Clean duck well, season with salt, black pepper, and add a tablespoonful of vinegar, to remove wild taste. Make a bread dressing, season with sage and chopped onion, stuff the duck, roast same as chicken. When done, cut gashes in sides of fowl, put salt and white pepper in, and pour over it 2 glasses of Burgundy, which has been warmed. Baste duck with wine, cover, and let seasoning soak in. Then serve.

Stewed Goose.

Clean, singe, and draw the goose; disjoint and cut in pieces, reserving the breast to pickle. Season well with salt, pepper and ginger, put on in a large deep boiler, cover well with water, add ½ onion cut in round slices, a tiny piece of garlic cut up, and a handful of cut-up celery, a little thyme if convenient. Cook until tender, then add some finely-chopped parsley, and thicken with flour wet with a little water; let boil a few minutes, and serve with the gravy poured over.

Goose Livers.

Soak livers for several hours in cold water with a little salt in it.

Put enough goose fat in saucepan to cover livers. When very hot, drain all the water off the livers, and put a tiny bit of sugar where the gall has lain. Lay them in the hot fat, baste constantly with a spoon until one side is brown, then turn and brown on other side. Do not cook too long, or they will be dry. If desired, some onion can be cut in fat before livers are added. Or the livers can be taken from the salt water, some of the soft or " linda " fat of the goose laid in a small round pan, lay the livers on top, and run in a hot oven. Baste often.

Pickled Goose Breast.

Take the breast of a fat goose, cover with the fat skin that has been removed from the neck, and sew on. Season covered breast well with salt, pepper, ginger, and a little garlic. Lay in a bowl, cover with a clean cloth and put weights on top. Put aside for a few days, turning occasionally. Saltpetre can be rubbed over the breast, if you want it red. When ready to be cooked, put 2 cupfuls goose grease in a covered skillet, let it get smoking hot, lay in the goose breast, pour a dipper of cold water over it and cover at once. Let cook, not too fast, until all the water is cooked out, then brown on both sides in same skillet. To be eaten hot or cold.

Stuffed Goose Neck.

Remove the fat skin from the neck of a fat goose, being careful not to put any holes in it. Clean carefully and sew up the smaller end and stuff through largar end with the following :

Grind fine some pieces of raw goose meat (taken from the breast or legs), grind also some soft or "linda fat," a tiny piece of garlic, a small piece onion, when fine add 1 egg, and a little soaked bread, season with salt, pepper, and ginger. When neck is stuffed, sew up larger end, lay it in a pudding pan, pour a little cold water over it, set in stove and baste from time to time. Let brown until crisp. Eat hot.

Goose Cracklings (*Greeben*).

Cut the thick fat of a fat goose in pieces as big as the palm of your hand, roll together and run a toothpick through each one to fasten. Put a large preserve kettle on top of hot stove, lay in the cracklings, sprinkle a tiny bit of salt over them and pour in a cupful or two of cold water ; cover with a top and let cook, not too fast, until water is cooked out. Then add the soft or "linda" fat, keep top off and let all brown nicely. About 1 to 2 hours is required to cook them.

Chicken Tamales.

Boil a chicken until tender and chop fine. Boil 6 red peppers until tender, then chop fine, and add one small chopped onion, 1 piece chopped garlic (can be omitted), soak the whole in ½ cup vinegar. Then mix with chicken meat, add 1 cupful bread crumbs, 1 cupful tomatoes, 1 egg, and if convenient spoonful soup stock. Add 2 olives for each tamale. Roll with hands into croquette shape, then roll in white corn meal. Put in corn husks, allowing four husks to each tamale. Tie with husks' strings. Steam in boiling water with vinegar 3 hours. Soak part of husks in cold water, put two moist ones next to meat, and two dry ones on outer part. Run in hot stove 1 minute to dry, when done serve hot.

Fricassee of Squirrel.

Clean as many young squirrels as required. Cut into joints and lay in salted water for an hour; then wipe each piece dry, season with salt, pepper and ginger, and sprinkle with a little flour.

Put on a fryer with a tablespoonful of butter; when hot, cut up an onion in it and fry light brown; then add the pieces of squirrel and brown slightly; add also 1 or 2 tablespoonfuls tomatoes and 1 tablespoonful Worcestershire sauce. Pour a pint of water over all, add some celery cut up, also a little parsley, cover with a lid and stew until tender, about 2 hours. If the gravy is too thin thicken with a little flour.

Fricassee of Rabbit.

Procure as many young rabbits as required. Clean them, cut into joints and soak in salted water for an hour. Prepare same as fricassee of squirrel. The tomatoes may be omitted if preferred.

Fried Rabbit.

Procure young rabbits, clean them and cut into joints. Lay in salted water for an hour. Wipe dry, season with salt, pepper, and ginger; roll each piece in cracker crumbs or flour, then in beaten egg, and fry in hot butter or lard until brown and tender. If not very young, cover the saucepan while frying.

Fried Squirrel.

Procure young squirrels and prepare same as "Fried Rabbit."

MEAT, FISH AND VEGETABLE SAUCES.

Hollandaise Sauce.

Melt 1 tablespoonful butter, then stir in 1 heaping tablespoonful flour until smooth, and add 1 cupful boiling water. When it boils remove from fire, and stir in one by one yolks of 4 eggs; return to fire, and boil 1 minute. Remove and stir in juice ½ lemon, 1 tablespoonful butter, and 1 teaspoonful of chopped parsley. Stir until smooth, then serve. Half the quantity can be made. To be used with fish, timbales, or croquettes.

Beárnaise Sauce.

Cream 2 oz. fresh butter with 1 scant teaspoonful each of salt and pepper, add the yolks of 4 eggs, stir until light, then add 1 tablespoonful finely-chopped onion, juice of ¼ lemon, and stir into the mixture 2 tablespoonfuls tarragon vinegar and 1 of water (which have been heated together).

Put on the stove in a double boiler, stir until it begins to boil, then add ½ teaspoonful "beef extract," stir until it thickens, then pour over the steak. Can be served hot or cold.

Mushroom Sauce. No 1.

Melt 1 tablespoonful fresh butter in a saucepan, stir in 2 tablespoonfuls flour; when light brown stir in the liquor from 1 can mushrooms. Add 2 teaspoonfuls Worcestershire sauce and 2 of Tomato Catsup, and a pinch of salt. Put in the mushrooms cut in half, and boil 15 minutes.

Mushroom Sauce. No 2.

Brown in a skillet on stove 1 tablespoonful butter with 1 tablespoonful flour. Add 1 cup liquor from mushrooms, pinch of salt and pepper. Let boil up once, then add the mushrooms, and 1 tablespoonful chopped parsley. Boil a few minutes longer and serve.

Brown Sauce.

Brown 1 tablespoonful butter or beef drippings in a skillet, stir in 1 small chopped onion, let brown, then add 1 tablespoonful flour, brown also, then add 1 cup soup stock or hot water. Let thicken and season with chopped parsley, salt, and pepper.

Tomato Sauce.

Brown 1 tablespoonful butter in saucepan with 1 onion, then add 1 tablespoonful flour. When brown stir in one pint tomatoes which have previously been cooked and strained, add also 1 teaspoonful sugar, 1 tablespoonful vinegar, a pinch of salt, pepper, and red pepper, also 1 tablespoonful Tomato Catsup.

Caper Sauce.

Melt 2 tablespoonfuls butter in a saucepan, then add 2 tablespoonfuls flour, ½ teaspoonful salt, then 1 cupful hot water, 1 cupful soup stock. Stir until thick and smooth, then add ½ cupful capers and serve immediately.

Mint Sauce.

Boil in saucepan ½ cupful vinegar with one tablespoonful sugar, chop mint fine, throw it in and let boil once. Remove from fire and set aside until time to use. Serve cold. Or chop mint fine and let stand in cold vinegar 2 hours.

Maitre d'Hotel Butter.

Cream 1 heaping tablespoonful of butter, add ½ teaspoonful salt, pinch pepper, and 1 tablespoonful of lemon juice, then 1 tablespoonful of chopped parsley. Put on ice until ready to serve. Serve with broiled steaks or chops.

Egg Sauce.

Dissolve in a saucepan on stove 2 tablespoonfuls butter, then stir in 2 tablespoonfuls flour, mix smooth and add 2 cupfuls boiling water, stir until smooth and thick. Remove from fire, and add yolks of 3 eggs and juice of one lemon (1 tablespoonful vinegar can be used instead of lemon, if preferred). Add also a little chopped parsley. Serve with boiled fish or tamales.

Apple Sauce.

Core, peel and quarter 6 tart apples. Put them in a saucepan with 1 cupful cold water, add ½ cupful sugar and boil until the apples are very tender and the water is almost all cooked out. Then strain through a colander, put in a bowl and sprinkle a little cinnamon and sugar on top. Serve cold. A little lemon juice improves the flavor.

Cranberry Sauce or Jelly. No. 1.

Get 1 quart nice cranberries, pick clean and wash them, put in a boiler with enough cold water to cover them thoroughly. Let them boil on a quick fire until soft enough to mash, about 45 minutes. Remove from the fire, and pass all through a colander, being careful to mash all the substance possible from the berries.

Put back in a clean saucepan, add 1 good pint sugar and boil on a quick fire until thick as jelly. Pour into small fancy glass dishes and set aside to cool. Serve cold with meat or fowls.

Cranberry Sauce. No. 2.

Put on 2½ cupfuls sugar and 1½ cupfuls water, and let it boil over a quick fire until it begins to get a little thick, or like honey. Add 1 quart of cranberries after they have been cleaned and washed. Cover with a lid until they begin to boil, then remove the lid and let them cook (not too fast) until they are clear or like preserves. If the water cooks out too fast, about half a cupful more may be added. The berries and syrup should look clear when done. About 15 or 20 minutes should be long enough to cook them after the berries are added.

Drawn Butter Sauce.

Put 2 tablespoonfuls fresh butter in a saucepan on the stove to melt (not brown), stir in 2 tablespoonfuls sifted flour until smooth, then stir in slowly 2 cupfuls boiling water, and let it simmer on the side of the stove until it thickens. Season with salt and pepper, stir continually and when it thickens squeeze in the juice of half a lemon.

Cream Sauce for Asparagus or Cauliflower.

Put in a boiler 1 cupful thin sweet cream, or rich milk, and a small lump of butter. When it commences to boil, stir in 1 teaspoonful flour (mixed until smooth with a little cold milk); stir constantly until it thickens, then pour over the well-beaten yolks of 1 or 2 eggs. Season with salt and pepper ; and if desired a little dry mustard may be added. Serve hot or cold.

Whipped Cream Sauce for Asparagus.

Put on to boil, 1 cupful sweet milk ; when it comes to a boil stir in 2 tablespoonfuls flour, that have previously been dissolved in a little cold milk. Stir until very thick, then season with salt and white pepper, and set aside to cool. When cold stir in 1 cupful thickly whipped cream. Serve cold.

Lemon Sauce for Asparagus.

In a fryer put 1 tablespoonful fresh butter, when melted stir in 2 tablespoonfuls flour until smooth, then add gradually the water from 1 can asparagus, being careful to keep smooth. When thickened stir in the beaten yolks of 3 eggs; stir a few minutes, remove from fire and add the juice of 1 or 2 lemons, according to taste Serve cold.

White Sauce for Asparagus.

Melt 1 tablespoonful butter, then stir in 1 tablespoonful flour, stir in ½ cupful water that the asparagus was boiled in, and ½ cupful hot water. Season with salt and pepper. Stir until smooth, let it come to a boil and thicken, then pour over the asparagus.

Cream Mayonnaise. No. 1.

Take 1 tablespoonful yellow mustard and 2 teaspoonfuls flour, and mix with 1 cupful vinegar until smooth, then add it slowly to 4 eggs well beaten. Put on the stove and stir continually until it thickens. When done add salt and white pepper to taste, and just before using, when cold, add ½ cupful sweet cream.

Cream Mayonnaise. No. 2.

Stir until light 5 eggs, a little pepper and salt; then add 1 teaspoonful butter, then 1 cupful vinegar which has been heated with 1 teaspoonful sugar in it. Mix well, put in a double boiler, and stir until thick. Remove from the stove, squeeze in the juice of 1 lemon, and when well mixed add 1 tablespoonful thick sweet cream.

The cream can be omitted if preferred.

French Mayonnaise.

Break 2 raw yolks in a shallow bowl and stir in slowly drop by drop 1 cup French olive oil. Do not beat but stir thoroughly and when it is a stiff, thick mass add gradually a pinch of salt and white pepper, 1 teaspoonful raw mustard and 2 tablespoonfuls lemon juice. Mix well and put on ice until ready to serve.

Mayonnaise Sauce. No 1.

Beat the yolks of 3 raw eggs until very light, add gradually 2 tablespoonfuls olive oil, beat constantly, then stir in the yolks of 2 hard-boiled eggs (which have been rubbed smooth), add a good pinch of pepper, salt, dry mustard, and cayenne pepper.

Heat 1 cup vinegar with 2 teaspoonfuls sugar in it, stir while hot into the egg mixture and when well mixed set back on the stove in a double boiler, and stir until thick. Serve cold.

Mayonnaise. No. 2.

Beat 3 whole eggs until very light, add 2 tablespoonfuls olive oil, stirring constantly, add a good pinch of salt, pepper, mustard, and cayenne pepper.

Heat ½ cup vinegar with 1 teaspoonful sugar in it, stir while hot into the eggs, and put back on the stove in a double boiler and stir until thick. Serve cold.

Tartare Sauce. No. 1.

Beat the yolks of 3 raw eggs until very light, add 2 tablespoonfuls olive oil, stirring constantly, add the yolks of 2 hard-boiled eggs (previously mashed smooth), season with a good pinch of mustard, salt, pepper, and cayenne pepper.

Heat 1 cupful vinegar with 2 teaspoonfuls sugar and pour while hot over the egg mixture. Put back on the stove in a double boiler and stir until thick.

Chop fine, a tiny piece of garlic, a small piece of onion, 2 tablespoonfuls capers, 6 olives, 1 large salt pickle and a little parsley. Add to the sauce after removing from the stove, stir in ½ teaspoonful lemon juice, mix thoroughly and serve cold.

Tartare Sauce. No. 2.

Beat 3 whole eggs until very light, add 2 tablespoonfuls olive oil stirring constantly, add a good pinch of salt, pepper, dry mustard and cayenne. Heat ½ cupful vinegar with 1 teaspoonful sugar, pour while hot over the egg mixture ; put back on the stove in a double boiler and stir until thick. Remove from the fire and add the following ingredients chopped fine, a tiny piece of garlic, a small piece onion, 6 olives, 1 large pickle, 2 tablespoonfuls capers and a little parsley. Add ½ teaspoonful lemon juice. Serve cold.

Tartare Sauce. No. 3.

Break into a bowl the yolks of 2 eggs, then stir briskly in, drop by drop, 1 cupful olive oil. When *perfectly stiff* add juice of ½ lemon, 1 saltspoonful each of salt, pepper and mustard, and a dash of cayenne. Add 2 tablespoonfuls capers, 1 small shallot, ¼ small onion, 2 cucumber pickles and 1 tablespoonful parsley, all chopped fine.

MEATS.

Beef Drippings.

Remove the fat from any kind of *beef* that comes to hand (mutton or veal will not do). Put the fat in a saucepan, add water enough to half cover it, place on the stove, and stew slowly until every bit of the water is cooked out and the pieces of fat are dried up. Then strain through a fine sieve and put aside to use when needed. Put in a glass or stone jar well covered.

Roast Beef.

Fill an iron meat skillet half full of beef drippings or fat, and let it get boiling hot. Lay in the roast without seasoning it, put inside the stove and bake from 45 minutes to one hour according to size. Baste often. Season after it is done.

Roast Beef with Potatoes.

Get what is called second cut, three ribbed piece near short loin part is best. Rub roast well inside and out with salt, pepper, ginger and if desired a tiny piece of garlic. Lay aside for 3 or 4 hours to season thoroughly. When ready to cook, lay in a baking pan, sprinkle a little flour on top, pour a dipper of water in the pan and put in a *hot* oven. Baste often. Allow 1¼ hours for 8 lbs roast or 1½ hours for 10 lbs if wanted medium rare—less if very rare, longer if wanted done.

When ready to serve, skim grease from pan, add a

little more flour, brown, and add a little water, cook a few minutes and serve gravy in sauce boat.

About 30 minutes before meat is done, peel and wash 8 or 10 sound Irish potatoes. Lay around the roast in the pan and baste often with gravy. It gives them a nice flavor.

Rolled Ribs of Beef.

Get 2 or 3 ribs of what is called second cut, have the bones taken out and the meat rolled up and tied.

Put a spoonful of drippings in a meat pan, put in your roast with a wire rack under it and put in the stove. The fire must be *very hot* so that the fat will form a crust outside and keep the meat rare and tender within.

When the top fat is a nice brown, cover with a piece of thin writing paper and baste often through the paper. Bake from ¾ to 1 hour. Do *not* add any water to the meat. Serve with Yorkshire Pudding.

Beef A la Mode.

Secure a nice Round Roast, about 6 lbs. Season well on both sides with salt, pepper and ginger. Heat about a cupful of drippings, or fat in an iron skillet that has a closely fitting top. When hot lay in the roast, add 3 bay leaves, 6 cloves and 1 large onion cut in round slices, keep the onion on top of the meat to prevent browning too quickly. Cover closely, cook over moderate fire 4 hours. Turn the meat occasionally. Keep closely covered and do not add any water. Should be thorougly done. When ready to serve, take up the roast, skim most of the fat from the skillet, and if necessary add a little water and pour the gravy over the meat before sending to the table.

1 glass claret can be added if desired to gravy, and let boil a few minutes.

Wiener Braten.

Secure a lean, round roast weighing 5 or 6 pounds. Put in a bowl, cover with white vinegar and set aside for 24 hours. Then put roast in an oven with a top to it, sprinkle with flour, cut 1 large onion in round slices and lay over it, stick 10 cloves in the meat, put in a little whole mace, ground ginger, and a tiny bit of garlic, a few bay leaves, a few cloves, 1 carrot cut in round pieces, ½ of a turnip cut in small pieces, squeeze the juice of one lemon over all, and cut up the peel and throw in. Put oven on top of stove, cover and let it cook. Do not add any water. Baste occasionally and turn meat when brown on one side.

Put on 1 pint tomatoes, cook well, then mash through sieve, season with salt, pepper, a little ground spice, some chopped parsley, add a small piece cooked ham cut fine, boil up once or twice to thicken, pour over the meat. When almost done, add 1 glass white wine, and let cook a few minutes longer. Must be thoroughly done. Serve with gravy poured over.

Serve with potato pancakes.

Brisket of Beef—Horseradish Sauce.

Cook in the soup as soup meat, but do not cook to pieces. When done, remove from the soup, and make the following

Horseradish Sauce.

Put a fryer on the stove and in it heat 1 tablespoonful fat ; when hot cut up ¼ of an onion in it and fry light brown, then brown in same fryer 1 tablespoonful cracker meal or flour, then add 2 tablespoonfuls grated horseradish, let brown some, then add some soup stock, 1 tablespoonful brown sugar, 2 cloves, 2 bay leaves, salt, pepper and 2 tablespoonfuls vinegar. Let cook a few minutes then add 1 more tablespoonful grated horseradish, and if necessary a little more sugar or vinegar.

Lay the brisket in this sauce and cover on back of stove until ready to serve.

Filet de Boeuf a la Jardinière.

Put filet in pan, with plenty of butter, and bake in oven about ¾ of an hour. Prepare cauliflower, French green peas, and mushrooms. Lay filet on platter, on either end place mushrooms piled, and on one side of platter, cauliflower, on the other, green peas. Garnish with celery tops. Pour mushroom sauce over filet.

GREEN PEAS.

Open can and let soak in cold water about fifteen minutes before cooking. Or put fresh peas in cold water, and cook until tender. Season with teaspoonful of butter, teaspoonful sugar, pinch salt, and pepper. Let come to a boil, drain off liquor, and put peas on platter.

MUSHROOMS.

Brown a bit of butter in skillet, add flour, and brown part of mushroom liquor, chopped parsley, pinch salt and pepper. Then cook mushrooms in it, until tender. Drain off sauce, and set sauce aside, and put mushrooms on either side of platter.

CAULIFLOWER.

Wash well, break head of cauliflower in pieces, cook in salt water until tender. Take cup of soup stock, pour over cauliflower, add pinch salt, pepper, and a bit of butter. Drain gravy, and put cauliflower on side of dish.

Filet or Broiled Tenderloin of Beef. No. 1.

Secure 2½ lbs. Tenderloin of Beef, remove all fat and skin, season with salt and pepper, rub with 1 teaspoonful butter or olive oil, lay on a broiler over moderate coal fire. When done on one side, brown on the other. Serve with slices of lemon.

Filet or Broiled Tenderloin of Beef. No. 2.

Secure 2½ lbs. Tenderloin of Beef, remove all fat and skin. With a sharp knife make two or three cuts across the top of the beef.

Take some of the fat that has been removed from the meat, rub it over a long fryer that has been heated, until well greased and very hot, lay in the tenderloin, cover and let cook 10 minutes, then turn and brown on other side. While meat is cooking, melt in a saucepan 2 tablespoonfuls fresh butter, add 1 teaspoonful salt and ½ teaspoonful pepper. Remove steak to hot platter, pour the butter over it on both sides, and garnish with parsley.

Filet de Boeuf au Champignons.

Prepare the Filet same as for Broiled Tenderloin of Beef No. 2, only do not pour the melted butter over it; instead, after laying on a hot platter, pour over it Mushroom Sauce No. 1.

Filet de Boeuf à la Beàrnaise.

Prepare and broil a 2½ lb. filet as for Broiled Tenderloin of Beef No. 2. Serve on a hot platter, and pour over it a Beàrnaise Sauce.

Broiled Beefsteak.

Have steak from 1 to 1½ inches thick. Remove skin and superfluous fat, but do not remove bone. Wipe with a damp towel. Place in the broiler, and butter each side quickly. Turn until sufficiently done. If broiler is not handy, steak may be put in flat skillet on top of stove, *without* any *fat*, and turned first on one side, then on the other. Spread with fresh butter, or Maitre d'Hotel butter. Serve immediately on hot platter.

Broiled Beefsteak, Mushroom Sauce.

Broil steak same as in foregoing recipe, and pour over it Mushroom Sauce No. 2 just before serving.

Broiled Steak with Tomato or Oyster Sauce.

Prepare steak same way as for plain broiled steak. Melt in saucepan 1 tablespoonful butter, add 1 tablespoonful flour, ½ chopped onion, and let brown. Then add 1 pint stewed tomatoes, teaspoonful sugar, pinch salt, pepper, and tiny pinch cayenne, and 1 tablespoonful chopped parsley. Pour over steak in platter.

OYSTER SAUCE.

Make tomato sauce same as above, adding ½ pint of small oysters to sauce. Let cook until beards of oysters curl, then pour over steak, and serve at once.

Fried Steak with Onions.

Season the steak with salt and pepper, and dredge with flour. If tough, chop on both sides with a sharp knife. Lay in a pan of hot fat, when brown on one side, turn and brown on the other. While the steak is frying, heat some fat in another fryer and drop in 4 or 5 white onions that have been cut up. Fry crisp but not black. Remove the steak to a hot platter, stir 1 tablespoonful flour in the fryer until smooth, add ½ cupful boiling water. Lay the crisp onions over the steak, then over all pour the brown gravy.

Baked Hamburg Steaks.

Soak ⅛ loaf bread in cold water, squeeze dry, mash fine and mix with 2 pounds finely-chopped raw meat. Season with salt, pepper, juice of 1 onion, and 3 eggs, dropped in one by one. Put in baking pan, with butter over, and bake until almost done. Then sprinkle grated bread crumbs over. Pour over 2 cupfuls of tomatoes which have been stewed, strained and seasoned with salt, pepper, and pinch sugar. Arrange meat in high cone shape. Let bake together about 5 minutes more, put on flat platter and serve. Garnish with parsley.

Hamburg Steak.

Chop 2 pounds of the round of beef very fine, season with ½ teaspoonful pepper, pinch salt and onion juice. Shape into flattened balls, and put on broiler, over clear fire. Broil 8 minutes. Can also be fried in hot fat. After balls are done, remove from skillet, brown 1 tablespoonful of flour in the remaining fat, add 1 cupful water, salt, pepper and let boil. Strain before serving. One or two eggs can be added to the meat balls if desired, if they are to be fried.

Filled Calf Shoulder.

Procure shoulder of a young calf, let butcher remove all bones except 2 inches in leg part.

Cut out all the meat, leaving only a little more than the skin so as to be able to stuff it.

Grind very fine the meat that has been removed, add some finely-cut up beef fat, salt, pepper and ginger, ½ of a small onion, a tiny piece garlic and 1 egg. Fill the shoulder with this mixture, sew it up. Put some fat in a meat pan, lay in the shoulder, sprinkle salt and pepper over, also a little flour, pour 2 cups water in, put in oven and bake until well done, basting often. Brown on both sides.

Stuffed Breast of Veal.

Clean veal same as in above recipe, and fill pocket of a 3½ pound breast with this dressing; soak ½ small loaf of white bread in cold water until moist, press dry. Put a tablespoonful of drippings or fat in a skillet, ½ grated onion, and dry the bread in this. Add pinch salt, pepper, ginger, saltspoonful of celery seed, teaspoonful finely-chopped parsley, 1 lb. of finely-chopped or ground raw veal. Mix well, then break in 1 whole egg. Bake veal same as above. The bread dressing can be used without the meat.

Spring Lamb, Mint Sauce.

Wash and clean the meat well, season with salt, pepper and a little onion. Put in a double meat pan, pour in 2 cupfuls water and 1 cupful vinegar. Bake until tender, basting often. Lard the sides of the meat either with meat drippings or fresh butter. Bake a crisp brown. Serve with Mint Sauce.

Spring Lamb with Tomato Sauce.

Prepare the lamb same as for mint sauce, only add 2 whole tomatoes while baking. Instead of mint sauce serve with Tomato Sauce.

Barbecued Lamb.

Get forequarter of lamb, have neck and shoulder cut out by butcher. Take rib part, put in a baking pan, pour 2 cupfuls salt water over it, put in oven and bake until brown, basting very often. When almost done pour ¼ cupful white vinegar over it and baste with it. 20 minutes before serving make the following:

SAUCE.

Put saucepan on fire with 1 tablespoonful fresh butter in it, when melted stir in 2 kitchen-spoonfuls Worcestershire sauce, 2 of Tomato Catsup, and 2 of Durkee's salad dressing. Mix well and send to table in separate sauce boat. Serve over each slice of lamb. Very nice.

Shoulder of lamb can be prepared same way.

Roast Lamb.

Secure a leg or loin of Lamb, must be young. Wash well, dry, and season well with salt, pepper, and ginger. Lay it in a baking pan. Sprinkle a little dry mustard over it. Cut up 1 onion in round slices, lay on top, also 2 or 3 tomatoes cut up, or 2 spoonfuls canned tomatoes. A little Tomato Catsup or Worcester Sauce adds flavor, but can be left out if preferred. Sprinkle a little flour over all, pour 2 cupfuls cold water in the pan and set in a hot oven; baste frequently. If necessary add more water, which must be boiling. Cook 3 hours if 6 lb. roast. Serve with the gravy in separate sauce boat.

Roast Mutton.

Prepare same as Roast Lamb.

Spring Lamb with Green Peas.

Get a quarter of young lamb. Wash and dry well, season with salt, pepper, and ginger and sprinkle with flour. Lay in a roasting pan, cut a few slices of onion over it, pour 2 cupfuls of water in the pan and set in a hot oven; baste frequently. It should be well done. Allow 20 minutes for each pound of lamb when young. Serve with Green Peas.

Stewed Spring Lamb. Piquante.

Season lamb well, cut in 3 inch pieces and put on to stew, with plenty of water. Pour ½ cupful of vinegar in pot, and cut up 1 onion. When lamb is tender stir a little flour in gravy, to thicken, pour 1 pint stewed tomatoes over, 1 small red pepper cut in pieces, and a little chopped parsley. Taste, and if necessary add salt and pepper. Let cook up well together, and serve.

Boiled Leg of Mutton, with Rice and Caper Sauce.

Wipe leg of mutton with a damp towel, remove skin and extra fat. Put in a pan, and cover with boiling water. Keep mutton covered with cloth dipped in flour, to prevent becoming discolored. Add ½ cupful rice to the water. When meat is almost done, add 1 teaspoonful salt. When done, put meat on a platter, and drain rice, and put in a border round meat. Make a caper sauce, and pour over leg before serving.

Pork Roast with Apple Sauce.

Wash well, and season a 5 lb. pork roast. Put in a pan with plenty water. Bake 2 hours, basting often. Dredge with flour, and brown nicely all over. Serve with Apple Sauce.

Veal Roast.

Secure a nice fat, white loin of veal. Wash and wipe dry. Season well with salt, pepper, and ginger, dredge with flour. Lay in a roasting pan, sprinkle bits of butter or some fat over, pour in 1 glass of water, cover tightly, and bake inside the stove basting frequently. Tomatoes can be added if desired. Must be well done.

Brown Hash.

Any kind of cold beef left from the table is palatable when served this way. Cold roast is particularly nice.

Cut the meat in square dice-shaped pieces. Heat 2 tablespoonfuls fat in a saucepan, then brown in it, 1 onion cut up, and 2 tablespoonfuls flour, then add the meat, also 3 or 4 Irish potatoes also cut dice-shape. Season with salt, pepper, and some finely chopped parsley. Cover with water and cook until done. About half an hour. A spoonful or two of tomatoes added to the hash while cooking, gives a nice flavor, but can be omitted if preferred.

Irish Stew.

For this purpose, brisket, bottom of the roast, or any of the less choice and cheaper cuts of meat will do. Season meat well and put on to stew with plenty of water. After it has cooked about an hour, add an onion cut up and 3 potatoes cut in one inch pieces. Stew until meat is tender and potatoes done, then put in 1 can of corn, 1 pint of tomatoes, season with salt and pepper, stew up once, and then serve all together. If fresh tomatoes are used about 6 large ones are necessary, and if fresh corn, the corn cut from 3 ears. Add 1 small red pepper, or $\frac{1}{4}$ of a large one, just before removing from fire, and let cook up once. If fresh vegetables are used, they must cook a little longer in the stew before removing.

Camp Stew.

This stew requires young meat, lamb or veal. Place on the bottom of the pot 3 or 4 slices of bacon. Cut the fresh meat into pieces about one-half the size of the hand, and add it to the bacon. Put in a layer of sliced Irish potatoes, a layer of corn, a layer of onions, a layer of tomatoes, a teaspoonful of butter, a tablespoonful of vinegar, a little parsley, and season highly with salt, pepper and Worcestershire sauce. Let this simmer slowly until done, without adding any water.

Casserole of Rice and Meat.

Boil 1 cupful rice until tender. Chop fine 3 cupfuls cold cooked meat, add 1 teaspoonful chopped onion, a pinch of salt and pepper, 1 egg, 1 saltspoonful celery salt, and 2 teaspoonfuls bread crumbs. If you have any soup stock on hand, add sufficient to moisten well.

Butter a mold, line with rice $\frac{1}{2}$ inch thick, put in meat, then cover with rice. Cover closely and steam 45 minutes. Serve with brown gravy or tomato sauce.

Boiled Ham.

Secure a nice lean ham, about 10 pounds, wash it, and dry thoroughly. Put in a large boiler and cover with water. Let boil until done, about 2½ hours. Remove from the water, lift off the upper skin, trim neatly, stick about 10 cloves in the upper surface, sprinkle granulated sugar over it lightly, place in a roasting pan, run in a hot stove, and brown quickly, and set aside to cool. Serve cold or warm.

Broiled Ham.

Cut from the boneless part, the number of slices required, having them as thin as possible. Pare off the skin, arrange on a hot broiler, and broil 2 minutes on each side. Lay on a hot platter, garnish with parsley, and serve.

Broiled Lamb Chops.

Secure as many rib lamb chops as required. Wipe dry, season with salt and pepper; place them on a broiler over a hot coal fire, first rubbing the broiler with butter, so that they will not stick. When done on one side turn on the other. Serve on a hot platter with thin slices of lemon and sprigs of parsley. Pour melted butter over each chop, and wrap the end of the bone of each chop with fancy cut writing paper.

Pork Chops.

Get nice, thick, pork chops, pare and flatten nicely. Season with salt and pepper, and sprinkle a little flour over each chop. Put on a fryer with some fat or beef drippings, when hot lay in the chops, brown well on one side, then turn and brown on the other side.

Spare Ribs. No. 1.

Secure as many pounds of spare ribs as required, wipe and dry well, season with salt and pepper; lay in a baking pan, and run in a hot oven. When brown on one side turn and brown on the other, and serve.

Spare Ribs. No. 2.

Secure as many pounds of spare ribs as required, wipe and dry well, season with salt and pepper, lay in a baking pan, sprinkle flour on top, and add a cupful of water. Run in a hot oven, and when brown skim off the grease, stir in 1 spoonful of flour, and if necessary add a little more water, and cook a few minutes longer, basting often. Serve with the gravy poured over.

Breaded Veal Cutlets.

Secure as many loin veal cutlets, if possible, as required. Wipe and dry them well, season with salt and pepper, dip them in beaten egg, then in cracker meal, and fry in a skillet with hot fat or beef drippings. Fry brown on both sides, and serve on a hot platter with sprigs of parsley.

Veal Cutlets Breaded with Tomato or White Sauce.

Cover the cutlets with boiling water, let stand 1 minute, drain and wipe dry.

Dip the cutlets first in beaten egg, then in bread crumbs. Put 2 tablespoonfuls drippings in a skillet, when hot lay in the cutlets and fry brown on both sides. Serve either with Tomato Sauce or White Sauce. Garnish with parsley.

Fried Brains.

Scald and clean the brains. Cut in pieces about the size of an oyster, wipe dry. Dip in beaten eggs, then roll in cracker meal seasoned with salt and pepper, and fry in boiling fat or lard.

Sweet Sour Brains.

Scald and clean the brains. Put in saucepan ¾ cupful vinegar and ½ cupful water, add one half onion cut in round slices, one half lemon cut in round slices, 3 cloves, 2 bay leaves and 12 raisins. When the mixture begins to boil, add the brains and cook until well done. Remove the brains, and to liquor add 3 tablespoonfuls white sugar (which have been melted and browned without water). Stir in one tablespoonful flour dissolved with a little water, add more sugar if wanted. Let boil a few minutes and when thickened pour over the brains. Serve cold.

Fried Sweetbreads.

Scald sweetbreads in hot water until tender, skin and clean them. Dip first in beaten eggs, then in cracker meal and fry in boiling fat. Serve with green peas.

Fried Calf Liver.

Cut liver in thin slices, season with salt and pepper, sprinkle a little flour over each slice. Put in a skillet which has been heated, with drippings or lard in it, cover with a top, fry slowly until both sides are done. Requires about 15 minutes.

Fried Tripe.

Scald and clean the tripe thoroughly. Cut in small square pieces, make a thin batter of flour, milk and eggs, season the tripe with salt and pepper, dip in the batter and fry in hot fat.

Stewed Tripe.

Scald and clean the tripe well. Cut in narrow strips as long as a finger.
Put on a saucepan with 1 tablespoonful butter or

drippings in it, drop in ¼ onion cut fine, let brown, then add 1 heaping tablespoonful flour, brown lightly, then stir in 3 cups of water. Add the tripe and boil until tender. Add some finely-chopped parsley before tripe is done.

Stewed Kidneys.

Wash kidneys well, and steam until tender in weak salt water. Make a brown gravy, cut kidneys in 1 inch pieces, cook up in gravy. Add one teaspoonful chopped parsley, and a few drops of lemon juice. The French cooks add a wineglassful of sherry wine, but it is not absolutely necessary.

Sausage Meat.

Procure as much ground sausage meat as required, season with salt and pepper if required, and form into flat balls.

Fry in a hot skillet, but do not grease the skillet much as they have enough grease in them. Serve very hot, garnish with parsley.

Liver Sausage.

Put on the sausages in cold water, and let it come to a boil, then remove the sausages, being careful not to break them, and put in a fryer with some warm fat, (not too hot or they will burst); put over a hot fire, cover with a lid and fry brown on both sides; about 20 minutes. Serve hot with potatoes.

Vienna Sausage.

Wash, and put on in boiling water. Boil 10 minutes, fill a deep dish with hot water, put sausages in, cover, and serve in hot water. To be eaten with grated horseradish or French mustard.

Smoked Sausages.

Prepare like Vienna sausages, only boiling 20 minutes instead of 10 minutes.

Pork Sausage.

Put in skillet with a little water to prevent scorching, and fry until water is absorbed and grease is drawn out from sausage. Brown on one side, then the other, and serve hot.

KITCHEN TIME TABLE AND TABLE OF WEIGHTS AND MEASURES.

Kitchen Time Table.
Boiling.

			Baked		
Potatoes,	30	minutes	Potatoes,	45	minutes
String Beans,	2	hours	Sweet Potatoes	1	hour
Lima Beans,	1½	"	Beans,	6	"
Sweet Potatoes,	¾	"	Biscuit,	20	minutes
Green Peas,	¾	"	Turkey,	2 to 3	hours
Green Corn,	20	minutes	Roast,	1½	"
Asparagus,	30	"	[medium rare 8 lbs.]		
Spinach,	20	"	Ducks,	2	hours
Fresh Tomatoes,	30	"	Fish,	¾	"
Canned "	20	"	Mutton, 8 lbs.,	3	"
New Cabbage,	1	hour	Veal, " "	3	"
Beets,	1	"	Lamb, " "	3	"
Squash,	¾	"			
Carrots,	1	"			
Cauliflower,	20	minutes			
Onions,	30	"			
Parsnips,	45	"			
Macaroni,	20	"			
Rice,	30	"			
Cucumbers,	20	"			

Table of Weights and Measures.

3 teaspoonfuls liquid,	equal	1 tablespoonful
2 gills, -	"	1 cup or ½ pint
2 cupfuls,	"	1 pint
4 tablespoonfuls,	"	1 wineglassful
8 "	"	1 gill
2 cupfuls granulated sugar,	"	1 lb.

2½ cupfuls powdered sugar,   equal   1 lb.
1½ tablespoonfuls granulated sugar,   1 ounce.
10 large eggs,   equal   1 lb.
2 tablespoonful flour,   "   1 ounce.
1   "   butter,   "   1   "
1 cupful   "   "   ½ lb.
4 cupfuls sifted flour,   "   1 qt. or 1 lb.

VEGETABLES.

Boiled Potatoes in Jackets.

Put potatoes on about half an hour before needed in cold water with a little salt ; cook steadily until a fork will easily pierce them. Then pour off every drop of water, cover tightly, set on back of stove to dry, shake the saucepan often and when dry serve at once.

Boiled Potatoes without the Skin.

Pare off as little of the skin as possible. Lay in cold water half an hour; put in a saucepan with just enough cold water to cover, add salt, and boil until tender. Pour off every drop of water, add a lump of butter, salt and pepper, shake the pot a few times on the stove, and serve at once.

Mashed Potatoes.

Prepare the potatoes same as for " Boiled Potatoes without the Skin "; when boiled, mash until perfectly smooth, add 1 teaspoonful butter, salt and pepper to taste, and ½ cupful milk or cream. Be careful to get perfectly smooth, and serve as soon as prepared. Potatoes prepared this way and put cone shaped in a pan, with beaten yolk of egg spread over, can be baked inside the oven and are very nice.

Potato Vermicelli.

Boil the potatoes same as for " Boiled Potatoes without the Skin." When done, run them lightly through a patent potato masher into the dish in which they are to be served. Sprinkle salt and pepper over, and serve at once.

Potato Cakes.

Boil 5 or 6 potatoes same as for "Boiled Potatoes without the Skin." When done, mash them and season with salt and pepper, add 1 or 2 eggs well beaten, a little butter, and a little flour. Form into small cakes, and fry them in very hot lard or fat.

Potato Croquettes.

Boil about 5 Irish potatoes same as for "Boiled Potatoes without the Skin." Mash smooth, then add yolks of 2 eggs, and a tiny piece of butter; season with salt and pepper, form them into croquettes, dip in beaten egg, and fry in hot fat.

Potato Soufle.

Boil five good-sized potatoes until done; mash them through a sieve or potato masher. Heat ½ cupful milk with 1 tablespoonful butter in it, and add to the potatoes; salt and pepper to taste. Then add 3 eggs, yolks and whites beaten separately. Mix lightly, pour in a buttered pan, and bake until brown in a quick oven.

Potatoes with Cream.

Boil 5 nice potatoes, cut them in squares. Melt 1 tablespoonful fresh butter in saucepan (not brown), stir in 1 tablespoonful flour until smooth, add 1 cupful sweet cream (or milk), pinch of salt and pepper, and some finely-chopped parsley. When it comes to a boil, add the potatoes, let boil up once or twice, and serve. Cold boiled potatoes are nice prepared this way.

Baked Potatoes.

Select smooth, large potatoes, and bake in a quick oven until soft, about ¾ of an hour. If a tiny piece is cut off both ends of the potatoes before putting in the stove, it will allow the steam to escape and make them more mealy.

Stuffed Potatoes.

Bake as many fine potatoes as desired, without cutting off the ends. Cut each potato in half, lengthwise, with a sharp knife. Scrape out the inside of each half with a spoon, being careful not to break the shells. Now run the scraped potato through a sieve or potato masher, season with salt and pepper, add half teaspoonful sweet cream or milk for each potato, add a lump of butter, mash smooth; then fill each half with this mixture, sprinkle cracker crumbs, and bits of butter over and brown them inside the stove. Serve at once.

Stuffed Potatoes with Meat.

Bake 6, fine, large, potatoes without cutting off the ends. Prepare same as "Stuffed Potatoes," and to the scraped insides add 1 large tablespoonful butter, season with salt and pepper, add ½ lb. finely ground raw meat, which has previously been seasoned with salt and pepper. Fill each half of shell with mixture, place in oven without putting together, and bake until meat is done. Serve hot.

Cold cooked beef ground fine can be substituted for the raw beef.

New Potatoes.

Scrape the potatoes and lay in cold water half an hour. Put on in cold water with a little salt added; when done pour off all the water, and pour over them 1 cupful milk or sweet cream, with 2 teaspoonfuls flour or cornstarch added, add 1 teaspoonful fresh butter, some finely-chopped parsley. Let boil up once or twice, and serve. Old potatoes can be prepared same way.

Imitation New Potatoes.

Secure a potato cutter, and with it cut the old potatoes (after they have been pared) to the size of nuts. Prepare same as in the above recipe, or they can be fried by dropping them in very hot fat.

French Fried Potatoes.

Peel and wash 4 large potatoes, cut them in slices $\frac{1}{4}$ of an inch in thickness. Drop them in a skillet of hot fat and cook (not too fast); when they are soft, remove from the fat, heat the grease to the boiling point, drop the potatoes back in and brown all over. Sprinkle salt over, and serve.

Lyonnaise Potatoes.

Cut cold boiled potatoes in small pieces, and season with salt and pepper. Melt 1 tablespoonful butter in skillet, and fry in it ½ onion chopped fine, until onion is yellow. Then add potatoes and fry brown, using a fork to stir to prevent breaking. Add a little chopped parsley, and serve on a hot dish.

Potatoes Browned Whole.

Select nice, sound, small potatoes, pare off as little of the skins as possible, lay in cold water half an hour. Have some fat or beef dripping very hot, lay in the potatoes, brown lightly, then pour in 1 or 2 spoonfuls cold water, cover tightly, and brown all over nicely.

Saratoga Chips.

Peel 3 large potatoes and cut them in very thin round slices with a patent potato knife or cutter. Lay in cold water for half an hour. Drain and dry thoroughly, and drop the pieces (a few at a time) into boiling lard or fat. Brown nicely, remove with a skimmer, lay on brown paper a few minutes to absorb the grease, sprinkle salt over them and serve.

Julienne Potatoes.

Wash and peel four large potatoes, slice and strip lengthwise in tiny strips, as fine as a straw. Soak in cold salt water half an hour, then drain, and fry in plenty of boiling fat until light brown. Fry carefully as they burn easily.

Stewed Potatoes.

Put a tablespoonful of beef drippings or butter in a spider, when hot drop in 1 onion cut in pieces, brown lightly, then add 1 tablespoonful flour and when slightly brown add the potatoes which have previously been peeled, washed, and quartered. Season with salt and pepper, cover closely, and stew until tender, add some soup stock, boil a few minutes longer and serve.

Hash Brown Potatoes.

Boil 6 large potatoes, and set aside until perfectly cold. Those boiled in jackets the day previously are best. Cut them in very small dice shape pieces, season with salt, pepper, and some chopped parsley. Heat some good butter in a spider, when hot, pour in the potatoes. Give them the shape of an omelet. Let them brown on the bottom, then run them in a hot oven and brown on top. Slip them into a platter, being careful not to disturb the shape, and serve.

Escalloped Potatoes.

Peel potatoes, and slice very thin, in round slices. Butter a baking pan, put a layer of potatoes, season with salt and pepper, and bits of butter, another layer of potatoes, then seasoning, and so on. Pour a scant cup of milk over whole, and bake in oven.

Potato Balls.

Boil 4 large Irish potatoes until done. Rub through a sieve or potato masher. Cream well in a bowl, add 2 whole eggs, 2 cupfuls flour, and salt to taste.

Fry some bread cubes or croutons in hot butter. Now make the potato paste into good-size balls, putting some of the fried bread cubes in the center of each ball. The dough must be rolled around the bread, same as apple dumplings. Boil the balls in boiling salt water in uncovered kettle for 15 minutes. Serve in dish with cream sauce over them.

CREAM SAUCE.

Put on one cup rich milk to boil, with one teaspoonful butter in it, thicken with one teaspoonful flour. Pour when boiling over beaten yolks of 2 eggs, and add a little salt. Pour over balls before sending to table.

Potatoes au Parmesan.

Peel Irish potatoes, and cut small with potato cutter. Put on to boil in salt water, cook until tender but not broken. Mix 4 tablespoonfuls of grated bread crumbs, 2 tablespoonfuls of grated cheese, 1 tablespoonful chopped parsley, and season with salt and pepper. Dip potatoes in beaten egg, then in the mixture, and fry in boiling fat. Drain, and dish up in hot napkin, decorated with fresh sprigs of parsley.

Baked Sweet Potatoes.

Select sound potatoes of uniform size, wash well, cut off a very small piece at each end, and bake in oven until done, about three-quarters of an hour. Remove from the oven, put in a pan, and keep in the warmer about half an hour. This will make them soft.

Boiled Sweet Potatoes.

Wash the potatoes well, put on in cold water and boil until done, then drain all the water off, and dry for a few minutes.

Sweet Potato Croquettes.

Boil 3 medium size potatoes until done, then peel them and mash until perfectly smooth. Add yolks of 2 eggs, a small lump butter, 1 tablespoonful sweet cream, salt and pepper. Form into croquettes, dip in beaten egg and fry in hot fat.

Fried Sweet Potatoes.

Take large potatoes, peel and slice about quarter of an inch thick. Lay in salt water about half an hour; fry in hot lard, browning on both sides. Boiled sweet potatoes can be sliced and fried this same way. Sprinkle lightly with sugar before serving.

Candied Yams.

Peel 4, large, sweet potatoes, selecting yellow yams, and slice lengthwise. Steam with a little butter, water, salt and pepper. When tender drain off water, and pour over potatoes, 1 cupful dark, New Orleans molasses. Put in baking-pan, and bake in oven until molasses candies over the potatoes. Serve in same dish it was baked in.

Sugared Yams.

Boil 4 large yellow yam potatoes until done, drain, peel, and cut them lengthwise in half inch slices. Put one half the potatoes in pudding dish, sprinkle with ¼ cupful brown sugar, cinnamon, and bits of fresh butter, put on other layer of potatoes, sprinkle with sugar, butter, and cinnamon same as before, pour ½ cupful cold water over all, and put in stove until brown. Serve in same dish in which it is baked.

Sweet Potato Puree.

Boil 5 medium size sweet potatoes. When done mash through a potato masher until perfectly smooth.

Add butter size of an egg, 2 whole eggs, ¼ teaspoonful cinnamon, 1 scant tablespoonful brown sugar, ¼ cupful milk. Cream well together, put in pudding dish in which it is to be served and bake in oven until brown.

Farina Dumplings.

Beat yolks of 4 eggs with 2 kitchen spoonfuls of goose fat, turkey or chicken fat, but if these are not convenient, clear beef drippings will do. Put in enough farina to make a good batter. Beat whites of 4 eggs to a stiff froth with pinch salt, and stir in batter. Put on in large boiler sufficient water to boil dumplings and add a handful of salt. When boiling drop in by tablespoonfuls. Boil 1 hour. This quantity makes 20 dumplings. Half quantity can be used.

Yorkshire Pudding.

Put 6 heaping tablespoonfuls flour in a bowl with 1 teaspoonful salt, stir gradually into it about ½ pint milk, which should make a thick batter, but fall easily from the spoon; when smooth add 3 well-beaten eggs, beat well together and bake in a shallow pan a little longer than it is broad. Bake until it is solid within and brown without. The grease from under a roast can be poured around the pudding, it should then be baked 15 minutes longer. This pudding is nice served with Roast Beef.

Rice Plain Boiled.

Clean and wash 1 cupful rice. Put in a saucepan and cover with cold water, add a pinch of salt, put on the lid and boil 20 minutes. Drain off the water, cover again, set on the back of the stove, and let steam until dry.

Sweet Rice.

Clean and wash 1 cupful rice. Put on to boil with cold water, add a pinch of salt. When done, drain off the water, if any, add 1 pint milk, stir in and let boil 5 minutes. Dish up, then sprinkle sugar and cinnamon generously over the top. The yolk of an egg can be added just before dishing up if desired.

Rice Croquettes.

Put on with cold water 1 cupful rice, and let boil until tender. Drain water off and mix with rice, 1 tablespoonful of butter, yolks 3 eggs, and pinch salt. About a tablespoonful of flour can be added to make croquettes hold together. Beat whites of 3 eggs to a stiff froth, mix in last; shape into croquettes, and fry in hot fat. Place on platter and put a lump of jelly on top of each croquette.

Pilaff.

Put 2 cupfuls of water on to boil, add juice of 2 tomatoes, and pinch of salt. When boiling, add 1 cupful rice, and let cook until water has evaporated. Then add melted butter, mix well, and keep in hot place, covered, until ready to serve.

Apples with Rice.

Peel and core 6 sound apples, put on in a saucepan with 3 tablespoonfuls sugar and ½ cupful cold water. Meanwhile, boil quarter of a pound of rice in a pint and a half of milk, add a little salt. When the apples are done, lay them in a pudding pan, being careful not to break them. Pour the boiled rice over them and put in a moderate oven for 10 minutes. Serve with

VANILLA SAUCE.

Put half a pound granulated sugar in a saucepan with 2 cupfuls cold water. Boil until it gets like syrup. Flavor with vanilla.

Green Corn Boiled. No. 1.

Select young, tender ears of corn, pare off the outer leaves, leave enough of the inner ones to cover the corn while boiling. Pull down the inner leaves, being careful not to break them off, and remove all the silk from the corn. Then straighten up the inner leaves and with a piece of corn shuck tie the leaves at the top so that the corn will be closely enveloped. Soak in cold water 1 hour, then boil for 20 minutes in boiling salt water. Serve on a folded napkin. Boiling the corn this way prevents it from turning yellow, and retains the sweetness.

Green Corn Boiled. No. 2.

Select tender young ears of corn, pull off all the leaves and remove the silk; soak in cold water 1 hour, then boil in boiling salt water for 20 minutes and serve.

Fried Corn.

To 1 pint of green corn cut from the cob, add ½ cupful milk, 1 tablespoonful butter, salt and pepper to taste. Put in a frying pan, let cook until tender, then fry a light brown. Canned corn can be prepared same way.

Stewed Corn.

To ½ dozen large ears grated green corn, or corn cut from the cob, add 1 cupful sweet milk, butter size of an egg, ½ teaspoonful sugar, salt and pepper to taste. Cook until done, about 30 minutes, beat in 1 egg and cook a few minutes longer. Canned corn can be prepared same way.

Succotash.

Boil 6 ears of green corn until tender, and scrape from the cob. Boil half the quantity of Lima beans that you have corn until tender. Drain off the water, mix with the corn, season with salt and pepper, ½ cupful milk and lump of butter; cook a few minutes. If necessary, thicken with a little flour. String beans can be prepared same way with corn.

Fresh Corn Fritters.

Grate corn from 6 ears, stir in yolks of 2 or 3 eggs, pinch salt and pepper. Beat whites separately, and mix lightly. Grease a hot skillet, put a spoonful of batter for every fritter, into the pan, brown on one side, then on the other, and serve hot. If corn is old and tough, 1 tablespoonful milk must be added to prevent starchiness.

Canned Corn Fritters.

Open 1 can of corn, and chop and mash very fine. Add 1 tablespoonful butter, 1 tablespoonful flour, pinch salt and pepper. Drop in 3 whole eggs, one at a time, stirring briskly as each egg is added. Grease frying pan, drop spoonful of batter in, brown on one side, then on the other, and serve hot.

Corn Pudding.

Grate corn from 8 ears, mix in 4 well-beaten eggs, 1 cupful sweet milk, 1 tablespoonful sugar, pinch salt and pepper, 1 tablespoonful fresh butter. Mix well, put in baking pan, and bake until it is firm. Brown on top.

Cream String Beans.

Cut off the tops and bottoms and "string" carefully, 1 pint tender *yellow wax beans*. Lay in cold water 15 minutes. Drain, then put on in cold water to cover them, and boil until tender. When tender pour off every drop of water. Stir 2 tablespoonfuls flour until smooth in 1 cupful milk; pour over the beans, add 1 teaspoonful butter, season with salt and pepper, and stir gently until thick, being careful not to break the beans. Do not let stand long after milk is added.

Stewed String Beans.

Boil for about 1 hour a small piece of fat meat, bottom of roast will serve, or a piece of the soup meat. Some prefer a piece of pork or bacon. Skim well. String the beans, cut them in half crosswise, then in half lengthwise, wash in cold water, and put on to boil in cold water. When water is boiling, remove beans and put in same pot with meat, and let cook from 1 hour to 1½ hours, according to the tenderness of the beans. Thicken gravy with a little flour, season with salt and pepper, and serve beans in same dish with meat.

String Beans Sweet and Sour.

String the beans, cut in half, crosswise, then in half, lengthwise. Put on to boil in cold water. Cook from 1 to 1½ hours, dependent on the tenderness of the beans. Brown in a frying pan, ½ cup granulated sugar, and when melted, stir in 1 tablespoonful flour, mix well, then add ½ cupful vinegar, pinch salt and pepper and 1 cupful of water beans were boiled in. Stir the whole smooth, add beans and let all come to a boil.

Sweet Potatoes cut in small squares, and steamed, can be prepared same way.

Lima Beans.

After soaking the beans in cold water 15 minutes, put on in cold water and boil until tender, drain off the water, season with salt and pepper, add 2 tablespoonfuls sweet cream for every pint of beans, a small piece of butter, cook up once or twice and serve.

Boston Baked Beans.

Soak 1 quart beans in cold water for 2 hours; then drain and add salt and pepper to taste, ½ teaspoonful mustard, and ½ teacupful molasses. Put in an earthen bean pot, put ½ lb of salt pork well streaked with lean, on top of beans, then pour in enough warm water to cover all.

Bake in oven of even temperature for 12 hours. As the water gradually evaporates, more should be added; care should be taken to keep the beans covered. This must be done until beans are almost ready to be taken out, when no more water should be added, so that they will not be so moist as to be mashed or broken. The pot may remain where it will simply keep hot for any length of time without injury. Half this quantity is sufficient for medium size family. Serve with Brown Bread.

Baked Yankee Beans.

Wash beans well, and if possible soak in cold water over night. If not, soak in cold water at least 1 hour before cooking. Drain water off, and put on to boil with fresh cold water. Boil 3 hours. Drain off water, put beans in baking dish, with a few small pieces of pork, bacon, or fat beef. Add pinch pepper, and if convenient 1 cupful soup stock. The last can be omitted. Put lumps of fresh butter over top, and bake in oven, at least 1 hour. Let top brown. If any of the dish is left, can be eaten cold next day, with vinegar poured over.

Spinach.

Pick well, clean, and cut off the stems of 2 bunches of spinach. Wash thoroughly and soak in cold water 1 hour.

Put on in cold water to cover it, boil until done, about 20 minutes. Remove from the fire, pour into a colander, let all the water drain off, and pour cold water over it five or six times, while it is in the colander. Or hold it under the cold water faucet, and let the water run over it. This takes out the strong taste. Now with the hands squeeze out every drop of water, lay on a board and chop the spinach as fine as possible.

Heat 1 spoonful beef drippings in a fryer, add a small piece of chopped onion; when brown, add 1 tablespoonful flour or cracker meal, brown lightly, then add the chopped spinach. Fry a few minutes, then add 2 cupfuls soup stock or water, if soup stock cannot be had.' Season with salt, pepper and ginger. Cook 10 minutes, stirring occasionally. Serve with hard-boiled eggs sliced over. Chopped sausage can be added if desired before dishing up.

Stuffed Egg Plant With Tomatoes.

Parboil the egg plant until tender, not soft (put on in cold water). Cut in half crosswise with a sharp knife; scrape out the inside, being careful not to put a hole in the frame.

Chop very fine half of a small onion, put in a saucepan in which 2 spoonfuls butter have been heated, cook until light brown, add the scooped out egg plant, and 2 spoonfuls tomatoes. Cook for 10 minutes. Remove from the fire, season with salt, pepper, and add 2 eggs, and if too soft a little cracker meal. Fill both halves with this mixture, sprinkle cracker crumbs and bits of butter over each one. Put in a covered pan, with a little soup stock over, put inside the oven, baste often and brown nicely.

Baked Egg Plant.

Parboil egg plant, drain off water, scoop meat from egg plant, being careful not to break the skin in any other place than opening. Brown a little butter on stove, add egg plant, some bread crumbs, pinch salt and pepper, and yolk of 1 egg. Mix well together, and refill shell of egg plant. Bake in a pan inside stove, and baste with butter.

Fried Egg Plant.

Peel and slice raw egg plant, and put in cold salt water, about 15 minutes before frying. Have fat very hot in frying pan, dry slices of egg plant, dredge with flour, and brown in fat. Serve hot.

The slices of egg plant can be dipped in batter instead of flour if preferred.

Egg Plant Fritters.

Boil egg plant until tender, putting it on with cold water. Remove meat from shell, mash fine, add pinch of salt and pepper, 2 tablespoonfuls of flour, and two well-beaten eggs. Mix well. Put a very little fat in skillet, and when hot, drop in the batter, a spoonful to every fritter. Fry brown on one side, then on the other. Serve hot.

Stuffed Squash.

Wash the squash, put on in cold water and parboil until tender, not soft. When tender cut each squash in half crosswise; take out the inside, being careful not to break the shells. Put on a fryer with 2 tablespoonfuls butter or fat, when hot lay in ½ onion cut fine, brown lightly, then put in a handful soaked bread from which all the water has been squeezed, add the squash which has been scraped out, fry all together for 15 minutes, stirring occasionally. Remove from the fire, season with salt and pepper, add 2 whole eggs, mix well and fill each half with the mixture. Sprinkle cracker meal and bits of butter on top, put in the stove and brown nicely.

Stewed Squash.

Peel squash, cut in quarters, put on to boil in cold water, and cook until tender. Drain water off, mash fine and smooth, add ½ cupful milk or cream, 1 tablespoonful of butter, pinch salt and pepper, and put back on stove to keep hot. Beat well with a spoon to make light and smooth.

Oyster Plant Fritters.

Scrape oyster plant, boil in salt water until very soft. Drain water off and mash very fine; add 2 beaten eggs, 1 tablespoonful of butter, 1 tablespoonful of milk, 1 tablespoonful of flour, pinch salt and pepper. Grease frying pan, drop spoonful batter, brown on one side, then on the other. Serve hot.

Fried Oyster Plant.

Scrape oyster plant and boil in weak salted water until tender. Cut in 4 strips lengthwise, dredge with flour, salt, and fry in hot fat.

Parsnips.

First scrape parsnips, then boil in weak salt water until tender, drain, and put in white sauce. Oyster plant may be prepared same way.

White Sauce.

1 cupful milk, heated. Melt 1 tablespoonful butter in saucepan, add 1 tablespoonful flour, pinch salt and white pepper, and then hot milk. Stir until smooth, add parsnips, and let whole boil up once.

Steamboat Cabbage.

Pare off the outer leaves from a medium sized cabbage; cut into quarters, wash thoroughly, and put in a saucepan covering it with salted hot water. Boil 10 minutes, drain off this water, then add more boiling water and boil until tender. Drain again, then add salt, pepper, 1 teaspoonful of butter and 2 tablespoonfuls sweet cream. Boil up once or twice and serve.

Stuffed Cabbage with Meat.

Use a hard head of white cabbage. Remove carefully half a dozen of the outer leaves. Cut a good sized circle in the top with a sharp knife; reserve a few pieces cut off the top, and then remove the inside of the cabbage leaving only a frame, but be very careful not to cut into it or the dressing will escape. Now put the frame in salted water and parboil for 10 minutes.

Chop fine as much of the inside of the cabbage as you think necessary to fill with, cover with water and boil until tender.

Take ¼ pound cooked pork or ham, chop or grind very fine, mix with the finely-chopped cabbage, season highly with salt, pepper, ginger and cayenne pepper. Rub the frame inside and out with pepper and salt, put in the stuffing. Cover with the top that has been reserved, and tie around on the outer leaves that have been removed.

Put the stuffed cabbage in a pan or oven with a top to it; pour some soup stock or water over it, put in stove, cover over, baste often and let cook until done and brown, about 1 hour.

Stuffed Cabbage With Bread.

Prepare the cabbage same as for "stuffed cabbage with meat." After parboiling fill with the following:

Cut up the inside of the cabbage in very small pieces, put on in cold water and boil until tender. Soak ⅛ loaf baker's bread in cold water and squeeze out all the water.

Put on a fryer with 2 spoonfuls butter; when hot

put in the soaked bread and the cooked cabbage, fry until it leaves the side of the fryer. Remove to a bowl, season with salt, pepper, ginger, add 2 eggs, mix well, fill in the cabbage, put on the top, tie the outside leaves around and bake same as with meat.

Stuffed Cabbage with Chestnut Dressing.

Prepare same as for above, only adding 1 cupful of cooked chestnuts chopped fine, to the filling.

Red Cabbage.

First cut the cabbage up fine with a sharp knife or slaw cutter, then put it in a colander and pour boiling water over it 2 or 3 times to take some of the coloring out, but not all.

Heat 1 tablespoonful fat in saucepan, cut up 1 onion and drop in, also add the cut up cabbage, put cover on saucepan for 10 minutes, then add enough cold water to cover the cabbage, add 2 bay leaves, a little salt, and boil until tender, then season to taste with sugar and a little vinegar, thicken with 1 spoonful flour mixed with the vinegar, and serve.

Kohlraben.

Peel and slice in slices like turnips. Lay in cold water half an hour. Drain and put on in a saucepan with cold water, adding a little salt. Boil until very tender, being careful not to break the slices.

Drain off every drop of water, put into the dish in which they are to be served, and pour over them the following

CREAM SAUCE.

Put on 1 cupful milk to boil, add 1 teaspoonful fresh butter, salt and pepper; thicken with 2 teaspoonfuls flour and pour over yolk of 1 egg well beaten. Pour over the kohlraben, and serve at once.

Kohlraben.

Wash kohlraben well, cut off bottoms, and let greens soak in cold water until ready for use. Peel the turnip-looking part, cut in quarters and boil in cold water until tender. Put greens on in another pan with cold water, and boil until tender. Drain through a colander, pour greens on a wooden board, and chop perfectly fine and smooth. Brown a tablespoonful of flour in a tablespoonful of fat in skillet, and when hot, put in chopped greens. Add the white part of the kohlraben cut in dice, pinch salt, and pepper, and cupful soup stock. Let cook up together, and serve hot.

Sauerkraut.

Get 1 quart best sauerkraut, also 3 lbs. of nice brisket with plenty hard fat on it.

Lay one-half of the kraut in the bottom of a large saucepan, sprinkle with flour, put the piece of brisket on top, then cover with the other kraut, sprinkle a little more flour over this layer. Cover the whole with cold water, add 2 bay leaves, put a top on, and boil until tender, about 2 hours. When tender, season with brown sugar to taste, add a little more vinegar if necessary, and thicken with 1 or 2 tablespoonfuls flour. Cook a few minutes longer, and serve with Mashed Potatoes, Potato or Farina Dumpling.

Sauerkraut.

Put a small piece of fat meat, brisket, or bottom of the roast will do, in a pot with cold water, and boil 1 hour, or can be put in the soup. Skim well. Put a pint of sauerkraut in with this, add 2 tablespoonfuls of granulated sugar, ½ cupful white vinegar, 1 teacupful wine, pinch salt and pepper. Cook 2 hours, and serve hot. To be eaten with Farina or Potato Dumplings.

Turnips.

Pare, and cut in round slices 6 white turnips. Lay in cold water half an hour. Drain, then put on in cold salted water and boil until half done; then add 2 sound Irish potatoes cut in round slices. Boil the whole until well done, then drain all the water off and with a potato masher mash until smooth. Heat 1 tablespoonful beef drippings or fat in a saucepan, brown in it 1 tablespoonful flour, then add the mashed potatoes and turnips. Stir in 1 spoonful soup stock, add 1 teaspoonful sugar, season with salt and pepper, cook a few minutes and serve.

Creamed Turnips.

Peel and cut turnips in small pieces. Put on in boiling water, and cook until tender. Drain water off, and set aside. Melt in saucepan 1 tablespoonful butter, add 1 tablespoonful flour, pinch salt, and pepper, and 1 cupful hot milk. Stir until smooth, add turnips, and let whole come to a boil.

Stewed Tomatoes.

Scald 8 sound tomatoes in boiling water for half a minute; drain and peel them, cut up in small pieces; put them in a saucepan with 1 tablespoonful butter, salt and pepper, half a teaspoonful of sugar and 1 tablespoonful bread or cracker crumbs. Cook slowly for 30 minutes, mash with a spoon while cooking.

Canned tomatoes can be prepared same way.

Baked Tomatoes.

Scald 10 or 12 sound tomatoes in boiling water, drain, then remove the skins and cut in small pieces; put them in a saucepan with half a cupful cold water and cook until very tender. Remove from the fire and run them through a fine sieve. Season with salt, pepper, 1 teaspoonful powdered sugar, 1 tablespoonful fresh butter, and add 1 tablespoonful cracker meal. Put in a small round earthern dish, place in stove and cook until brown, about 20 or 30 minutes. Canned tomatoes are nice prepared this way; only do not add any water when first cooking them.

Deviled Tomatoes.

Cut 4 large tomatoes in slices, and lay aside. Rub yolks 2 hard-boiled eggs with 1 tablespoonful of vinegar, 1 tablespoonful melted butter, 1 teaspoonful of sugar, pinch salt, mustard and cayenne. Put whole on stove, and when boiling, stir this into beaten yolk of 1 raw egg. Let come again to a boil. Broil the slices of tomatoes, lay on dish, and pour dressing over. Serve hot.

Stuffed Tomatoes.

Select as many sound ripe tomatoes as required. Wash and dry well. Cut off the top of each without detaching, so that it will serve as a cover. Scoop out the inside of each, and put aside until needed. Be very careful not to cut or break the tomatoes.

Chop very fine ½ of a small onion, brown in a saucepan with 1 spoonful of butter or drippings, add 1 handful of bread that has been soaked and squeezed out, fry a few minutes; then add the tomatoes that were scooped out; fry all together for 5 minutes, and with the mixture fill the tomatoes; cover with the tops, put them in a small pan, pour in 1 spoonful of the top of the soup stock, and place in oven to cook and brown, about 20 minutes. Baste often.

Stuffed Tomatoes with Meat.

Cut off tops of tomatoes, and scoop out insides, being careful not to break the tomatoes.

Melt in saucepan 1 tablespoonful butter, and brown 1 small onion in it, 1 cupful chopped meat (cooked), and inside of tomatoes that were scooped out, season with salt and pepper, and add ½ cupful fresh bread crumbs. Mash smooth, and remove from fire; add beaten yolk of 1 egg. Rub all through a sieve. Fill the raw tomatoes with the mixture, put tops on, and bake in pan inside of stove, with bits of butter over. Bake 30 to 45 minutes, basting often.

Escalloped Tomatoes.

Peel the tomatoes, slice, but not too thin.

Line a pudding dish with cracker crumbs, sprinkle bits of butter over, then a layer of tomatoes, sprinkle with salt and pepper, or sugar, as preferred, do not use both. Put another layer of cracker crumbs and butter, then tomatoes, etc., until all is used up. Have cracker crumbs and bits of butter on top. Bake half an hour.

Stuffed Green Peppers.

Wash green peppers, cut off tops, remove seeds and all inside matter, being careful to leave outer shell whole. Soak in cold water with salt until ready for use, at least three hours. Soak a few slices of stale bread in cold water until moist, squeeze dry, and mash through colander to make smooth. Brown ½ chopped onion in skillet with a small tablespoonful of fat, stir in bread, until thoroughly dry, and add tablespoonful chopped parsley. Remove from fire, fill peppers, put tops back on, and place in flat pan. Put bits of fresh butter over, and a very little water in bottom of pan. Baste frequently. Bake from 35 to 45 minutes.

Stuffed Green Peppers with Meat.

Secure nice large peppers. Slice off the tops, remove the seeds and all the inside. Rinse in cold water.

Prepare dressing same as for "Stuffed Tomatoes." adding 2 tablespoonfuls tomatoes to the dressing while cooking.

Canned Green Peas.

Empty contents of 1 can green peas in a saucepan, add 2 teaspoonfuls butter, salt and pepper to taste, and 1 teaspoonful sugar; put on the stove and cook 20 minutes. Dissolve 2 teaspoonfuls flour in ½ cupful milk, stir into the peas and cook 10 minutes longer.

Green Peas.

Drain liquor from can of French peas, and rinse in cold water. Drain again. Put peas in saucepan, add small lump of fresh butter, pinch salt and pepper, 1 teaspoonful sugar, and 1 cupful strained soup stock. Let come to a boil, stir in a little chopped parsley and serve hot. If fresh green peas are used, boil in cold water until tender, then add soup stock, etc., to the peas, leaving water in which they were cooked.

Carrots—Sweet and Sour.

Peel carrots, and cut in 1 inch pieces. Put on to boil in cold salt water, and cook until tender. Drain off water. Brown ½ cupful sugar in skillet with 1 tablespoonful of flour, add ½ cupful vinegar (if vinegar is very strong less is needed), and rub smooth. Add ½ cupful soup stock if convenient, if not cold water will do, and put carrots in. Let whole boil up together.

Carrots and Peas.

Prepare carrots and peas separately, same as in above recipes, only using ½ cupful of the gravy from peas instead of soup stock. Drain peas, mix in with the carrots, let whole boil up well, and serve.

Baked Onions.

The large Bermuda onions are best for this purpose. Remove the outer skin and boil onions in salt water and milk until tender. Place in baking pan with butter on top, and a little fresh milk. Bake until brown in oven.

Boiled Onions.

Select large white onions, remove the outer skin; put on to boil in salt water, season with salt and pepper, and 1 tablespoonful butter. When tender, and just before serving, add 1 spoonful sweet cream; boil up once and serve.

Boiled Okra.

Wash okra, cut off sharp points of ends, and put on to boil with weak, cold, salt water. When tender, drain off all water and pour over 1 large tablespoonful of fresh melted butter and pinch pepper. Serve hot.

Chestnuts and Raisins.

Remove the outer shells from 1 quart of chestnuts. Then pour boiling water over them and remove the skins; put in cold water for half an hour, then drain and put on in a boiler with cold water and boil until tender. Do not add any salt as it toughens them.

In another boiler put 1 cup raisins which have been stemmed, cover with cold water, add 2 bay leaves and some stick cinnamon; boil until tender, then pour them into the boiler containing the chestnuts. Add a pinch of salt, and 1 teaspoonful butter and continue to boil until chestnuts are done, then add 2 tablespoonfuls white wine, 2 teaspoonfuls sugar, ½ teaspoonful of vinegar and thicken with 1 tablespoonful flour dissolved in water. More sugar or vinegar can be added to suit the taste. Boil a few minutes then serve.

Puree of Chestnuts.

Peel, and skin chestnuts, and boil until tender. Drain off water. Mash chestnuts smooth with potato masher, mix in 1 tablespoonful fresh butter, pinch salt, and pepper. Put chestnuts in baking dish, bake in oven and serve in same pan that it was baked in.

Chestnuts and Prunes.

Peel 1 pint chestnuts and skin, then boil until tender. Boil 1 pint prunes and remove stones when prunes are tender. Mix chestnuts in with prunes, leaving water prunes were cooked in, season with sugar, cinnamon, and lemon juice, and cook together. Add a little soup stock, then a wine glass of sherry. Serve hot. Be careful not to break the chestnuts or prunes.

Fresh Asparagus with Sauce.

Wash the asparagus carefully, tie in bunches having the heads all one way, cut the stalks off even. Put the bunches in boiling salt water; boil steadily for 20 minutes. When done, untie the bunches, lay on a hot platter and serve with drawn butter sauce, or any of the sauces for asparagus.

Fresh Asparagus on Toast.

Tie the asparagus in bunches as for above recipe. Boil in boiling salt water for 20 minutes. Have ready some nice pieces of hot buttered toast; lay 5 or 6 pieces of asparagus on each piece of toast, pour drawn butter sauce, or cream sauce for asparagus, or white sauce, over the tips, and serve on hot platter.

Fresh Asparagus.

Wash asparagus in cold water, and scrape only the stem part. Tie in small bundles, and boil in salt water until tender. Remove from water, and untie. Put in saucepan 1 cup soup stock or chicken gravy, thicken with a little flour, add teaspoonful fresh butter, pinch salt and pepper, and let come to a boil. Drop asparagus in, and let whole cook together. Serve hot.

Canned Asparagus.

Open one end of the can, stand can up in *boiling* water on stove for 20 minutes. Be careful not to get any water in. Empty the contents on a hot platter, remove all the liquor, sprinkle a little table salt over and serve hot with any of the sauces for asparagus.

Canned Asparagus on Toast.

Prepare the asparagus as above. Have ready some nice pieces of buttered toast, cover the toast with cream sauce for asparagus, lay 4 pieces of asparagus on each piece of toast and serve hot. Canned "asparagus tips" are nicest served this way.

Stewed Celery.

Cut celery stalks in pieces 1½ inches long, and boil in salt water. Then drain off water. Boil in another saucepan 1 cupful milk, with tablespoonful butter, add a little flour which has been dissolved in milk, pinch salt and pepper. Let boil up, put celery in, and let all come to a boil together. Serve hot.

Stuffed Mushrooms.

Wash and skin mushrooms. Remove hearts and stems, and chop fine. Put butter in saucepan, and chopped part of the dry chopped mushrooms in it. Soak 1 slice white bread, squeeze dry, and add soft part to this, 1 egg, a little cream, salt and pepper. Mix well together, and put back in place in mushrooms where other parts were taken out. Bake in flat pans, and moisten with a little soup stock or water.

Artichokes with Sauce.

Wash and trim neatly as many French artichokes as required. Place them in a boiler, cover with cold water, add a handful of salt and 2 tablespoonfuls vinegar. Boil until very tender, test by drawing out one leaf. Take them from the water and drain and serve on folded napkin with the following

ARTICHOKE SAUCE.

1 cupful milk, butter size of an egg, a little salt and pepper, let boil in double boiler. While boiling stir in 1 cupful sweet cream in which 2 tablespoonfuls flour have been dissolved. When it begins to thicken stir in the juice of ½ lemon and ½ teaspoonful vinegar, stir constantly and pour over the well beaten yolk of 1 egg. Is best eaten cold, but can be served hot.

Artichokes with Tartare Sauce.

Prepare and boil as many French artichokes as desired, same as for the foregoing recipe. When very tender, drain and serve on a folded napkin. Serve with them in a separate sauceboat, any of the Tartare Sauces given under "sauces."

Cauliflower with Sauce.

Pick off the leaves and cut the stalk close to the flower, examine well to see that nothing adheres to it. Be careful not to break the bunch. Lay in cold water half an hour; drain, then tie the cauliflower in a piece of clean white cloth and drop in boiling salt water. Boil 20 minutes. Have ready any of the sauces given for cauliflower, and either pour over the cauliflower before sending to the table, or serve in a separate sauce boat, hot or cold as preferred.

Baked Cauliflower.

Prepare and boil the cauliflower as above. Then lay the head of cauliflower in an earthen dish, sprinkle 1 cupful of bread crumbs over it, pour 2 tablespoonfuls fresh melted butter over the crumbs, and place inside the stove to brown. Then serve in same dish or remove very carefully to another so as not to break the head.

Creamed Cucumbers.

Peel cucumbers with a silver knife, halve crosswise (if cucumber is large), then cut into about 8 pieces lengthwise. Scald with boiling water, for 1 minute, then drain off water. Be sure and discard ends, as they are apt to be bitter. Put cucumbers on in a sauce pan with cold water and a pinch of salt. Cook for about 20 minutes, then drain off water, retaining it. Melt in another saucepan 1 tablespoonful of butter, add 1 tablespoonful of flour, rub smooth, and add 1 cupful of the water the cucumbers were boiled in. Season with salt, pepper, and strained juice of ½ lemon. Put cucumbers in and let come to a boil. Serve hot. If desired, freshly buttered toast can be prepared. Arrange three pieces of cucumber on each piece, pour sauce over, and serve.

Macaroni with Tomatoes.

Steam macaroni in boiling water until tender. Stew ½ pint tomatoes, strain and season with 1 teaspoonful sugar, pinch salt and pepper. When macaroni is done, drain water off, and mix with heaping tablespoonful fresh butter, pinch salt and pepper. Put a layer of macaroni in baking dish, a layer of tomatoes, a layer of macaroni, and so on. Bake in oven until brown on top and serve in same pan it was baked in.

Macaroni au Gratin.

Break 8 sticks of macaroni or spaghetti into 3 inch pieces, put on in cold salt water and boil 20 minutes from the time it begins to boil. When done, pour in the colander and let every drop of water drain out.

Grate quarter of pound of Parmesan or American cheese.

Put half of the macaroni in a baking dish in which it is to be served, then sprinkle half of the cheese over, then a layer of cracker crumbs, sprinkle salt, pepper and bits of butter over, put in another layer of macaroni, cheese, crumbs, and seasoning with bits of butter on top.

Beat the yolk of 1 egg with 1 cupful milk or sweet cream, pour over the whole, put in oven and bake until a nice brown.

Noodles and Mushrooms.

Beat 4 whole eggs very light and sift in sufficient flour to make a very stiff paste. Work until smooth, break off small piece, and roll out on board very thin. Break off another piece, and so on until whole is used up. Let rolled out dough dry, then cut all, except 2 pieces, in long strips 1 inch wide. Fold these 2 pieces in layers, and cut very fine noodles. Boil large noodles in pot of salt water, drain in colander when tender, and stir in 1 heaping tablespoonful of butter. Put in baking pan. Heat a tablespoonful of fat in skillet, and brown fine noodles in fat. Sprinkle over top of large noodles, pour a cup of soup stock over whole, and brown in stove. Serve in same dish it was baked in.

MUSHROOMS.

Brown a spoonful of butter in skillet, add ½ tablespoonful of flour, then liquor of mushrooms, pinch salt, and pepper. When smooth add mushrooms. Let boil, and serve in a separate dish from noodles. When dished, a spoonful of mushrooms is to be put over each portion of noodles.

Puree of Chestnuts.

Put 1 lb. of chestnuts in a pan and run in an oven for a few minutes to loosen shells, then remove, and peel and skin. Put on to boil in 1 pt. milk, and cook until tender, then mash smooth. If necessary add more milk while boiling. Strain and season with salt, and pepper, and 1 teaspoonful of fresh butter. Serve hot.

SALADS.

Sauce for Asparagus Salad.

Cream a piece of butter the size of an egg, add 5 eggs well beaten with a little salt and pepper.
Heat 1 cupful vinegar with 1 teaspoonful sugar added. When hot, stir briskly into the eggs and butter. Put back on the stove and stir constantly until thick. If desired a little sweet cream may be added and is an improvement.

Mayonnaise Dressing for Salads. No. 1.

Beat 3 whole eggs until light, then pour in 2 tablespoonfuls olive oil stirring constantly, add a large pinch salt and white pepper and a dash of cayenne pepper. Stir into this ½ cupful vinegar, which has been heated with 1 teaspoonful sugar in it. Stir well, put back on stove, and stir until thick. Set on ice until cold.

Mayonnaise Dressing. No. 2.

Mash the yolks of 2 hard-boiled eggs until perfectly smooth, add yolks of 3 raw eggs, cream well, then pour in 2 tablespoonfuls olive oil, stirring constantly, add a large pinch of salt and white pepper and a dash of cayenne pepper. Stir into this ½ cupful white vinegar, which has been heated with 2 teaspoonfuls sugar in it, mix well, put back on stove and stir constantly until thick. Set on ice until cold.

French Mayonnaise.

Break yolks 2 raw eggs in a shallow bowl, and stir in slowly drop by drop 1 cupful imported French olive oil. Do not beat but stir steadily, and when all is a stiff thick mass, add gradually, pinch fine salt, pinch white pepper, teaspoonful raw mustard, 2 tablespoonfuls lemon juice. Mix well, and put on ice until ready to serve.

Tartare Sauce.

Make mayonnaise same as above, then add 2 tablespoonfuls capers, 2 sprays chopped parsley, 8 olives chopped, and ½ salt pickle chopped fine. Mix well and put on ice until served.

French Dressing.

Put 1 saltspoonful salt, ½ saltspoonful white pepper, in a bowl, and stir in 3 tablespoonfuls of olive oil, then add ¼ teaspoonful onion juice, and 1 tablespoonful of vinegar. Mix well.

Chicken Salad. No 1.

Boil until *very* tender 1 large hen.

Now remove all skin, fat and bones, and with a sharp scissors cut up the chicken in small pieces. Cut up 2 white stalks of celery (that have been cleaned) in pieces same size as chicken, add to chicken; also add ½ cupful capers and 4 hard-boiled eggs chopped fine, put all in a bowl, season with a little salt and pepper, and moisten (not wet) with some of the water in which the chicken was boiled, and set aside until you make the following
DRESSING.

Beat until light the yolks of 3 eggs, drop into it 2 tablespoonfuls olive oil, stir well, add ½ teaspoonful each of salt, pepper, and dry mustard, 1 teaspoonful sugar and a pinch of cayenne pepper, then stir in the smoothly mashed yolks of 2 hard-boiled eggs, pour over all 1 cupful hot vinegar, stirring all the time; put on stove in double boiler and stir until thick. Pour while hot over the chicken mixture, reserving some dressing to decorate the dish. Mix dressing and chicken together with a fork, and if not seasoned enough add more pepper, salt or sugar.

Lay lettuce leaves on salad dish, put in the salad lightly with a fork, and dress the top with the cold dressing that has been left out.

Chicken Salad. No 2.

Boil a fat hen until thorougly done, then remove meat from bones, take away every bit of fat and skin, and chop meat fine. Have 1 large stalk of celery soaked in ice-water, then cut in small pieces and add to chicken. Dress a salad dish with lettuce leaves, and lay chicken and celery on it and pour over it the following

DRESSING.

Mix well together 1 teaspoonful white sugar, 1 teaspoonful flour, a pinch of cayenne pepper, and ½ teaspoonful table salt; add 4 whole raw eggs, beat well, then add 1 glassful vinegar, and 1 tablespoonful butter that has been rubbed soft. Stir well, put on the stove and continue stirring until thick. Set aside to cool, and when cold add ½ cupful whipped cream and pour over the chicken. Some capers and cut up pickles can be added to the chicken if desired.

Chicken Salad. No. 3.

Put on to boil with cold water, one old hen, which has been cleaned and seasoned the day previous. Boil until tender, not stringy. Skim off the grease from the top when done and set aside. Remove bone, fat, gristle, etc., from chicken, and chop the meat in 1 inch pieces. Allow half as much celery as you have chicken, cut in ½ inch pieces. Mix with the chicken; add ½ salt pickle, and 6 olives chopped fine.

Mash in separate bowl yolks of 4 hard-boiled eggs, add gradually the grease skimmed from the chicken until the mixture is smooth and thick, then add 1 teaspoonful prepared mustard, a large pinch pepper and salt, 1 tablespoonful sugar, 1 teaspoonful each mustard and celery seed, and ½ cup white vinegar. Mix well, then add to the chicken, stirring with a fork to prevent mashing. Serve on lettuce leaves and cover with French Mayonnaise Dressing.

Veal Salad.

Prepare same as Chicken Salad No. 3. Half chicken and half veal can be used if preferred.

Beets Stuffed with Salad.

Boil large beets in water until tender, but not to pieces. Peel and soak the whole beets in vinegar until cold and firm; then hollow out the inside, being careful to leave a thick shell. Stuff either with chicken or celery salad, and serve on lettuce leaves. Pour a tablespoonful of either mayonnaise or French dressing over each beet just before serving.

Tomatoes with Chicken Salad.

Plunge the tomatoes in boiling water 1 minute, and remove the skins. Allow 1 large red tomato for each person. Put in an earthen platter on ice until very cold. Make a "chicken salad" by any of the foregoing recipes, and just before ready to serve, cut the top off of each one of the tomatoes, scoop out the insides, and fill the cavity with the chicken salad. Lay the tomatoes on lettuce leaves, and pour "French Mayonnaise" over each one, and serve at once ice cold.

Tomatoes with Shrimp Salad.

Prepare the tomatoes as for the "Chicken Salad," or they can be left with the skins on; place on ice and when cold scoop out the insides.

Shell the shrimps, sprinkle with a little salt and pepper, and place on ice till needed.

Make a "French Mayonnaise dressing." When ready to serve, mix half of it with the shrimps, fill the cavities of the tomatoes, and pour the other half of the mayonnaise over, after placing the tomatoes on lettuce leaves. Serve ice cold. Two stalks of celery can be cut in ¼ inch pieces and added to the shrimps if desired.

Tomato Salad—French Dressing.

Take 6 firm red tomatoes, wash and wipe them neatly, slice them in thin slices with a very sharp knife. Line a salad bowl with lettuce leaves, lay the sliced tomatoes in, and sprinkle salt and pepper over, add ½ teaspoonful olive oil, and 3 tablespoonfuls of vinegar. Serve very cold.

Tomato Salad—Mustard Dressing.

Take 6 firm red tomatoes, and slice as above. After placing in a salad bowl lined with lettuce leaves, pour over them the following dressing: Take 2 tablespoonfuls prepared French mustard, or Durkee's salad dressing, stir ½ cup white vinegar in it, add pepper, salt, and a little sugar, pour over the tomatoes and serve ice cold. Tomatoes that have been scalded, skinned, and left whole are nice prepared this way.

Whole Tomatoes—Mayonnaise Dressing.

Take as many firm red tomatoes as desired, wipe them neatly, plunge them into boiling water one minute; drain and remove the skins, and place on ice till wanted. Line a salad bowl with lettuce leaves, lay in the ice cold tomatoes, and pour a mayonnaise dressing over them.

Baldwin Salad.

Secure sound Baldwins or any fine, large red apples. Wash the apples, cut off the tops, and hollow out the insides, being careful not to break the shells. Make a French mayonnaise, mix with the inside of apples, and fill the shells. Serve on individual plates.

Celery Salad.

Two large bunches of celery stalks make 1 pint cut up. Cut in ½-inch pieces as much celery as required for salad, sprinkle with salt and white pepper. Prepare either a French dressing or mayonnaise, mix well and serve either on lettuce leaves or decorated with celery tops.

Waldorf Salad.

Peel and cut in ½ inch pieces 5 large apples, add 4 cupfuls of celery-stalks cut in ½ inch pieces. Season with two tablespoonfuls of white wine vinegar, pinch of salt. Mix well, then stir in 1½ cupfuls of French mayonnaise dressing (the other mayonnaise can be used if desired). Serve individually on lettuce leaves or in a glass bowl, and decorate with celery tops.

Fruit Salad. No. 1.

Slice 1 pineapple, 3 oranges, and 3 bananas. Pour over it a French mayonnaise, put on lettuce leaves and serve at once. For those who do not care for the mayonnaise, make a syrup of 1 cupful of sugar and ½ cupful of water, boil until thick, add juice of lemon, let slightly cool, then pour over fruit. Let stand on ice 1 to 2 hours. Another nice dressing is 1 cupful of claret, ½ cupful sugar, and piece of lemon. Always use lemon juice in preference to vinegar in fruit salads. All fruits that go well together may be mixed. This is served just before desert.

Fruit Salad. No. 2.

Peel and slice 5 yellow peaches, 1 dozen yellow pears, and 1 small bunch white grapes cut in half and seeds removed. Serve either with mayonnaise or with syrup prepared as above.

Potato Salad.

Boil 5 large sound potatoes in their skins. When done peel them at once while hot, and slice in thin, round slices; slice an onion in thin, round slices over the potatoes, sprinkle generously with salt and pepper; add 1 tablespoonful mustard seed, ½ tablespoonful celery seed, ½ tablespoonful sugar.

Beat 2 eggs until light, pour two tablespoonfuls hot goose fat or fresh butter, melted, over the eggs, stir well, add ½ cupful vinegar, pour over the seasoned potatoes; then add ¼ cupful hot water, and if necessary add a little more vinegar, salt or pepper. 1 or 2 chopped hard-boiled eggs added, improves the salad.

Line a salad dish with lettuce leaves, pour in the salad and decorate the top with grated hard-boiled eggs.

Potato and Oyster Salad.

Make a potato salad same as in above receipe, omitting the onion. Scald in their own liquor 2 dozen oysters, with a teaspoonful of butter, pinch of salt and pepper. Cook oysters done, then drain and lay in vinegar for a few minutes. Line bottom of salad dish with potato salad, while warm yet, and then layer of oysters, another layer of potatoes, and so on until bowl is full. Pour vinegar, oysters were lying in, over whole. Decorate with celery tops or parsley sprays, and slices of hard-boiled eggs.

Cucumber Salad.

Procure sound large cucumbers. Pare thickly from end to end. Cut in thin round slices, strew *thickly* with salt, put in a bowl, press down heavily with pieces of marble or brick for 3 hours. Then press, or with a lemon squeezer, squeeze out every drop of water; put in a salad bowl, lay thin slices of onion over, season with white pepper, 1 teaspoonful olive oil, pour over enough vinegar to wet well, and serve. A tiny bit of sugar and some cut up parsley can be added if desired.

Lettuce Salad. No. 1.

Use nice white heads of lettuce; pare off the outer leaves and stems; cut the remaining part in 4 pieces, lay in cold water until just before needed. Put in a colander, drain off all the water, lay the pieces nicely in a salad bowl. Mix a pinch of salt and pepper together, add 2 tablespoonfuls vinegar, and ½ teaspoonful olive oil; pour this seasoning over the lettuce, and decorate with slices of hard-boiled eggs. Lettuce salad should only be dressed when ready to be served, as it wilts from standing.

Lettuce Salad. No. 2.

Cut and clean the heads of lettuce as for No. 1, and before serving, pour a mayonnaise dressing over.

Chicory Salad.

Wash clean, and drain nice heads of chicory, and before serving, prepare a dressing as for "Lettuce Salad No. 1," and decorate with slices of hard-boiled eggs.

Cold Slaw.

Cut up 1 small, firm, head of white cabbage very fine, with a sharp knife or slaw-cutter, put in cold salt water 1 hour. Drain and put in salad bowl.

Beat yolks of 2 eggs until light, add 1 tablespoonful sugar, 1 teaspoonful pepper, ½ teaspoonful salt and dry mustard; pour 1 cupful vinegar over, stir well, and pour over the slaw.

Cold Slaw With Mustard Sauce.

Select a nice, white, hard-head cabbage, peel off loose outer leaves, and cut in half. Half a cabbage is sufficient for a moderate sized family. Shave fine with a cabbage cutter, and sprinkle with a little salt. Put in a small bowl 1 tablespoonful olive oil, 1 teaspoonful prepared mustard (French), 1 saltspoonful salt, 1 saltspoonful sugar, ½ cupful white vinegar; pinch black pepper. Mix all well, and stir lightly with the cold slaw. Have salad very cold.

Cold Slaw With Cream Sauce.

Prepare cabbage as for plain slaw. Put on to boil in a sauce-pan 1 cupful white wine vinegar. Break in a bowl 3 yolks of eggs, and stir in gradually 1 cupful sweet milk. When well mixed, stir the boiling vinegar into eggs and milk, very carefully and slowly. Season with salt, pepper, 1 tablespoonful of sugar, 1 teaspoonful butter, and 1 teaspoonful cornstarch dissolved in a little cold milk.

Put back on stove, and boil, stirring constantly to prevent curdling, and as soon as thick remove immediately. Mix with the slaw while hot, and serve when cold. Double the quantity of sauce must be used if a larger amount of salad is required.

String Bean Salad.

String and wash 1 pint fresh string beans. Put on in cold salt water and boil until tender. Drain and when cold, put in a salad bowl, season with salt and pepper, pour ½ teaspoonful olive oil over, also ½ cupful vinegar and serve. If preferred the olive oil can be left out.

Okra Salad.

Wash and put on to boil 1 pint fresh okra; when tender, cut off the ends, season same as " String Bean Salad " and serve.

Beet Salad.

Wash the beets thoroughly, cut off the stems except about 3 inches to keep from bleeding. Put on in cold water and boil until tender; remove from the fire, slip the skins off and slice in round slices, season with salt, pepper, and white sugar; pour enough white vinegar over to cover them, and set aside to cool. If the beets are put in a jar and well covered with vinegar they will keep for some time. Grated horseradish can be added if desired.

Asparagus Salad. No. 1.

Use canned asparagus. Set the can in boiling water and boil 20 minutes, then place on ice. When cold, sprinkle salt and pepper over, and pour ½ cupful white wine vinegar over, and serve ice-cold.

Fresh asparagus can be prepared same way, and 1 tablespoonful olive oil can be added to the dressing.

Asparagus Salad. No. 2.

Use canned asparagus; boil in the can for 20 minutes, place on ice until wanted. Make the following sauce, and when cold and ready to serve, pour it over the asparagus.

SAUCE.

Cream a piece of butter size of an egg, then add 5 eggs well beaten with a little salt and pepper.

Heat one cupful vinegar with 1 teaspoonful sugar, and pour over the eggs, stirring well. Put back on the stove in double boiler and stir until thick. Add enough sweet cream to thin a little. The cream can be omitted if desired.

Fresh Asparagus Salad with Mayonnaise.

Tie the asparagus in bundles, boil in cold weak salt water until tender, drain, and put in a china dish. Pour 1 cupful white vinegar over, also pinch of salt and pepper, and put on ice to get cold. When ready to serve place the asparagus on a platter. Have a cold mayonnaise dressing in a separate bowl, and serve the asparagus with a spoonful of mayonnaise on the side of each plate.

Brazilian Salad.

Prepare 1 cupful string beans broken in halves, 1 cupful green peas, 1 cupful Lima beans, 1 cupful turnips cut in cubes, 1 cupful carrots cut in dice, and 1 cupful cauliflower. Put each on to boil separately in cold weak salt water, and cook until tender. Drain water off and mix all together lightly, and put in an ice-box to get cold. Pour the following dressing over, mix well and put in a salad bowl.

DRESSING.

Grate a little onion in a bowl, add 1 teaspoonful salt, ⅓ teaspoonful pepper, then beat in gradually 3 tablespoonfuls of olive oil, and 6 tablespoonfuls vinegar.

Lobster Salad.

Boil the lobster and when cold, pick out all the meat from the shells, carefully abstracting the gall. Cut the meat into small square pieces. Or use a can of lobster. Cut 1 stalk of white celery in small pieces and add to the lobster. Boil 2 eggs hard and chop very fine, and also add to the lobster. Season with salt and pepper. Line a salad bowl with crisp lettuce leaves, put in the lobster, celery, and eggs well mixed, and pour a mayonnaise dressing over it. Decorate the top with capers and set in a cool place till wanted.

Herring Salad.

Soak 4 herring in cold water over night, and then rinse several times in fresh cold water. Skin, bone, and cut in ½ inch pieces. Peel two apples, and cut in dice. Mix with herring, then add a handful of coarsely-chopped almonds and 1 onion chopped fine. Remove the milsiner or soft egg from the inside of herring, and mash perfectly smooth. Add ½ cupful vinegar, 1 teaspoonful of sugar, pinch of pepper. Mix well, and then pour over herring, stirring with a fork to prevent mashing. Set in ice-box until ready to serve. Put sliced lemons on top. Herring can be left whole, dressing made and poured over whole herrings, and served at table.

Salmon Salad.

Procure a nice piece of salmon. Put on to boil in cold salt water with ½ cupful of vinegar added. Cook half an hour, and set aside to cool; then skin and remove all bones, and tear the salmon in small pieces. Or use canned salmon. Line a salad bowl with crisp lettuce leaves; put in the salmon, cut one or two white sound onions in round slices and lay over, sprinkle salt and pepper over, and over all, pour enough white vinegar to moisten well.

Mackerel Salad.

Procure a nice fat mackerel, boil, and when cold, proceed same as for "Salmon Salad," only do not cut the pieces quite as small.

Shrimp Salad. No. 1.

Get 1 quart boiled shrimps, shell, and put in a salad bowl lined with lettuce leaves. Make a mayonnaise dressing, and when cold, pour over the shrimps and serve.

Shrimp Salad. No. 2.

Take 1 quart boiled shrimps, shell, and put in a salad bowl lined with lettuce leaves. Make a dressing as follows and pour over the shrimps:

Beat the yolks of 2 eggs until light, add ½ teaspoonful salt, ¼ teaspoonful pepper, and ¼ teaspoonful dry mustard; stir in 1 tablespoonful Durkee's salad dressing. Add ½ cupful white vinegar.

Decorate the top with two hard-boiled eggs sliced, and serve.

Fish Salad.

Take 1 pound cold boiled fish left over from the day previous, or boil fresh fish and let cool, then skin, bone and flake. If fresh fish is used, mix 2 tablespoonfuls of vinegar, a pinch of salt and pepper with the fish. Make a mayonnaise dressing (French mayonnaise preferred), and mix half with the fish, leaving other half to spread over top of salad, after it is put in bowl. Serve either with or without lettuce leaves.

Crab Salad.

Boil 12 crabs in boiling water for 20 minutes, clean them and pick the meat from the shells and claws. Make a mayonnaise dressing; mix half of it with the crabs, and after laying the salad on lettuce leaves in a salad bowl, pour the other half of the mayonnaise over it.

Tomatoes with Crab Salad.

Skin whole tomatoes, cut off stem end, scoop out insides. Set in cold place until ready. Make crab salad as above, fill tomatoes, place tops back on, cover with a spoonful of mayonnaise, and serve on lettuce leaves.

Brain Salad.

Scald brains with boiling hot water to cleanse thoroughly. Boil until tender, in fresh cold salt water, being careful to remove from water while it is yet firm. Slice lengthwise and lay in dish. Pour over ½ cupful vinegar, which has been sweetened with a pinch of sugar to remove sharp taste, pinch of salt and pepper. Garnish with parsley and serve cold. Can also be served with mayonnaise.

Sweetbread Salad.

Lay sweetbreads in cold water 1 hour before cooking. Boil in weak salt water, until tender, then remove from water, skin and clean. Cut in slices, lay on lettuce leaves, and pour over a French dressing or French mayonnaise. Put on ice until ready to serve. If desired, celery cut in ¼ inch pieces can be added to the sweetbread.

Oyster Salad.

Scald the oysters in their own liquor, only let boil up once. Put them on ice until perfectly cold, then cut each one in four pieces, cut up some celery in small pieces, add to the oysters, and put all in a salad bowl lined with lettuce leaves. Sprinkle with a little salt, and pour a mayonnaise dressing over all and serve at once ice cold.

COMPOTES.

Baked Apples.

Take nice, large, sound apples, wash and core them. Put them in a long pan, fill the hole in each apple with plenty of white sugar, sprinkle more sugar over the apples, add a little lemon rind and a little cinnamon, pour in enough water to fill the bottom of the pan, put them in the oven and bake until the apples are done and tender. Baste the syrup over them *very often*. If the apples are done before the syrup is thick, remove the apples to a dish and continue cooking the syrup on top of the stove until it is thick, then pour it over the apples.

Filled Apples.

Cut off the tops from as many apples as required. Scrape out the inside of each one, remove the seeds and core, and add to the scraped apple a handful of raisins and chopped almonds, the rind and juice of 1 lemon, a little cinnamon and sugar to taste. Fill each apple with this mixture, replace the tops and stew the apples in wine and water that has had a little sugar added. Baste often. When the apples are done without being broken, lay them in a glass dish, and if the syrup is not thick enough, continue cooking until thick and pour over the apples.

Jellied Apples.

Pare and core 10 small sound apples.

Put in a wide porcelain kettle 2 cupfuls sugar and 1½ cupfuls water, let boil until it begins to get syrupy, then lay in the apples, being careful not to crowd them too much, cover with a top and cook for 5 minutes; then remove the top and let the apples simmer slowly until they are very tender, but not broken, turn them occasionally. Remove the apples to a glass dish, fill the holes with apple jelly, and when the syrup has boiled down thick, pour it over the apples. Serve cold.

Stewed Apples.

Pare, core, and quarter, 8 nice tart apples, put on to boil with very little water, add a piece of cinnamon bark, and enough sugar to sweeten. Cook until the apples are soft, then mash though a sieve. Serve cold. A handful of raisins and blanched almonds can be added if desired.

Apple Float.

Prepare 8 apples as for foregoing recipe, and shortly before serving, beat the whites of 4 eggs to a stiff froth, then add 4 tablespoonfuls sugar to them, mix the apples in lightly and serve cold.

Baked Pears.

Core large pears, Laconte are best for baking, and fill with butter and sugar. Stick a few spice in each pear. Pour a cupful of claret over whole, and bake in oven, basting with its own sauce.

Fresh Pear Compote.

Pare, core, and quarter, 8 large sound cooking pears, put them in a saucepan with water enough to barely cover, add 1 cupful sugar and 4 pieces of cinnamon bark, let them cook slowly until the pears are tender, but not to pieces, remove the pears to a glass dish, and, if the syrup is not cooked down enough, continue cooking it until it forms a syrup, then pour it over the pears.

If the pears are very small, use double quantity, and core them without cutting them. Leaving a little of the peeling on each pear gives them a pretty red color when cooked. Serve cold.

Fresh Peach Compote.

Pare 2 dozen sound peaches. Make a syrup of 1 cupful sugar and 1 cupful water, then drop in the whole peaches or sliced ones, cover, and cook until tender. Add a little cinnamon bark to the syrup. Serve cold. A few peach kernels added gives a nice flavor.

Canned Peach Compote.

Put on to boil the liquor from 1 can of California peaches, add 2 tablespoonfuls sugar, a few drops of lemon juice, 1 tablespoonful citron cut in small dice shaped pieces, and about 2 dozen raisins. Let all boil until it has boiled down to a syrup; lay in the peaches, cover with a top for a few moments until the syrup begins to boil again, remove the top and let the peaches cook about five minutes longer, pour into a glass dish and let cool. Serve cold.

Canned Pear Compote.

Prepare same as peach compote.

Canned White Cherry Compote.

Prepare same as peach compote.

Canned Green Gage Compote.

Prepare same as peach compote.

Canned Pineapple Compote.

Cut 1 can of sliced pineapple in quarters, and prepare same as peach compote.

Stewed Plums.

Wash 1 quart sound plums, and put in a saucepan with enough water to barely cover them, add two cupfuls sugar, and let cook until the plums are done. Remove the plums, and if the syrup is not thick enough, cook a few minutes longer and pour over the plums. Set aside to cool ; when cold, make a syrup of 1 cupful sugar, and 1 cupful water, and when almost thick, pour the plums and syrup in again and cook about ten minutes. This takes away the bitter taste of the plums. Serve cold.

Stewed Blackberries.

To 1 quart of blackberries add a cupful of sugar. Put on to boil with stick cinnamon. Stew until berries are cooked tender. Serve cold.

Stewed Strawberries. No. 1.

Wash and pick 1 quart strawberries. Put in saucepan with 1 cupful sugar or 1½ cupfuls according to the acidity of the berries, and a very little water. Cook until water has left strawberries ; remove from fire and serve cold.

Stewed Strawberries. No. 2.

1 cupful sugar and ½ cupful water, let boil until syrupy, add 1 quart freshly picked and washed strawberries, boil for 20 minutes, pour in fancy bowl. Serve cold.

Stewed Prunes.

Soak for half an hour, then wash 2 cupfuls nice prunes. Put them in a saucepan with water enough to cover them well, add 3 slices of lemon and 3 pieces of cinnamon bark; boil until the prunes are about half done and swell, then add ¾ cupful sugar; continue boiling (not too fast) until the prunes are done, and the syrup is somewhat thick. They should cook all together about 1½ hours. Pour into a glass dish and serve cold.

Filled Prunes.

Prepare and cook the prunes (they must be fine ones) same as for the foregoing recipe. While they are still warm, remove the seed from each prune with a sharp knife; be careful not to mash the prunes. Put a blanched almond, or a pecan meat inside of each prune, lay in a glass dish and pour the syrup over. Serve cold.

Stewed Rhubarb.

Break stalks of rhubarb in pieces and put in saucepan with cold water to stew. When tender, strain, sweeten to taste, put back to dissolve sugar, and when it has boiled, remove, and set in a cool place until ready to serve. Can be used for pie if desired.

BAKED PUDDINGS.

Farina Pudding.

Put on 1 cupful milk to boil. While boiling stir in 1 good tablespoonful farina, gradually, and continue stirring until thick as pap; add a pinch of salt and set aside to get cold.

Stir 4 whole eggs with ½ cupful sugar, add 1 level tablespoonful butter, then stir in the cold farina; when well mixed add 3 cupfuls milk and ½ teaspoonful vanilla. Put in a pudding pan in a moderately hot oven, and bake until brown on top, and set; about 25 or 30 minutes. If it takes too long it will get watery.

Farina Chocolate Pudding.

Thin 1 cupful cooked farina with 1 pint milk, stirring until smooth. Dissolve ⅛ pound chocolate in 1 cupful milk. Beat 4 eggs very light with 1 cupful sugar, add farina, then chocolate. Add 1 cupful milk. Flavor with vanilla. Pour in pudding pan, bake until firm, and serve in same pan as it was baked in. Serve with caramel sauce.

Ante Farina Pudding.

Get ¼ pound macaroons, and ¼ pound lady-fingers. Dip ½ the macaroons in a little wine and put them in the bottom of a pudding dish. Lay ½ the lady-fingers on top of the macaroons, after separating in halves and spreading each with a little jelly. Put in the other half of macaroons dipped in wine, then the balance of the lady-fingers, after separating and spreading with jelly, and over all pour a boiled custard made of 1 pint of milk, the yolks of 3 eggs and 1 tablespoonful cornstarch. When thick, flavor with vanilla and pour over the cake. Spread over the whole a meringue made of the whites of the 3 eggs and 6 level tablespoonfuls sugar. Put in the oven and brown nicely. Serve cold.

Dandy Pudding.

Beat the yolks of 6 eggs and 6 tablespoonfuls sugar very light.

Let 1 quart milk come to a boil, then stir it into the beaten yolks, add 2 tablespoonfuls cornstarch which have been dissolved in a little cold milk, add also half of the stiffly-beaten whites. Put in a pudding pan and set in another of boiling water on the top of the stove, and stir until thick. Remove from the fire, flavor with vanilla, spread over the top a meringue made of the balance of the whites and 5 tablespoonfuls sugar. Put in the oven and brown nicely on top. Serve cold, with or without cream or fruit sauce.

Kiss Pudding.

Get ½ lb. stale lady-fingers (stale sponge cake will do). Put one-half the cake in the bottom of a pudding pan. (If lady-fingers are used, separate the halves). Now put in a layer of peaches (canned are best), then the other half of the cake, then another layer of the peaches.

Make a boiled custard of 1 pint of milk, the yolks of 3 eggs, and 1 tablespoonful cornstarch. When thickened, pour it over the peaches and cake, and put the pudding in the oven for about 10 minutes. Remove from the oven, pour over it a meringue made of the whites of the 3 eggs and 6 even tablespoonfuls sugar. Put back in the oven, and brown lightly. Serve cold.

Delightful Pudding.

Take stale lady-fingers, split in half, spread with jelly, and arrange in pyramid form in a platter or glass dish. Make a custard of 1 pint milk, 4 yolks of eggs beaten with ½ cupful sugar, and whole boiled until thick. Flavor with vanilla, and pour over lady-fingers. Make a meringue of 4 whites beaten with ¼ cupful granulated sugar, spread over whole, and place in oven a few minutes to brown. Decorate with red jelly. If desired, the jelly can be put over custard, then meringue added.

Peach Pudding.

Take 1 can of peaches, or if fresh, use 1 quart, pare and stone them, put on to stew in ½ cupful white wine and ½ cupful sugar, add about a dozen blanched almonds. When the peaches are tender, and the wine has cooked syrupy, pour them in a pudding pan, and pour over them the following:

Beat the yolks of 9 eggs with 1½ cupfuls sugar until light, add the grated rind of ½ lemon, half of the stiff-beaten whites of eggs. Pour over the peaches, and bake in a moderate oven until light brown. Then cover with the remaining whites of eggs beaten with 6 tablespoonfuls sugar. Brown lightly again.

Serve cold with whipped or sweet cream.

Fruit Custard.

Cook fruit almost to a jelly, strain, and sweeten to taste. Measure 1 pint juice, and let get cold. Beat 4 whole eggs with 2 tablespoonfuls of granulated sugar, and add 1½ pints boiling milk. Mix well, then add fruit juice. Put in individual cups, or one pudding pan, place in a larger pan containing hot water, and bake in oven until firm. If desired, 2 whites can be left out, and beaten with 2 tablespoonfuls of sugar to make a meringue. Must be put on when custard is done, then browned. Can be eaten cold.

Rice Custard.

Beat 4 eggs light with 1 cupful sugar. Add 1 cupful cooked rice, 2 cupfuls sweet milk, juice and rind of 1 lemon, ½ teaspoonful of cinnamon. Pour in pudding pan, and bake in oven in a pan filled with hot water until firm. Serve with lemon sauce.

Cream Rice Pudding.

Use ⅓ cup rice, pour enough *boiling* water over to cover thoroughly, put aside to soak in a bowl 1 hour.
When soaked, pour off every bit of water, and add 1 quart cold milk to the rice, stir in ¾ cupful sugar, a good pinch of salt and ½ teaspoonful vanilla. Mix well and pour in a pudding pan. Drop bits of fresh butter all over the top and put in a moderate oven and bake until done, about ¾ to 1 hour.

Indian Meal Pudding.

Boil 1 quart milk with 1 cupful corn-meal, stirring constantly until all milk is absorbed. Add a piece of butter size of an egg, 1 cupful sugar, and a pinch of salt. Stir until sugar is dissolved, remove from stove, and let cool. Beat 4 whole eggs very light, stir the corn-meal in, add 1½ pints sweet milk, 1 teaspoonful vanilla. Bake in pudding pan until firm. If made properly, the corn-meal is hardly noticeable, tastes more like a custard pudding. Serve with cream sauce.

Sago Pudding.

Boil in saucepan ¼ lb. sago with 1 quart of milk, until sago is transparent and has absorbed all milk. Stir to prevent burning, remove, and let cool. Beat yolks 4 eggs with 1 cupful sugar, add to sago, add pinch salt. Beat whites separately, stir in gently, and flavor with vanilla. Butter 12 individual molds, or 1 large one ; pour in mixture. Place in a large pan filled with hot water to ½ the depth of the mold. Bake in oven 35 to 50 minutes. Serve with cream sauce.

Tapioca Pudding.

Soak ¼ lb. tapioca in cold water over night, then prepare and bake same as Sago Pudding.

Queen Pudding.

Beat well together the yolks of 4 eggs with 1 cupful sugar, add grated rind of 1 lemon, 1 teaspoonful fresh butter, and 2 cupfuls grated bread crumbs, and then stir in 1 quart sweet milk. Bake. When done spread a layer of jelly over the top, and cover with a meringue made of the stiffly-beaten whites of the 4 eggs and 1 cupful sugar, and juice of ½ lemon. Put back in oven on top rack until browned lightly. Eaten cold.

Caramel Pudding.

Melt in saucepan ½ cupful granulated sugar, then add ¼ cupful cold water. Stir until thick and smooth. Take a pudding mold holding 1 quart, and pour caramel over bottom and sides. Or line individual dishes with caramel. Let get cold. Make a custard of 2 cupfuls milk, ½ cupful sugar, 4 eggs, and flavor with lemon extract. Put in mold, over caramel. Put mold in pan with hot water, and bake in oven until firm. Remove, and serve with its own sauce.

Grated Pineapple Pudding.

Cream ½ cupful butter, with 1 cupful sugar, then add one by one yolks of 6 eggs, 1 cupful grated bread crumbs, 1 can grated pine-apple. Beat whites stiff, add to batter, bake in pudding pan, and serve in same pan it was baked in.

Sliced Pineapple Pudding.

Put on 1 quart milk to boil. Beat the yolks of 4 eggs with ¾ cupful sugar until light. Dissolve 2 heaping tablespoonfuls cornstarch in a little milk.

Mix the eggs and cornstarch together, pour the boiling milk over the mixture, and put back on the fire, stirring all the time until thick. Remove from the fire, add a few grains of salt, and flavor with vanilla.

Drain all the liquor off a can of sliced pineapple, cut the pineapple in small pieces and cover the bottom of a pudding pan with it. Pour the thick custard over, and cover the top with a meringue made of the whites of the 4 eggs beaten stiff with 8 level tablespoonfuls sugar added. Put on the rack in the oven and brown nicely. Serve cold.

Orange Pudding.

Make the same as pineapple pudding, substituting 3 oranges pared and cut in pieces 1 inch square, and covered with sugar, in place of the pineapple.

Cocoanut Pudding.

Make the same as pineapple pudding, substituting half a grated cocoanut for the pineapple, and sprinkling a little sugar over the cocoanut.

Cream and Banana Pudding.

Beat the yolk of 3 eggs and 3 heaping tablespoonfuls sugar very light, then add 1 pint rich, sweet cream. Pour into a pudding dish, and sprinkle lightly over with grated bread-crumbs. Set in a larger pan of boiling water, and put in the stove to set, from 20 to 30 minutes. When done put on a layer of thinly sliced bananas, then spread the top with a meringue made of the whites of the 3 eggs beaten stiff, and 5 level tablespoonfuls sugar. Put in the oven on the top rack and brown lightly. Serve cold.

Orange Pudding.

Make same as banana pudding, substituting thinly sliced oranges.

Pineapple Pudding.

Make same as banana pudding, substituting thinly sliced canned pineapple.

Sweet Potato Pudding.

Grate 3 good-sized raw sweet potatoes in a bowl, stir in 3 eggs, 1 cupful sweet milk, 2 tablespoonfuls syrup, 1 heaping tablespoonful fresh butter, 1 cupful brown sugar, 1 teaspoonful cinnamon, ½ teaspoonful allspice, and a pinch of salt. Mix well together, pour into a pudding pan, and bake in a moderate oven until done, from ¾ to 1 hour. Serve cold.

Bird's Nest Pudding.

Pare 8 sound apples, 6 if large, cut off tops carefully. Scrape out the inside of each one, being careful not to break the apples. Now season the apple that has been scraped out, with sugar, cinnamon, a few seeded raisins, a little grated almonds and a little white wine. Fill each apple with some of this mixture and put the tops back on. Pour 1 cupful sugar and ½ glass water and ½ glass wine over the apples, put in oven in a pan and bake, basting often. Be very careful not to break the apples. When tender, not soft, put apples in bottom of a pudding pan. Make sponge by beating until light yolks of 6 eggs and 1 good cupful sugar, add ½ cupful matzos or cracker meal and stiffly-beaten whites, pinch salt, pour over apples and bake until brown. Serve cold with sweet cream.

Plain baked apples can be substituted for the filled ones.

Grated Apple Pudding. No. 1.

Soak ½ stale loaf in milk until moist, squeeze dry and mash through a sieve. Grate 5 large tart apples. Beat yolks 6 eggs light with ¾ cupful sugar, add ½ cupful grated almonds, pinch salt, mashed bread, juice of ½ lemon, grated rind, and 6 whites beaten to a stiff froth. Mix apples in, and bake in pudding pan, about 30 minutes.

Grated Apple Pudding. No. 2.

Beat the yolks of 8 eggs and 1½ cupfuls sifted powdered sugar until very light, then add 2 cupfuls grated apple, ½ cupful matzos meal, the grated rind of 1 lemon, and lastly the stiffly-beaten whites of the 8 eggs with a tiny pinch of salt added. Mix well, pour in a large, greased spring form, and bake in a moderately slow oven. Serve cold with sweet cream.

Apple Pudding.

Bake 8 apples that have previously been peeled, cored, and cores filled with jelly. Beat yolks 6 eggs with ¾ cupful sugar, ¾ cupful grated almonds. Beat 6 whites stiff, add to batter. Flavor with vanilla. Pour over apples, and bake 30 minutes in oven. Serve with sauce.

Apple Chocolate Pudding.

Beat very light 5 eggs with 1 cupful sugar. Dissolve ¼ lb. chocolate with 1 pint milk on stove until smooth. Pour into eggs, then add ½ cupful cracker meal or 1 cupful bread crumbs. Stew 6 apples, sweeten, and pour in bottom of pudding pan. Pour chocolate mixture over apples. Bake in moderate oven.

Baked Chocolate Pudding. No. 1.

Boil 3½ cupfuls milk. Beat the yolks of 4 eggs with ¾ cupful sugar until very light. Dissolve 2 tablespoonfuls cornstarch in ¼ cupful milk. Dissolve ¼ lb. grated sweet chocolate in ¼ cupful milk. Mix the dissolved cornstarch and chocolate together, pour the boiling milk over them, put back on the stove and boil until thick, stirring all the time. Remove from fire, flavor with vanilla, pour into a pudding pan. Beat the whites of the eggs to a stiff froth, add ½ cupful sugar, then spread the meringue over the pudding, put in the oven and brown nicely on the top rack. Serve cold with whipped cream.

Chocolate Pudding. No. 2.

Melt ¼ lb. sweet chocolate in 1½ cupfuls milk, then stir in 1½ cupfuls grated bread crumbs. Remove from stove, and cool. Beat in, one by one, yolks of 5 eggs, add 1 tablespoonful of butter, 1 cupful sugar, 1 cupful sweet milk. Beat 5 whites stiff, add to batter, flavor with vanilla, and bake in oven in pan of hot water 1¼ hours. Serve with cold cream or sauce.

Lemon Pudding. No. 1.

Beat 6 yolks light with 1 cupful of sugar, add 1½ cupfuls stale bread crumbs, 2½ cupfuls of milk, grated rind of 1 lemon, and put in pudding dish. Bake until firm. Beat 6 whites stiff, add ½ cupful sugar, and juice of 1 lemon. Put a layer of tart jelly on top of pudding, pour meringue over, put in oven until meringue is brown.

Lemon Pudding. No. 2.

Melt in saucepan ⅓ lb. butter, ⅓ lb. of powdered sugar, 6 yolks, grated peel and juice of 1 lemon. Stir with egg beater until well mixed. Remove from stove, let cool, then add 6 beaten whites. Put in individual molds which have previously been buttered, place in pan of hot water, and cook inside oven for 40 minutes. In a large mold takes from 1 to 1½ hours. Very fine. Serve with cream sauce.

Orange Pudding.

Make same as above using only orange instead of lemon.

Cottage Pudding.

Cream ½ cupful butter with 1 cupful sugar. Beat 4 eggs light, add to butter. Then stir in 2 cupfuls flour, 1 teaspoonful yeast powder, and 1 cupful milk. Bake in cake pan, and turn out when done. Serve with any kind of sauce.

Macaroon Pudding.

Take 1 lb. macaroons, dip them in sweetened wine, put on a dish in pyramid form. Pour over them a meringue made of whites of 4 eggs and sugar, flavored with lemon. Decorate with candied cherries, and set in stove to brown lightly. Serve with wine sauce.

Macaroon Apple Pudding.

Soak ½ lb. macaroons in white wine until ready for use. Stew 6 apples, strain and sweeten to taste. Flavor with wine. Grate ¼ lb. almonds. Put a layer of apples in bottom of pan, a layer of macaroons, a layer of grated almonds, then apples, and so on until pan is filled. Beat 3 eggs light. Pour over whole, and bake in stove until set. Serve with wine sauce.

Almond Custard.

Make a custard of 1 quart milk, yolks 6 eggs, whites of 4, and 1 cupful sugar. When thick remove from stove. Grate ¼ lb. blanched almonds and mix with 2 tablespoonfuls of rose water. Mix with custard, put in pudding pan, or custard cups, put a meringue made of the two remaining whites, and 2 tablespoonfuls of sugar on top, and bake in oven until meringue is brown.

Tipsy Pudding.

Beat the yolks of 6 eggs and 1 cupful sugar until light, add a pinch of salt, 1¼ cupfuls sifted flour, ½ teaspoonful baking powder, the stiffly-beaten whites, and vanilla to flavor. Bake in a biscuit pan, and when cold, cut lengthwise in 3 equal pieces.

Put one piece on a flat dish, spread the top with apple jelly, then saturate with white wine, put another piece of cake on top of the first, and put on jelly and wine as before. Put the third piece of cake on the top of the second, saturate with wine, and cover the whole top and sides of the layers with a raw icing made of the whites of 2 eggs beaten stiff with powdered sugar. Drop bits of jelly or crystallized cherries on top of the icing, and set in a cool oven or the sun to dry. Serve cold with a custard sauce.

Kugle.

Soak half a five cent loaf of white bread in cold water; when soft, squeeze out every bit of water, put it in a bowl, add 1½ cups "linda" or soft goose fat cut in small pieces, 10 whole eggs, 2 cupfuls flour, ½ cupful sugar, 1 handful cracker meal, 3 apples and 2 pears cut in small pieces, 2 dozen raisins with the seeds removed, salt to taste, a tiny pinch of pepper, ¼ teaspoonful each of cinnamon and allspice. Mix all well together, and pour into an iron pan that has the bottom well covered with goose fat, stick a few pieces of cut apple or pear in the top of the pudding. Pour a dipper full of cold water over all, place in the oven to bake. Bake slowly, usually 5 or 6 hours. If the water cooks out before it is ready to brown, add more. Bake brown top and bottom.

BOILED PUDDINGS.

The tin molds are best for this purpose, either melon, round, or brick. If the mold is buttered first, then sprinkled with granulated sugar, a nice crust will form. Have a large, deep pan filled with boiling water. Place mold in, let water come up to rim, put a heavy weight on top of mold to keep down, and boil steadily. The pan must be constantly replenished with boiling water, if the pudding is to be done in time. Always place paper in top of mold to prevent water from penetrating. When puddings are boiled in bags, a plate must be placed in bottom of pan to prevent burning. Only certain puddings can be boiled in bags. Always grease inside of bag, so puddings will slip out easily. A bag made of two thicknesses cheese-cloth, stitched together, will do. Always leave room in mold or bag for pudding to rise, using a smaller or larger mold according to quantity of pudding. If not boiled *steadily*, and emptied as soon as done, puddings will fall and stick.

Almond Pudding.

Beat 8 yolks of eggs light with ½ lb. sugar, then add 1 cupful grated walnuts or almonds, 1 cupful grated white bread-crumbs, then stiffly beaten whites of 8 eggs. Put in pudding form, and steam from 1½ to 2 hours. Can be also baked in oven 1 hour. Serve with wine or fruit sauce.

Chocolate Pudding. No. 1.

Beat the yolks of 8 eggs and 1½ cupfuls powdered sugar until light, add ¼ lb. grated chocolate, 2 tablespoonfuls cracker meal, and 1 scant teaspoonful baking powder, add last the stiffly-beaten whites of the eggs. Boil in mold about 1 hour. If desired, ½ cupful grated almonds can be added to the pudding, and ½ cupful flour be substituted for the cracker meal. Serve with whipped cream, or any preferred sauce.

Chocolate Pudding. No. 2.

Beat yolks 5 eggs very light with 1½ cupfuls sugar. Sift ½ cupful cracker meal, add to eggs, then 1½ cupfuls grated chocolate, ½ teaspoonful yeast powder, grated rind of 1 lemon, and juice of ½ lemon. Boil 2 hours in mold. Serve with cream or caramel sauce.

Individual Chocolate Puddings.

Cream well ¼ lb. powdered sugar and ¼ lb. butter, add ¼ lb. chocolate (grated), and yolks of 5 eggs. Put whole in saucepan on stove, and stir quickly for 5 minutes. Remove and let cool, and add stiffly-beaten whites 5 eggs. Butter and sugar well 6 small pudding molds, and fill. Place in shallow pan, half filled with water, ½ height of molds. Cook 30 minutes. Can also be placed in large form, and boiled 2 hours. Serve with chocolate sauce or whipped cream.

Chocolate Pudding. No. 3.

Cream a piece of butter size of an egg, with 1 cupful sugar, then break in one by one 6 yolks, stirring all the time. Then add ⅜ lb. grated chocolate, pinch salt, ½ teaspoonful cinnamon, 1 cupful grated bread crumbs, 1 ounce chopped citron, and ½ cupful grated almonds. (If desired almonds and citron may be omitted.) Flavor with 1 wineglassful Madeira or sherry wine, and 1 teaspoonful vanilla. Mix well, then stir in lightly 6 stiffly-beaten whites. Serve with cold or whipped cream.

Rye-Bread Pudding.

Dry ½ cupful rye-bread crumbs in oven. Beat yolks 4 eggs very light with ½ cupful sugar, then add a pinch of cloves and allspice, ½ teaspoonful of cinnamon, grated rind of ½ lemon, and ¼ lb. chopped almonds. Moisten crumbs with 3 tablespoonfuls of whiskey or brandy, add to eggs, then add stiffly-beaten whites 4 eggs. Put in mold and boil 3 hours. Serve with a brandy or whiskey sauce.

Prince Albert Pudding.

Cream ½ lb. butter with ½ lb. sugar, until light, add 6 beaten yolks, ½ cupful stoned raisins, ¼ cupful cut citron; mix well. Sift ½ lb. flour 4 times, add to batter, then add 6 whites beaten stiffly. Put in mold, and boil 3 hours. Serve with sauce.

Prune Pudding.

Stew 35 prunes until tender, then stone, and mash fine and smooth, with 1 cupful sugar. Beat 9 whites very lightly, stir gently into prunes, and put in ungreased molds. Steam 2 hours.

Potato Pudding.

Beat 6 yolks light with 1 cupful granulated sugar, then add ½ lb. grated cold Irish potatoes. Mix well, then add 1 teaspoonful melted butter, 1 tablespoonful grated almonds, which have previously been blanched,

Flavor with a few drops of almond extract, and add the stiffly beaten whites of 6 eggs. Sugar and butter the pudding mold, and steam from 1½ to 2 hours. Serve with cream sauce.

Cherry Pudding. No. 1.

Soak 2 cupfuls of stale white bread in 1 cupful milk until moist. Place in saucepan on stove, add 2 tablespoonfuls butter, and stir until well dried, and loosens freely from the pan. Let cool. Beat 6 yolks light with 1 cupful sugar, and add to mashed bread. Stone cherries, and weigh 1 lb., either canned or fresh. Beat whites stiff, and stir in lightly. Flavor with grated rind of a lemon, and ½ teaspoonful cinnamon. Put in mold and boil 2 hours on top of stove. Serve with a sauce made of juice of cherries, or if fresh ones are used, a jelly sauce.

Cherry Pudding. No. 2.

Cream together ½ cupful sugar and 1 tablespoonful butter until light; add 2 eggs, ½ cupful milk, 1½ cupfuls sifted flour with 1 teaspoonful baking powder, add last 1 pint canned cherries that have been stoned, drained, and floured. Put mixture in greased jelly glasses set in a pan of boiling water, cover and steam 1 hour.

Or steam in a large mould 2 hours.

SAUCE.

Sweeten the juice of the cherries to taste, boil and thicken with 1 teaspoonful cornstarch.

Napkin Pudding.

Soak ½ loaf stale white bread in water until moist, squeeze perfectly dry. Put in skillet 2 tablespoonfuls of clear fat or butter, and when hot add bread, and stir until smooth and dry. Beat 5 eggs light with 1 cupful sugar, stir bread in, mix well, and flavor with rind (grated) and juice of 1 lemon. Grease a bag or very large napkin, tie, leaving plenty room to rise, place in boiling water, and boil 2 hours. Make a jelly sauce, not as thin as usual, and pour over just before serving. If desired ½ cupful currants can be added to pudding.

Cabinet Pudding.

Butter and sugar a pudding mold holding 3 pts. Mix 1 cupful seedless raisins, ½ cupful cleaned currants, 3 oz. citron, cut fine, and 3 oz. candied cherries (if desired, can be omitted). Cover bottom of mold with layer of mixed fruit, then put a layer of stale cake sliced, or fresh sponge cake sliced, or lady-fingers, another layer of fruit, then cake and so on. Make a custard of 3 cupfuls sweet milk, 3 eggs, ½ cupful sugar, and flavor with lemon extract. Boil on stove until slightly thick, being careful not to curdle, then pour over cake in mold. Put in water and boil 2 hours. Turn out on platter and decorate with red jelly. Serve with Wine Sauce, No. 2. Can also be baked in oven 1 hour by placing mold in a large, shallow pan half filled with hot water. Have a moderate fire.

Old-Fashioned Plum Pudding.

Beat yolks 2 eggs light with ½ cupful sugar, add ½ teaspoonful each, salt, cinnamon, cloves, spice, and 3 tablespoonfuls molasses. Soak ¼ lb. bread crumbs in 1 cupful milk, add to eggs, then mix in ½ lb. clean beef suet, chopped very fine. Mix ½ lb. raisins, ½ lb. currants, 1 oz. candied citron, chopped fine, 1 oz. candied lemon peel. Lastly 2 teaspoonfuls baking powder. Put in buttered bag, leaving plenty of room for pudding to rise, and boil for 4 hours. Serve with brandy sauce. Pour rum over pudding, light, and dish while burning.

English Plum Pudding.

Stone the day previous ½ lb. raisins. Add, ½ lb. seedless raisins, ½ lb. currants, ⅛ lb. citron, cut very fine, 1 teaspoonful each, cinnamon, cloves, and spice. In the morning, beat yolks 8 eggs light with 1 cupful granulated sugar. Flour fruit well, to prevent sinking to the bottom, and add to eggs. Then stir in ½ lb. sifted flour, and 1 teaspoonful salt. Mix well, then add sufficient sweet milk to make a stiff batter. Rub pudding bag with butter. Put pudding in, and tie neck tightly, leaving plenty room for the pudding to rise. Put plate in bottom of kettle of hot water, and boil 4 hours. When done turn out on platter, put rum over, light, and serve immediately. Serve with brandy sauce. Is very good cold. In winter a sprig of holly can be stuck in top of pudding. Double quantity can be made for very large dinner party.

Suet Pudding.

1½ cupfuls flour, 1½ cupfuls chopped suet, 1½ cupfuls bread crumbs soaked in 1 cupful milk, 1 cupful sugar, 1 cupful raisins, 2 teaspoonfuls cinnamon, ½ teaspoonful cloves, 2 teaspoonfuls baking powder, salt to taste. Mix well together and steam in pudding mold 3 hours. Serve with following

SAUCE.

Cream 1 cupful sugar and ½ cupful butter together, add 1 egg and 3 tablespoonfuls cold water, boil a few minutes and when cold flavor with vanilla.

Noodle Pudding.

Sift ½ cupful flour on a biscuit board, make a hole in the center of the flour, break in the yolks of 2 eggs, and gradually work in the flour until the dough is very stiff. Divide the dough in half, and roll each piece out as thin as possible without tearing it, put aside to dry, then fold and cut into very fine noodles with a machine for that purpose, or a sharp knife. Boil the noodles in boiling salt water for 10 minutes, drain and put aside.

Beat the yolks of 8 eggs with 2 cupfuls powdered sugar until light, add a handful pounded almonds, a pinch of salt, the drained noodles, and the whites of the eggs beaten to a stiff froth. Mix well, pour into a large greased pudding form, and leave in boiling water 1½ hours. Use half quantity for small family.

Pineapple Pudding.

Boil 2 cupfuls milk with 2 tablespoonfuls of butter. Add 2 cupfuls of sifted flour and ½ cupful powdered sugar, and stir until perfectly smooth. Remove from stove, cool, and add one by one, yolks of 4 eggs, beating steadily. Whip whites very stiff, then stir in. Butter and sugar a mold holding 1½ quarts. Put a layer of batter in mold ½ inch thick, then a layer of finely-sliced stewed or canned pineapple, then batter, and so on. Boil on top of stove for 3 hours or bake in oven in pan of water from 1 to 1½ hours. Serve with a sauce made from juice of fruit.

Peach Pudding.

Make same as above, only use 8 peaches, sliced, or a 2 lb. can.

Apricot Pudding.

Same as above, using 12 apricots, or a 2 lb. can.

Apple Pudding.

Make batter same as above, only mix 5 sliced apples with batter, and 1 teaspoonful of cinnamon. Mix whole together.

PUDDING SAUCES.

Chaud Eau Sauce.

Cream ½ cupful butter and 1 cupful sugar until very light, add ½ cupful boiling water, mix well, put on to boil in a double boiler. Boil as thick as honey, then pour over the well-beaten yolk of 1 egg, stir constantly or it will curdle. Flavor with white wine. Serve warm. Serve with puddings, cakes, or fritters.

Lemon Sauce.

Boil 1 cupful sugar with ½ cupful water, rind of 1 lemon, juice of 2, ½ teaspoonful of butter. When boiling stir in scant teaspoonful of cornstarch dissolved in a little cold water. Serve hot. Serve with puddings or fritters.

Caramel Sauce. No. 1.

Put 1 cupful cut loaf sugar in a saucepan on the stove, without adding a drop of water. Let it melt slowly, and get a nice brown without burning.

Beat the yolks of three eggs until light, stir in 1 pint sweet milk, and when the sugar is melted, stir all into the saucepan, and continue stirring until the sugar is dissolved and the sauce is somewhat thickened; then remove from the fire, add 1 teaspoonful vanilla essence, put in a bowl and put the stiffly-beaten whites of eggs on top. Serve with puddings, cakes, or fritters.

Caramel Sauce. No. 2.

Melt 2 cupfuls white granulated sugar in skillet on stove, and when liquid stir in ½ cupful cold water. Dissolve all lumps, then add 1 cupful sweet milk, stirring briskly to prevent curdling. Let boil, remove from fire, then pour boiling sauce on 1 raw yolk. Mix, then add beaten white. Pour in sauce-boat and keep in a warm place until ready to serve, but do not put back on fire. Flavor with vanilla.

Wine Sauce. No. 1.

Put on stove to boil 1½ glassfuls white wine, with ½ glassful cold water, add 2 or 3 small pieces of cinnamon bark, and 2 slices of lemon, and ½ cupful sugar. While boiling add 1 teaspoonful corn-starch which has first been dissolved in a tiny bit cold water. Boil a few minutes, then pour over the well-beaten yolks of 2 eggs. Beat the whites to a stiff froth, add 1 teaspoonful sugar, beat again then pour over sauce. Serve cold.

Wine Sauce. No. 2.

Put 1 cupful white wine, madeira or sherry, on to boil. Beat 2 whole eggs light with ¾ cupful sugar, stir in boiling wine, and return whole to stove to thicken. When sufficiently thick, remove, pour in sauce-boat, and keep warm until ready to serve.

Wine Sauce. No. 3.

Melt 1 tablespoonful of butter in saucepan, stir in 1 tablespoonful of flour, then add ½ cupful cold water, stirring constantly until smooth. Then add 1 cupful white wine, 1 oz. chopped citron. Remove from fire, let cool, flavor with teaspoonful each pistache and vanilla. If desired, 1 teaspoonful red Curaçoa or Maraschino liquor, can be added for flavoring.

Hard Sauce.

Cream together until perfectly smooth and white, 1 cupful sugar and ½ cupful fresh butter, flavor with brandy, vanilla or nutmeg.

Cream or Vanilla Sauce.

Boil 1 pt. milk with sugar to taste. Beat light 2 whole eggs, then stir boiling milk in eggs. Put whole back on stove, and add 2 teaspoonfuls cornstarch, dissolved in a little cold milk. When sufficiently thick, remove from fire, let cool, and flavor with teaspoonful vanilla.

Sherry Sauce. No. 1.

Boil 1 cupful milk, with ½ cupful sugar, and stir in 1 teaspoonful dissolved cornstarch. When boiling stir this into 3 whole well-beaten eggs ; mix well. Boil 1 cupful sherry wine, and pour into eggs. Mix well, put whole back on stove to come to a boil, remove, and keep in a warm place until ready to serve.

Sherry Sauce. No. 2.

Beat 2 yolks with 1 cupful sugar, then add ½ cupful sherry. Put whole on to boil in double boiler, or farina kettle, and cook until thick. Beat whites, and just before serving add to sauce.

Roman Sauce.

Boil 1 cupful brandy with 1 cupful sugar, and grated peel of 1 lemon. Beat 4 yolks light, and stir the boiling brandy in. Keep in a warm place until ready to serve. If not quite thick, when stirred in eggs, it can be placed a minute on stove to boil up.

Fruit Sauces.

Wash the fruit well, then put on the stove in a saucepan without adding any more water. Cover with a lid, and let the fruit get thoroughly heated all through until it comes to a boil, but do not boil it. Stir occasionally.

When well heated, mash the fruit well with a wooden potato masher, then strain through a fine sieve, being careful to get every drop of substance from the fruit.

Sweeten the juice with sugar to taste, add a few drops of wine or lemon juice, put back on the stove, and cook until it thickens, stirring occasionally. Serve with cake, fritters or puddings.

Blackberries, strawberries, or raspberries, make a nice sauce.

Orange Sauce.

Whip whites 3 eggs very stiff, then add 1 cupful powdered sugar. When smooth and thick, add strained juice of 1 lemon and 2 oranges. Serve as soon as possible. If blood-oranges are used, will make sauce a pretty color.

Foam Sauce.

Cream ¼ cupful butter with 1 cupful powdered sugar, until very light. Add one by one unbeaten whites of 2 eggs, stirring briskly, and beat again. Add 1 teaspoonful vanilla and ½ cupful hot water. Pour in sauceboat, and place boat in a pan of boiling water on stove, until it becomes frothy, then serve immediately.

Chocolate Sauce.

Dissolve ⅛ lb. chocolate in 1 cupful water, add sugar to taste, boil somewhat thick and flavor with vanilla.

Jelly Sauce.

Put ¼ cupful water with 1 cupful fruit jelly, put on the stove, and melt, if the jelly is very acid, add a little sugar.

Custard Sauce.

Put on 2 cupfuls milk to boil. Beat 4 whole eggs with 4 tablespoonfuls sugar uutil light, pour the boiling milk into this, and put back on the fire and stir until it thickens, not too thick. Remove from the fire and flavor with vanilla. Serve cold.

PASTRY, PIES, CUSTARDS, ETC.

Puff Paste.

Sift ½ lb. flour and a pinch of salt on a biscuit board, make a hole in the center, put in 1 ounce of butter, add a scant ¾ cupful ice water gradually and mix together. Put on ice for 5 minutes. Have ready 7 ounces more of cold firm butter, making ½ lb. in all.

Roll the cold dough on the slightly floured biscuit board to the thickness of ½ inch.

Lay the 7 ounces of butter in the center, fold the edges together so as to enclose the butter, flatten with a roller and put on ice for 10 minutes longer. Roll again lengthwise on the board in a different direction from the last time, fold it, and put on ice 5 minutes, then roll once more and put on ice 5 minutes, when it will be ready for use.

Roll the dough out ¾ inch thick, cut it all with a biscuit cutter. Take one half the pieces and cut the center out of them with a smaller cutter or small glass. Lay the whole biscuits in a flat pan, lay one of the pieces, from which the center has been cut, on top of each whole piece. With a fork prick a few holes in the small space that is not covered to prevent puffing, lay the small pieces that were cut out of the center, in the pan, and bake all in a quick oven. When done fill the holes with the oysters or sweetbreads, or any other mixture, and cover with the small pieces, and serve. If the patties are baked and cold, they must be heated again before filling, and serving.

This pastry can be used for patties, tartlets, pies, and many other things.

Paste for Pies. No. 1.

Put 1 cupful sifted flour on a biscuit board, add a tiny pinch of salt, and 1 *heaping* tablespoonful firm butter and lard mixed. Rub together until mixed, then make a hole in the center, pour in 2 tablespoonfuls ice water, and with a knife work until well mixed (never use the hand). Flour the biscuit board, roll the dough out thin, put a thin layer of fresh butter over, then sprinkle a little flour on top. Fold the dough over, and roll out thin again; put another layer of butter, then flour, roll the dough out, not too thin, and line a pie plate with it.

This makes 1 large pie in a deep pie plate.

If the crust is to be baked first, prick the bottom and sides to prevent puffing.

Paste for Pies. No. 2.

Sift flour, then measure 3 cupfuls. Sift again with ½ teaspoonful salt, measure 1 cupful of fresh butter and lard mixed (or 1 cupful butter if preferred), and cut in the flour with a sharp-bladed knife. Never use hands or a spoon in working, and work as little as possible. Then add ½ cupful cold water (ice water in summer), mix and roll out on board. If dough is stiff add a little more water. Much better if put on ice some time before using. This amount of dough will make 2 pies. A deep pan is better for pies than a shallow one. Remove pies from pan as soon as done, otherwise they will adhere to pan. Use wooden board or marble slab to roll and work dough on. When hot, never put pastry on china or oil-cloth, as this will cause crust to sweat and become moist. Press the prongs of a fork around the edge of pie crust before baking, as this gives a pretty appearance and causes them to come out more easily. If crust is to be baked first prick bottom and sides to prevent puffing.

Paste for Tartlets.

Cream ½ lb. butter, ¾ cupful sugar together, then add yolks of 4 eggs, rind of ½ lemon, and 1 teaspoonful lemon juice and ½ lb. flour. Mix well, then pour on a thickly floured board, and roll out not too thin, using as little more flour as possible. Cut with a saucer or large tin top, and line patty cases or plain muffin rings with the dough. Press into shape with the hands.

This recipe makes 18 tartlets. If you do not wish so many, take the dough that is left over, roll out very thin, cut into shapes, moisten the top with some beaten yolk of egg, sprinkle with pounded almond and powdered sugar and bake. When this pastry is used for tartlets, it is best to let them cool a little in the rings before removing, as they are then not so apt to break.

Charlotte Dough.

Mix 1 quart of flour with 1 cupful shortening (lard or butter), ½ cupful cold water, teaspoonful salt, yolk of 1 egg, 1 tablespoonful sugar, and ¼ teaspoonful baking powder. For charlotte, a deep iron pot is best, but a deep round pudding-pan can be used.

Fruit Rissolettes.

Make a rich pastry as for rich pie crust, roll it out very thin. Cut out in round pieces with a small biscuit cutter.

In the center of half of the pieces lay ½ teaspoonful of jelly or marmalade, around the edges of the dough wet with some beaten yolk of egg. Cover the pieces with the jelly on, with the other half of the dough that was cut and laid aside, press down around the edges with a small fork, to keep the two pieces together. Put in a greased pan and bake in a moderately hot oven until light brown, then sprinkle powered sugar over each one and put back in the oven to glaze.

Apple Charlotte. No. 1.

Put 3 cupfuls of sifted flour, a tiny pinch of baking powder, ½ teaspoonful sugar, and ½ teaspoonful salt on a biscuit board, make a hole in the center of the pile, lay in ¾ cupful fresh butter; with a knife, work the butter and flour together for a few minutes; make a hole in the mixture again, pour in gradually ¾ cupful ice water and mix all together with a knife. Work the dough as little as possible. Roll out a piece of the dough ½ inch thick and large enough to cover a deep iron skillet on the bottom and sides. Grease the skillet and line with the dough. Fill the skillet about ⅓ full with apples that have been peeled, cored and cut in small pieces, sprinkle generously with white sugar, lightly with cinnamon, lay in about a dozen raisins, pour a thin stream of syrup over, and put in tiny bits of butter, sprinkle just a little water over the whole. Roll out another piece of the dough very thin and cover the apples with it. Now put in another layer of apples, not so thick as the first, and proceed with the seasoning same as for the other layer. Then cover with the remaining dough rolled about ¼ inch thick. Melt a little rendered butter or lard on the stove, dip in the blade of the knife, and with it draw the dough from the sides of the skillet, and fasten down over the top dough so as to prevent the juice from cooking through. Pour some rendered butter or lard around the sides of the charlotte in the skillet, and put it in a moderately hot, steady oven and bake about 1¼ hours.

In emptying the charlotte, lay a wide, flat dish over the skillet, and turn the skillet quickly upside down.

Apple Charlotte. No. 2.

Line bottom and sides of pan with a crust of charlotte dough, rolled ½ inch thick. Pare 2 dozen apples, cut in dice, add cinnamon and sugar to taste, ¼ cupful blanched and coarsely chopped almonds, 1 cupful seeded raisins, ½ cupful cleaned currants. Mix well, then add juice and grated rind of 1 lemon. If preferred 1 wine glassful of white wine can be used instead. Fill pan with this, then add top crust. Put lumps of butter over crust. Bake in oven from 50 to 60 minutes.

Apple Strudel.

Sift 1 pint flour, add pinch salt, and 1 teaspoonful powdered sugar. Stir in slowly 1 cupful of lukewarm water, and work until dough does not stick to the hand. Flour board, and roll dough as thin as possible. Do not tear. Place a tablecloth on table, put rolled out dough on, and pull gently with the hands to get as thin as possible. The thinner the dough, the finer the strudel, but care must be taken not to tear. Have ready apples chopped fine, and mixed cinnamon, sugar, ½ cupful seedless raisins, ½ cupful currants. Spread this over the dough, cut up plenty fresh butter, all over apples. Take the tablecloth in both hands, and roll the strudel, over and over, holding the cloth high, and the strudel will almost roll itself. Grease a baking pan, hold to the edge of cloth, and roll the strudel in. Bake brown, basting often with butter. Can be served with cold cream, or whipped cream if desired, but is good without it.

Noodle Charlotte. No. 1.

Prepare same as for apple charlotte, only cutting up 12 apples. Make large noodles out of 3 whole eggs. Boil 15 minutes, drain, then mix with two tablespoonfuls of fresh butter. Add some sugar and cinnamon to noodles. Put a layer of noodles, then apples and so on until pan is filled, being careful to have noodles on top. Make no top crust. Put bits of fresh butter on top. Bake until apples are tender, and crust thoroughly done, then turn out on a large platter, with crust side on top.

Noodle Charlotte. No. 2.

Make noodles out of 3 eggs, dry, cut very fine as for soup, boil 15 minutes in salt water, drain, add two tablespoonfuls of fresh butter. In the meantime, pare and core 8 large apples. Mix chopped blanched almonds, raisins, currants, cinnamon and sugar together, fill the cores of apples with this mixture, and bake until tender. Bake in pudding pan. Beat yolks 5 eggs, with 1 cupful sugar, until like sponge, add noodles, mix well, and pour whole over baked apples in pan. Put back in oven, and bake until custard is hard and firm, and charlotte brown on top. Serve in pan it was baked in.

Strawberry Shortcake. No. 1.

Sift flour, measure 3 cupfuls, add 2 level teaspoonfuls baking powder, ½ teaspoonful salt, then cut in ½ cupful butter, then add 1 whole egg. Mix, then add 1 cupful sweet cold milk, and 1 tablespoonful sugar. This makes a soft dough. Roll in two layers, and spread in two pans both same size, baking each layer separately, in a very hot oven until light brown. Mash and sweeten ½ pt. strawberries, put on one layer, then add the other. Sweeten 1 pt. whole strawberries, spread on top layer; whip ½ pt. sweet cream, and spread on top. A meringue of whites of 2 eggs, and 3 tablespoonfuls of sugar, can be used instead if preferred.

Strawberry Shortcake. No. 2.

Sift into a bowl 1 quart flour, 1 teaspoonful salt, 2 teaspoonfuls baking powder, rub in 3 tablespoonfuls cold butter, add 1 egg slightly beaten, then 2 tablespoonfuls sugar, and mix into a smooth dough with about 1 cupful sweet milk; roll out into 2 pieces the size required, lay one on top of the other in a long pan, bake in a greased pan in a hot oven, and separate while warm. Butter well; use 1 layer for the bottom crust, cover with a layer of sugared strawberries, put on top layer, cover with more strawberries, and serve cold with sweet cream.

The strawberries can be left off the top if preferred. This makes a large cake; use ½ quantity for small family.

Roly Poly.

Make a pie crust No. 1, adding to the usual recipe, 1 yolk egg, 1 tablespoonful sugar, a pinch of baking powder. Roll out on board ½ inch thick, spread thickly with jam or jelly, roll over and over, until it is shaped somewhat like a loaf of bread. Bake in a flat biscuit pan, with 1 cupful of cold water. Baste often. The jelly makes its own sauce. When brown serve hot.

Fruit Tartlets.

If canned fruit is used, take a large can of any kind of fruit, drain all the syrup off and put in a saucepan with an equal quantity of sugar. Cook until it forms a syrup, then pour in the fruit, which has been stoned (if necessary), and cook until the whole is a syrupy mass.

If fresh fruit is used, put on two parts of sugar to one of water and cook until syrupy, then add the fruit, which has been peeled, sliced and stoned, and cook until the whole is a thick, syrupy mass.

Line the patty cases or plain muffin rings with the "pastry for tartlets," or "puff paste." Put a spoonful or two of the fruit in each one, and bake a nice brown. Peaches, white cherries, Malaga grapes, huckleberries, and apples make nice tartlets.

1 large can California fruit, fills 12 tartlets.

Cheese Tartlets.

Cream 1½ cupfuls clabber cheese until very smooth, add 1 tablespoonful flour, 1 tablespoonful thick cream, and a pinch of salt.

Beat the yolks of 3 eggs and three tablespoonfuls sugar together until very light, add 1 tablespoonful butter.

Mix the contents of both bowls together, flavor with a few drops of vanilla, and add the stiffly-beaten whites of eggs. Line patty cases or plain muffin rings with "paste for tartlets," or a rich pastry, fill with the cheese and bake in a moderately hot oven.

Cocoanut Tartlets.

Put on to boil 1 cupful sugar, and 1 cupful water; when it begins to get syrupy, add ½ lb. dessicated cocoanut, boil a few minutes longer, stirring occasionally, remove from the fire, add a few drops of lemon juice, a little of the grated rind, and the well-beaten yolks of 2 eggs.

Line patty cases or plain muffin rings with "paste for tartlets," put in the cocoanut mixture, and bake in a moderately hot oven. This makes about 10 tartlets.

Cream Tartlets.

Line patty tins or plain muffin rings with "paste for tartlets," or rich pastry. Bake, and when cold fill with whipped cream that has been sweetened and flavored to taste, put a bit of jelly or some crystalized cherries on top.

Almond Tartlets.

Beat until light the yolks of 3 eggs and ¼ lb. sugar; add ½ lb. grated almonds, 1 teaspoonful almond extract.

Line tart tins or plain muffin rings with "paste for tartlets," fill with the almond mixture and bake 10 minutes.

Orange Pie.

Beat the yolks of 3 eggs with 3 heaping tablespoonfuls of sugar, add 1 level tablespoonful butter, then add ¼ cup milk in which 2 level teaspoonfuls corn starch have been dissolved. Now add ¾ cup of the juice of oranges. Line 1 pie plate with rich pastry, pour in the orange mixture and bake a light brown, then spread with a meringue made of the whites of the 3 eggs beaten stiff and 6 tablespoonfuls sugar added. Brown lightly again.

Lemon Pie. No. 1.

Make a pie-crust after recipe No. 1, using half the quantity, line a deep pie plate, prick bottom, and bake crust a very light brown. Remove from oven and cool. Put on to boil 1 cupful sugar with 1 cupful water, and juice of 1 large lemon or 2 small ones. Cook until syrupy, and pour this into well-beaten yolks of 4 eggs. Put whole back on stove in saucepan, stir in 1 teaspoonful butter, then 1 teaspoonful cornstarch dissolved in a little cold water. Let thicken, remove from fire, and get cold. Beat whites of 4 eggs stiff, mix half with lemon custard. Pour lemon custard in crust, set in stove 1 minute to settle. Beat 3 tablespoonfuls of sugar in remainder whites, spread on top of pie, bake until a golden brown, and remove immediately from pan. Serve cold. This makes one pie.

Lemon Pie. No. 2.

Beat the yolks of 4 eggs with ¾ cupful sugar until very light, add 1 tablespoonful butter, the juice and rind of 2 lemons, then add the whites of the eggs beaten to a stiff froth. Mix well, put in a pie plate lined with rich pastry, and bake in a hot, steady oven.

Lemon Custard.

Put on to boil 1 pint milk, less 2 tablespoonfuls. Dissolve 1 heaping tablespoonful cornstarch in the 2 spoonfuls of milk, and when the milk on the stove begins to boil, stir in the dissolved cornstarch, and stir until it is thickened; remove from the fire, and immediately add a lump of butter size of a small egg. Beat until light the yolks of 4 eggs with ½ cupful sugar, then pour in the thickened milk and mix well. Line a *deep* pie plate with rich pastry, cover with a layer of jelly, then pour in the custard, put in a quick oven, and bake until light brown. Make a meringue of the whites of eggs and 6 level tablespoonfuls sugar, spread over the custard and brown nicely again.

Cocoanut Lemon Pie.

Beat the yolks of six eggs and 1 cupful sugar until very light, squeeze in the juice of 3 lemons and the rind of 2 of them, stir well, then add ½ of a cocoanut grated, and lastly, add the whites of the 6 eggs beaten to a stiff froth.

Line a *deep* pie plate with rich pastry, sprinkle a little flour over it, pour in the lemon mixture and bake. This makes 1 pie in deep pie plate. Very nice.

Lemon Tart.

Make a rich crust and bake in small spring form. Beat 3 whole eggs, and yolks of 3 very light, with 1 cupful sugar. Add juice and rind of 4 lemons, and juice of 1 orange. Put whole on stove, and stir until it comes to a boil. Put on baked crust, spread a meringue made of the remaining 3 whites and 3 tablespoonfuls of sugar on top, and put in oven to brown.

Cocoanut Pie.

If fresh cocoanut is used, grate ½ of a large cocoanut for 1 pie. If shredded cocoanut, soak 1 cupful in

1 pint milk until it is moist and soft. Beat 3 whole eggs stiff, with ¾ cupful sngar. Add 1 cupful cocoanut, 1 pint milk (or the milk and shredded cocoanut) and juice of ½ orange. Line pie plate with crust, pour in mixture, and bake in quick oven. This makes 1 pie.

Transparent Pie.

Cream 1 large tablespoonful of butter with 1½ cupfuls sugar. Add yolks 6 eggs, one by one, then add stiffly-beaten whites. Mix well, then stir in 2 heaping tablespoonfuls sifted flour, a pinch of cinnamon, cloves, allspice, and nutmeg. Then add 1½ cupfuls sweet milk, mix, then juice of 1 lemon. Make a rich crust, line 2 small pie plates, or 1 large one, and bake until light brown. Make a meringue of whites of 3 eggs with 3 tablespoonfuls of sugar, spread on top, and bake a golden brown.

Custard Pie.

Beat together until light 3 whole eggs with 3 heaping tablespoonfuls sugar, then stir in 1 scant pint of milk, add a tiny pinch of salt, a little grated nntmeg, and a little vanilla.

Line a *deep* pie plate with a rich pastry, pour in the custard, place in a moderately hot oven, and bake until the pastry is brown, and the custard is firm and set. If it stays in the oven too long it will become watery. Serve cold.

Cream Pie.

Make a pie crust, line a deep pie plate with it, prick with a fork and bake a light brown. Remove from oven and let cool. Boil 1 pint milk, and stir when boiling into the yolks of 4 eggs beaten with ⅓ cupful sugar. Put whole back on stove, add 1 tablespoonful cornstarch dissolved in a little cold milk. Let thicken, remove from fire, and flavor with vanilla. Pour cus-ard in crust. Put in stove 1 minute to settle. Beat 4 whites to a stiff froth with 6 tablespoonfuls of sugar. Spread on top of pie, and bake a golden brown. Remove immediately from pan. This makes 1 pie.

Apple Pie. No. 1.

Line 1 pie plate with nice short pastry, cut 5 small apples or 4 large ones in quarters, then in half again. Lay the apples lengthwise on the pie in a circle, and fill up all the empty spaces with small pieces of apple. Sprinkle thickly with sugar, then cinnamon over, and drop bits of butter over the top. Beat 1 egg with $\frac{1}{4}$ cupful milk, pour over the pie and bake until the apples are done and the pie a nice brown.

Apple Pie. No. 2

Put in saucepan $\frac{1}{2}$ cupful sugar, and $\frac{1}{4}$ cupful water, let it boil a few minutes, then lay in 5 large apples or 6 small ones, which have previously been peeled and quartered; cover with a lid and steam until tender but not broken.

Line 1 pie plate with rich pastry, lay on the apples, sprinkle with sugar and cinnamon and bits of butter, drop a few drops of syrup over, and bake.

Grated Apple Pie.

Beat together until light and creamy the yolks of 3 eggs and $\frac{1}{2}$ cupful sugar, then stir in 1 cupful of freshly-grated apple, mix well, then add $\frac{1}{4}$ cupful sweet thick cream, add also the grated rind of 1 small lemon, a few grated almonds, and seeded raisins may be added if desired, but the pie is nice without them.

Line a flat pie plate with rich pastry, pour in the apple mixture, and bake in a moderate oven until light brown, then spread with a meringue made of the whites of the 3 eggs beaten stiff and 6 level tablespoonfuls sugar added. Brown lightly. Serve cold,

Grated Pineapple Pie.

Line 2 *deep* pie plates with nice short pastry, prick the sides and bottom with a fork to prevent puffing, put in a hot steady oven and bake a *very* light brown. Remove from the oven, spread with a layer of some nice jelly, pour in the following mixture and bake a nice brown:

Beat the yolks of 8 eggs and 4 tablespoonfuls sugar until light, add ½ cupful milk or sweet cream, then 1 can of grated pineapple, and lastly the stiffly-beaten whites of the eggs. Mix well, and pour on the pie crusts.

This makes 2 deep pies. Use half quantity for 1 pie.

Fresh Strawberry Pie. No. 1.

Line 1 pie plate with rich pastry and cover with a layer of macaroon crumbs. Pick and wash ¾ of a quart of fresh strawberries, drain them well. Lay them on the pie crust, sprinkle thickly with sugar, then a little cinnamon, and put bits of butter on top. Bake in a steady oven.

Fresh Strawberry Pie. No. 2.

Wash and stem ¾ quart of fresh strawberries, cut them in half, pour 2 tablespoonfuls sugar over, and set aside half an hour.

Beat the yolks of 2 eggs and 2 heaping tablespoonfuls sugar until light, add 1 tablespoonful milk, then the sugared berries and juice they may have drawn. Mix, then pour into a pie plate lined with rich pastry. Bake a light brown, then spread with a meringue made of the whites of the 2 eggs beaten stiff, and 4 tablespoonfuls sugar added.

Canned Strawberry Pie.

Take 1 pint can of strawberries, drain all the liquor from them, and proceed same as for " Fresh Strawberry

Pie No. 2," only do not add sugar to the berries as they are already sweetened.

Line 1 pie plate with rich pastry, pour in the strawberry mixture, bake a light brown, spread with a meringue made of the whites of the 2 eggs and 4 tablespoonfuls sugar; put back in the oven, and brown nicely.

Huckleberry Pie. No. 1.

Line 1 pie plate with rich pastry. Pick, clean and wash 1 pint of huckleberries, drain and lay them thickly on the crust. Sprinkle thickly with sugar, lightly with cinnamon, and drop bits of butter over the top. Bake a nice even brown.

Huckleberry Pie. No. 2.

Clean, pick, and wash 1 pint of huckleberries, then drain them.

Beat yolks of 2 eggs and 4 heaping tablespoonfuls sugar until light, add 1 tablespoonful milk, then the drained berries.

Line 1 pie plate with rich pastry, pour on it the berry mixture, put in the oven and bake light brown; remove from the oven, spread with a meringue made of the whites of the 2 eggs beaten stiff, and 4 tablespoonfuls sugar added. Brown nicely. The whites can be beaten with the yolks and sugar if preferred.

Canned Peach Pie.

Line 1 pie plate with rich pastry. Take 1 small can of peaches, or ¾ of a large one, drain the liquor from it. Lay the halves of the peaches thickly over the pie crust, sprinkly thickly with sugar, lightly with cinnamon, and drop bits of butter over the top. Bake a nice brown. If desired, make a meringue of 2 eggs and 4 tablespoonfuls sugar, spread over the pie, and brown lightly again.

The liquor from the can of peaches, if strained and added to ¾ as much sugar, and cooked until thick, will make a nice glass of jelly.

Fresh Peach Pie. No. 1.

Make same as canned peaches, substituting freestone peaches, and breaking them in half after they are peeled. Use more sugar than for the canned ones.

Peach Pie. No. 2.

Make a pie crust. Divide peaches in half, peel, remove kernel, and line bottom and sides of a deep pie plate first with crust, then cover entirely with peaches. Sprinkle with sugar, and bake in quick oven. Just before removing, add ¼ cupful sweet cream to pie.

Blackberry Pie.

Line a pie plate with rich pastry. Pick, wash and drain the blackberries, spread thickly on the pie crust, sprinkle thickly with sugar, lightly with cinnamon, and put bits of butter on top. Bake a nice brown.

Pumpkin Pie.

Stew pumpkin in just enough water to keep from burning. When soft drain off water, and stew about 5 minutes longer. Mash fine, strain through a sieve, and measure 1 pint strained pumpkin for 1 pie. Beat 3 eggs with ½ cupful sugar very light, mix the pumpkin in with this. Then add 1 teaspoonful cinnamon, ¼ teaspoonful ginger, ¼ teaspoonful grated nutmeg, 1 teaspoonful salt, and 1 tablespoonful brandy. Mix well and taste. If not quite sweet enough, add a little more sugar. Line a deep pie plate with crust, fill with mixture, and bake in a very hot oven.

Sweet Potato Pie.

Measure 1 pint of mashed, boiled sweet potatoes. Thin with 1 pint sweet milk. Beat 6 whole eggs very light, with 1 cupful sugar. Mix with sweet potato. Season with ½ grated nutmeg, teaspoonful cinnamon, and 1 teaspoonful lemon extract. Line 2 pie plates with crust, fill with mixture, and bake in quick oven. Half the quantity makes 1 pie.

Mince Pie.

Boil 2 lbs. lean, fresh beef. When cold, chop fine. Add ½ lb. chopped suet, shredded very fine, and all gristle removed. Mix in a bowl 2 lbs. seeded raisins, 2 lbs. currants, ½ lb. citron chopped very fine, 2 tablespoonfuls cinnamon, 2 tablespoonfuls mace, 1 grated nutmeg, 1 tablespoonful each cloves, allspice, and salt. Mix this in with meat and suet. Then take 2 cupfuls white wine, 1 cupful brandy, juice of 4 lemons, and mix with 2½ lbs. brown sugar. Let stand. Chop fine 4 lbs. apples, and add meat to fruits. Then mix wine with whole, stir well, and put up in small stone jars. This will keep all winter in a cool place. Let stand at least two days before using.

Line pie plates with a rich crust, fill with mince meat mixture, put a puff paste crust on top, or strips, if preferred, prick slightly and bake. Serve warm, not hot.

Mock Mince Pie.

Pare, core, and chop fine, 8 tart apples. Add 1 cupful seedless raisins, ½ cupful currants, 1 oz. chopped citron, ½ teaspoonful each, cinnamon, cloves, spice and mace, a tiny bit of salt and grated nutmeg. Pour over whole 1 tablespoonful brandy, and juice and rind of 1 lemon. Sweeten to taste. Make as you need it. This makes 1 pie. Line bottom and sides of plate with crust, fill in with mixture, and put strips of dough across.

Cranberry Pie.

Stew 1 quart cranberries in sufficient water to cover them until tender. Strain and mash well through a sieve. Sweeten with two cupfuls sugar. Put whole back on stove; let come to a good boil. Make a pie-crust, line a pan and pour in cranberry mixture. This makes 1 large pie. Put fancy strips across and bake in a hot oven.

Cheese Pie.

Make a pie crust, only rolling a little thicker than usual. Line pie plate. Drip clabber the night before in a clean bag of cheese cloth, squeeze perfectly dry and measure 1 pint to a pie. Mash perfectly smooth and soft, add three whole eggs beaten in one by one, $\frac{1}{4}$ cup sugar, $\frac{1}{4}$ cup milk. Pour whole in pie plate, sprinkle $\frac{1}{2}$ teaspoonful cinnamon on top, and 1 teaspoonful fresh butter, broken into bits. Bake in a quick oven until custard is firm and brown on top.

Chocolate Pie.

Line a deep pie plate with a rich crust. Dissolve in saucepan $\frac{1}{4}$ lb. chocolate in $\frac{1}{2}$ cup milk. Beat yolks 3 eggs light with $\frac{1}{2}$ cupful sugar, stir in hot chocolate. Put whole back on stove, add a teaspoonful of butter, and tablespoonful cornstarch dissolved in a little milk. Let come to a good boil, remove, let get cold. Bake crust first, and when chocolate mixture is cold, mix in $\frac{1}{2}$ of the whites beaten to a stiff froth. Put the other half on top as a meringue. Put in hot oven and bake a golden brown.

MISCELLANEOUS DESSERTS.

Cream Puffs. No. 1.

Put on fire in deep skillet 2 cupfuls milk with two heaping kitchen spoonfuls fresh butter, stir until it begins to boil, then stir in 2 heaping cupfuls sifted flour, stir until batter does not stick to the sides of skillet. Remove from fire and let cool, then add 8 eggs each one separately, and put by spoonfuls in muffin rings. Bake in moderately hot oven. When cold, open 1 side of each puff with a sharp knife and fill with whipped cream that has been sweetened and flavored with vanilla. Or with custard made of 1 quart milk, 4 tablespoonfuls sugar, 4 whole eggs and two tablespoonfuls flour and 1 tablespoonful butter.
This quantity makes 22 cream puffs.

Chocolate Eclairs.

Make batter same as for Cream Puffs, No. 2, using only one-half quantity.
Instead of baking in muffin rings, drop with a spoon in greased pans, making each one as long and broad as a lady finger; leave space between each one to rise. Or us eeclair pans; when baked, let cool, then make an incision in each one with a sharp knife and fill with the following

CUSTARD

Put on 1 pint milk to boil, drop in butter size of walnut. Beat up yolks of 3 eggs with 3 scant tablespoonfuls sugar, when light, pour the boiling milk over, stirring constantly. Put back on stove, stir in 1 tablespoonful flour rubbed smooth with cold milk, and stir until thick. Let it get cold, then fill eclairs. Ice the top of each eclair with

CHOCOLATE ICING.

Put on 1 cupful sugar and ½ cupful water, boil until it ropes, remove from fire, stir until it begins to get white, then add 2 tablespoonfuls grated bitter chocolate (that has been melted over hot water), stir in thoroughly. Then set bowl over a boiler of hot water, add 2 teaspoonfuls cold water, stir until thin and smooth again, and with a stiff feather or knife put a thin coating on each eclair.
This recipe makes 20 eclairs.

Cream Puffs. No. 2.

Put in a deep skillet on the fire, 2 cupfuls water with 1 cupful butter in it; when it comes to a boil stir in 2 cupfuls of sifted flour, and stir until the dough leaves the sides of the skillet, set aside to cool, then add 9 eggs one by one and a pinch of salt. Bake in muffin rings, and when cold fill either with whipped cream flavored and sweetened to taste ; or a custard made of 1 quart milk and 4 whole eggs and 2 tablespoonfuls cornstarch.
This makes 24 cream puffs.

Chocolate Eclairs. No. 2.

Make pastry same as for Cream Puffs No. 2. using half quantity and bake in a long pan, drop in pieces about as long as a finger and 1 inch wide, leaving a space between each one, or use eclair pans. When baked set aside to cool ; then with a sharp knife open each eclair on one side and fill with a custard made of 1 pint milk, 3 whole eggs and 1 teaspoonful corn starch.

ICING.

Put ¼ lb. sweet chocolate in an agate boiler over another vessel with boiling water, add 1 tablespoonful sweet milk and 1 teaspoonful butter, let chocolate dissolve thoroughly, stirring occasionally, then cover the top of each eclair with a thin coating of the chocolate, let them cool and they will then be ready to serve.

Orange Baskets.

Cut 12 oranges in baskets.

Remove all pulp with a teaspoon. Soak ¾ box Cox's gelatine in enough orange juice to cover it, 1 hour. Strain the balance of the juice from the oranges, add 1 glass curaçoa to it and sweeten to taste. After the gelatine has dissolved, put on the stove just long enough to get thin, mix with the orange juice, strain and fill the orange baskets, put on ice to congeal when they are ready to be served.

Maraschino Punch.

Select as many large oranges as the number of guests requires, and prepare them by giving each one a transverse cut, about half an inch from the top. The interior, and this sliced part also, are then nicely scooped out, and the pulp is pressed in a sieve, until all the juice is extracted. This is sweetened to taste and weakened with a little water, until a strong orangeade is made. Into this is finally poured a sufficient quantity of Maraschino cordial to flavor the mixture agreeably, and the empty oranges are filled with it. Two straws are then prettily tied to the tops by narrow ribbon drawn through two punctures. These ribbons must match the other table decorations. When the cap is fitted again, they are ready for serving. They may be prevented from upsetting and spilling the contents by being put in paper cases upon small decorated plates.

Queen of Trifles.

Make a rich custard of 6 eggs, 1 cupful granulated sugar and 1 quart milk and one teaspoonful cornstarch. Boil until thick.

Have ready ½ lb. macaroons, ½ lb. lady-fingers, ¼ lb. dried figs cut fine, ¼ lb. blanched almonds, and ¼ lb. crystalized cherries.

Line a deep glass dish with macaroons that have been dipped in sherry wine, then make a layer of the mixed fruit, then a layer of lady-fingers, and so on until all is used. Then pour the boiled custard over all. Set on ice, and when cold, fill the bowl with whipped cream that has been sweetened and flavored with vanilla.

Macaroon Island.

Fill a glass bowl with alternate layers of macaroons and lady-fingers, sprinkle a layer of finely-chopped nuts over the cake, then a layer of crystalized cherries.

Boil 1 cupful wine, 1 cupful sugar and ½ cupful water together until syrupy and thick, pour it over the contents of the bowl, then spread a thick layer of thickly-whipped sweetened, and flavored cream over all. Serve very cold.

Syllabub.

Mix 1 quart of cream with ½ lb. powdered sugar, flavor to taste with sherry or white wine. Put in a deep bowl, churn with a syllabub churn, and as the foam rises, skim it off with a spoon, and serve at once.

Whipped Cream.

To 1 quart of rich thick cream, add ½ lb. powdered sugar, and 1 teaspoonful vanilla. Put in a large platter in a cool place, or on ice, and whip with a wire egg whip until perfectly smooth and velvety. Use half quantity for small family.

Neapolitan Cream.

Mix 1 pint thick rich cream with ¼ lb. powdered sugar, add ½ teaspoonful vanilla and whip until smooth and thick.

Beat the whites of 4 eggs to a dry froth, then beat in ½ cup currant jelly. Put a layer of whipped cream in a glass bowl, then a layer of egg, and so on until all is used. Keep on ice.

Eiderdown Cream.

Whip stiff 1 pint rich cream with ½ cupful powdered sugar and 1 teaspoonful vanilla.

Beat to a dry froth the whites of 4 eggs with a wire whip, mix lightly the egg froth and cream together, put in a glass bowl, and serve ice cold.

Boiled Custard.

Beat together until light the yolks of 4 eggs and 4 large tablespoonfuls sugar, add to this 2 tablespoonfuls cornstarch that have been dissolved in a little cold milk, pour over the whole 1 quart boiling milk, mix well, put back on the stove and stir until it thickens. Flavor with vanilla. Put aside to cool, then pour into a glass bowl. Beat the whites of the eggs to a stiff froth, add 1 tablespoonful sugar, pour over the custard, and put on ice to get very cold.

French Float.

Line a glass bowl with lady fingers or stale sponge cake. Dampen the cake with a little sherry wine (the wine can be omitted if preferred). Make a boiled custard of 4 eggs, pour it over the cake, then heap the stiffly-beaten eggs on top. Serve ice cold.

Baked Custard.

Beat 6 whole eggs and 6 large tablespoonfuls sugar until light, then add a tiny pinch of salt, ½ teaspoonful vanilla, and stir in 1 quart cold milk; put in a pudding pan, set in a larger one of boiling water, and bake inside a hot oven until set; about 20 minutes. If the custard is left in the oven after it is well set, it will become watery. Serve in same pan in which it is baked.

Cup Custards

Are made same as baked custard, only divide the mixture equally in cups, set the cups in boiling water and place inside a hot oven until set.

Floating Island.

Boil 1 qt. sweet milk. Beat the whites of 6 eggs to a stiff froth, drop in the milk by spoonfuls, and when firm, remove, and put on a platter. Beat yolks of 6 eggs with ½ cupful sugar, stir in the boiling milk, and place whole back on stove to thicken. If a thicker custard is desired, 1 teaspoonful cornstarch should be dissolved in cold milk, and stirred in. When cold, flavor with vanilla, pour in a glass bowl, put whites on top, and set aside in a cool place until ready to serve.

Marshmallow Custard.

Beat whites of 6 eggs very stiff, then add ¾ cupful granulated sugar, and ¼ box gelatine dissolved on the stove in a little cold water. Mix quickly, flavor with vanilla, pour in individual molds or egg cups, and set aside in a cool place to stiffen. Make a custard of the yolks of six eggs, ½ cupful of sugar, 1 qt. milk. Boil until thick, and if desired, 1 teaspoonful of cornstarch dissolved in a little cold milk can be added. Remove from fire, let cool, and pour in glass bowl. When ready to serve, empty molds, place contents on top of custard, and serve.

St. Honoré Torte.

Make cream puffs by the recipe for "Cream Puffs No. 1," using half quantity. Make a thick "Boiled Custard" by the recipe given, beating the 4 whole eggs with the sugar instead of reserving the whites.

When the puffs are cold, make an incision in each one, and fill with the custard, sprinkle powdered sugar over. Arrange the filled puffs on a large flat cake stand in a circle.

Whip 1 pint rich, sweet cream, that has been sweetened and flavored, until very stiff. Pile the cream in the center of the glass stand, with the puffs in a circle around it.

Peel 1 sound orange, and separate the sections carefully so as not to break the skin. Wipe 12 sound Malaga grapes and leave a small stem on each one. Dry the orange slices by putting them on a sheet of paper in the warmer.

Boil ½ lb. cut loaf sugar, and ½ cupful cold water until it ropes. Then carefully dip each slice of orange and each grape into the syrup, and lay them carefully on a piece of buttered marble or platter. The syrup should form a crust over the fruit. Lay 1 slice of orange on top of each cream puff, then lay 1 grape on top of each slice of orange. Serve very cold.

Ambrosia.

Peel, slice, and remove seeds from 4 oranges. Grate ½ fresh cocoanut. If cocoanut is small, use a whole one. Put a layer of oranges in bottom of a glass dish, sprinkle with sugar, then a layer of grated cocoanut, then oranges, sugar, and cocoanut, and so on. Let stand at least 2 hours in a cool place.

Fruit Salad.

Peel 5 large oranges, quarter, and cut quarters in half, 5 bananas peeled and sliced round, 1 pineapple sliced and quartered, and ½ lb. white grapes halved and seeded. Arrange fruit prettily on a large fruit dish, or in individual saucers. Mix juices of fruits with 2 tablespoonfuls of rum or brandy, and sweeten with powdered sugar to taste. Pour this over whole, and decorate top with red maraschino cherries. Can be used after dessert at a large dinner.

Banana Salad.

Slice 4 bananas, put in a fancy dish, pour over 1 glass claret. Slice a pineapple thin, add to bananas. Boil 1 cupful sugar, juice of 1 orange, ¼ cupful water, until thick and syrupy, let cool and pour over fruit. Let stand on ice at least 2 hours.

Strawberry Salad.

Wash and stem 1 quart strawberries, sugar with powdered sugar and put in a glass bowl. Pour over it the strained juice of 2 oranges and ½ cupful claret. Let stand on ice until ready to serve.

Iced Watermelon.

Select a fine ripe watermelon. Stand it on end, and cut off the top and bottom end of melon to the meat.

Take the tin bucket of an ice cream freezer, remove the dasher, put the open end over one end of the melon, press heavily until it cuts right through the centre of the melon, taking out the red meat and leaving the rind, give one long cut lengthwise through the rind and remove it from around the freezer. Put the top on the bucket, put it in the wooden freezer, pack with salt and ice, and give a few turns to the handle. This must be done not more than 15 minutes before serving, or the melon will be too cold.

Tipsy Watermelon.

Secure a fine ripe watermelon, and with a sharp knife plug it by cutting out a square piece of the melon. Pour in a pint bottle of champagne, put back the plug, lay the melon on ice for 5 hours, then serve in round slices.

Claret can be used instead of the champagne.

Charlotte Russe. No. 1.

Soak ¼ box gelatine in ¼ cupful cold water for 20 minutes.

Beat the yolks of 4 eggs and 4 heaping tablespoonfuls sugar until very light, then strain in the soaked gelatine which has been set on the stove a moment to dissolve, then add 1 pint cream which has been whipped stiff; lastly add the stiffly-beaten whites of eggs. Mix well, flavor with vanilla, rosewater, or wine, pour into a mold, and set on ice to get firm.

Charlotte Russe. No. 2.

Beat yolks of 5 eggs with 1 cupful fine granulated sugar, until all the grain is thoroughly dissolved, and eggs spongy. Dissolve on stove ⅓ box gelatine in a little cold water. Whip 1 pint sweet thick cream perfectly stiff, add cream to eggs then pour in gelatine, which must be slightly cool, not cold. Flavor with vanilla. Line a glass bowl, or individual glasses, with lady-fingers, split in half. Fill with mixture. Grate 2 lady-fingers over top, and set bowl away in a cool place to harden.

White Charlotte Russe.

Whip perfectly stiff 5 whites eggs with 1 cupful powdered sugar. Dissolve ⅓ box of gelatine on stove. Whip 1 pint cream stiff, add to eggs, then stir in gelatine, then flavor with rose water. Line a bowl with lady-fingers split in half and pour in mixture. Put in cool place until stiff and ready to serve.

Chocolate Charlotte Russe.

Boil ¼ lb. chocolate in 2 cupfuls water until smooth and thick. Put aside to cool. Whip 1 pint sweet thick cream with ½ cupful sugar until very stiff, mix with cold chocolate, flavor with vanilla, and put in separate cups, or a large glass bowl. Do not make more than a half hour before serving.

Charlotte Polonaise.

Make the day previous a sponge or angel food cake, and bake it in a brick or square form. The next day, cut off top 1 inch thick and hollow out cake, leaving crust 1 inch thick. Make a yellow charlotte russe of 3 eggs (yolks), ½ cupful sugar, ⅙ box gelatine, ¼ pint cream whipped stiff. Make a white charlotte russe of 3 whites, ½ cupful powdered sugar, ⅙ box gelatine, and ½ pint cream whipped stiff. Divide yellow charlotte russe in 2 portions. Put ⅛ lb. grated chocolate in one portion, mix well, and flavor with vanilla. Line bottom of cake with chocolate layer. Divide white charlotte russe into two portions. Flavor one half with rose water and put on top of chocolate. Color the other half of white charlotte russe with pink coloring, and flavor with strawberry extract. Put on top of white layer. Flavor remainder of yellow charlotte russe with vanilla and put on top of pink layer. Then put top of cake back on. Ice either with white or chocolate icing. Let stand in cool place about two hours before serving.

Fruits a la Creme.

Soak 1 heaping tablespoonful gelatine in 4 tablespoonfuls cold milk for half hour. Boil together until a thick syrup, ½ lb. cut loaf sugar and ½ cup water.

Have ready 1 lb. macaroons; dip the edges of the cakes in the thick syrup, one at a time, and with them form a square or a round form. The easiest way to do this is to have a tin spring form with a movable bottom and sides, put the macaroons together inside the form, and before serving, the tin form can be opened and taken off.

Whip stiff 1 pint thick, sweet, cream with ¼ cupful sifted powdered sugar and 1 tablespoonful vanilla; add ¼ lb. crystalized red and white fruits cut fine. Set the soaked gelatine over boiling water, and when dissolved stir into the thick cream. Pour the whole in the center of the macaroon basket, and when cold decorate the top with crystalized cherries.

Bavarian Cream.

Soak ⅓ box gelatine in cold water 20 minutes, then pour over it 1 pint boiling hot, sweet cream. Beat the yolks of 4 eggs with 1 cupful sugar until light, then add the hot cream and gelatine; put back on the stove in a double boiler, and stir until it begins to thicken. Remove from the fire. and while hot, stir in 1 pint of cream whipped stiff, flavor with vanilla. Pour in molds and set on ice to harden.

Strawberry Bavarian Cream.

Sugar 1 quart of strawberries with 1½ cupfuls sugar. Let stand 1 hour, then strain through a sieve. Dissolve ⅓ box of gelatine in ½ cupful water 1 hour, then melt over hot water, mix with strained berries, and put on ice, stirring constantly until it begins to harden. Whip 1 pint cream, mix with berries, and keep in icebox until hard. Serve with whipped cream.

Blanc Mange.

Put on 1 quart milk to boil.

Dissolve 4 large tablespoonfuls cornstarch in a little cold milk. Beat 2 whole eggs with ½ cupful sugar until light, and add a tiny pinch of salt.

When the milk begins to boil, add a piece of butter

size of a hickory nut, then pour it over the well-beaten eggs and sugar, mix well, and put back on the stove. Stir until it begins to boil, then stir in the dissolved cornstarch until the custard is very thick. Remove from the fire, flavor with vanilla or lemon, pour into a mold, and set on ice till very cold and firm. Serve with cream.

Chocolate Blanc Mange.

Dissolve ⅓ box gelatine in a little cold water. Dissolve ¼ lb. chocolate, with ½ cupful milk, then add 2 cupfuls sweet milk, 1 cupful sugar, and the dissolved gelatine. Boil 10 minutes, remove from fire, and let get cold. Beat 3 whites to a stiff froth, add to the chocolate, and flavor with vanilla. Put in mold, and set in ice-box until stiff. Make a custard of the 3 yolks, ½ cupful sugar, and 2 cupfuls milk. Let get slightly thick, pour in glass bowl, and set in ice-box until cold. Serve with blanc mange as a sauce.

Neapolitan Blanc Mange.

Soak 1 ounce of gelatine in 1 cupful cold milk for 20 minutes until thoroughly dissolved.

Put on 3 cupfuls milk to boil, when it begins to boil, stir in ¾ cupful sugar, and boil a few minutes.

Pour the boiling milk over the dissolved gelatine, and put on the fire in a double boiler, stir while boiling five minutes. Remove from the fire, strain, flavor with vanilla, and divide in 4 equal portions. Put 1 portion in a mold, and set on ice to congeal.

To another portion, add enough fruit coloring to make a pretty pink, flavor with strawberry.

To the third portion, add 2 tablespoonfuls chocolate. To the remaining portion, add the beaten yolk of an egg. When the layer in the mold is very firm, pour in the pink, then the chocolate, and last the yellow; allowing each layer to get perfectly firm before adding the next. Serve with cream.

Italian Cream.

Soak ⅓ box of Cox's gelatine in 1 pint cold milk over night; next morning pour 1 pint boiling milk over it and stir until dissolved, then sweeten and flavor to taste. Put on ice until congealed; then add the whites of 2 eggs beaten stiff, mix well, and let it congeal again.

Spanish Cream.

Soak ⅓ box of gelatine in cold water enough to cover it, for 1 hour; add 1½ pints cold milk to it, put in a boiler, and set on the stove in a pan of boiling water.

Beat yolks of 3 eggs and 1 cupful sugar together until light, add ½ pint cold milk and a pinch of salt. When the gelatine and milk begin to boil, stir in the egg mixture, and continue stirring for 5 minutes, then add the stiffly-beaten whites of eggs, stir well, remove from the fire, flavor, and put in molds on ice until congealed.

Lemon Cream Pudding.

Soak ¾ of an ounce of gelatine in enough cold water to cover it, for 10 minutes. Beat the yolks of 4 eggs and 1 cupful sugar until light, add the juice of 3 lemons, and the rind of 1, add also 1 wineglass of brandy or wine, place all together in a double boiler, and stir until it comes to the boiling point, then remove at once from the fire. While the mixture is cooling, whip stiff 1 pint cream, add the cream to the other mixture, then add the gelatine which has been dissolved on the stove and strained. Mix well together, put in a mold on ice until congealed, then turn into a fancy dish.

Lemon Gelatine Pudding.

Soak ½ box gelatine in 1 glass white wine, until gelatine is moist, then pour over it 1 pt. boiling water. Beat yolks 7 eggs with 1½ cupfuls sugar, add juice of

2 lemons. Pour hot gelatine over yolks. Let whole mass get cool, then stir in beaten whites of 7 eggs. Mix well, put in mold in ice-box until ready to serve. Let stand at least 3 hours. Can be made the night before if desired.

Cold Cream Pudding.

Beat yolks 8 eggs with 1 cupful sugar until spongy, then stir in 1 cupful boiling milk. Dissolve ½ box gelatine on stove. Whip very stiff 1 pt. sweet, thick cream, add to eggs, then stir in cooled gelatine. Mix well, flavor vanilla. Pour whole in a mold, and set on ice three hours before serving.

Jaune Mange.

Soak 1 oz. gelatine in ½ cupful cold water, and when water is absorbed, stir in 1 cupful boiling water. Boil in saucepan on stove, 1 cupful white wine, juice 1 orange, juice 1 lemon, grated rind of both, and ½ teaspoonful cinnamon. Beat yolks of 4 eggs with 1 cupful powdered sugar, then stir the hot wine into eggs. Mix well, then add gelatine. Put whole in saucepan back on stove, let boil up. Strain through a fine sieve, put in mold, and set in ice-box until stiff and cold.

Snow Pudding.

Soak ¼ box gelatine in 1 cupful cold water until dissolved, then pour 2 cupfuls boiling water over and stir until thoroughly dissolved, add 1 cupful sugar and juice of 2½ lemons. Strain and put on ice until *thoroughly* cold, then add the stiffly-beaten whites of 2 eggs, mix well with an egg whip, pour into a pudding mold, and set on ice until thoroughly congealed.

Before serving, empty on a fancy dish, and pour over it a custard made as follows:

CUSTARD.

Beat the yolks of 3 eggs with 3 tablespoonfuls sugar,

pour into it 1 pint boiling milk, put back on the stove and stir until thickened (not too thick), flavor with vanilla, and set on ice until very cold.

Chocolate Gelatine Pudding.

Dissolve ½ lb. grated chocolate in 1 cupful milk, and stir in saucepan on stove until smooth and thick. Beat yolks of 6 eggs with 1 cupful sugar until spongy, and add chocolate. Dissolve ⅓ box of gelatine on stove in a little cold water. Beat 6 whites stiff, add to eggs and chocolate, then stir in gelatine. Mix well, flavor with vanilla, then put in mold, and set in icebox until ready to serve.

Coffee Pudding.

Soak ¾ oz. of gelatine in enough cold water to cover it.

Beat the yolks of 2 eggs with 1 cupful sugar, then gradually add ¾ cupful of cold strong coffee, stirring all the time. Next 1 quart of whipped cream, and the white of 1 egg whipped to a stiff froth. Lastly add the soaked gelatine that has been put on the stove to be melted, and then strained. Mix thoroughly, pour into a pudding mold, and set on ice 3 hours.

Macaroon Wine Pudding.

Dissolve ⅓ box gelatine on stove in cold water. Beat yolks 6 eggs very light with 1 cupful powdered sugar. Put on to boil 1½ glasses white wine, with juice and rind of ½ lemon. Pour hot wine into eggs, put whole in saucepan back on stove, and stir constantly until stiff. Let cool, then beat whites of 6 eggs stiff, and add ½ beaten whites to custard. Add gelatine, and flavor with vanilla. Soak some macaroons in white wine, line a glass bowl with macaroons, sprinkle over a few seedless raisins, then custard, put another layer of macaroons, raisins, and custard until bowl is full. Beat the remaining whites with 3 spoonfuls sugar, spread over top, and decorate with crystalized cherries.

Macaroon Custard.

Beat the yolks of 8 eggs light with 1 cupful sugar. Boil 1 pint white wine and stir into eggs. Dissolve 1 heaping tablespoonful gelatine and when cool stir into this. Line a glass bowl with macaroons, and when the custard is cool pour over. Put another layer of macaroons, then a layer of custard and so on. Beat whites of eggs very stiff, with 8 tablespoonfuls sugar, spread on top and decorate with bits of jelly.

Wine Jelly.

Soak 1 ounce gelatine in 1 cupful cold water until thoroughly swelled, then pour over it 1 pint boiling water, to which a small piece of cinnamon and a few cloves have been added if desired. Add 1 cupful sugar, juice of 2 lemons and 1½ cupfuls white or sherry wine. Strain through a thin cloth or fine sieve, put in molds on ice till thoroughly congealed, then turn out on fancy glass dishes.

Ribbon Jelly.

Prepare the wine jelly same as for above receipe and color one half the jelly with fruit coloring. Place first a layer of light jelly, then a layer of red, and so on until all is used, allowing each layer to stiffen before adding the next. Set the mold on ice each time to harden it quickly.

Lemon Jelly.

To 1¼ ounces of gelatine add 2 cupfuls cold water and juice of 4 lemons. Let it stand 1 hour. Then add 2 cupfuls boiling water, 2 cupfuls sugar and two small pieces cinnamon bark; put on the stove, let it come to a boil, then strain through a fine sieve or thin cloth into molds, put on ice until perfectly congealed.

Orange Jelly.

Make same as lemon jelly, substituting 3 oranges and 1 lemon.

Strawberry Jelly.

Soak 1 ounce of gelatine in 1 cupful cold water for 1 hour.

Mash 1 quart fresh ripe strawberries through a fine sieve so as to obtain all the juice.

Pour 1 cupful boiling water over the dissolved gelatine, stir until melted, add 1 cupful sugar, juice of 1 lemon, then stir in the strawberry juice. Strain all through a piece of thin cloth. Put into molds and put on ice to congeal.

Nice to serve with meats or fowls. Or if served with whipped cream is nice for dessert.

Pineapple Charlotte.

Soak ⅓ box gelatine in ⅓ cupful cold water until soft, pour over it ⅓ cupful boiling water, 1 cupful sugar, juice of 1 lemon, and 1 cupful pineapple juice, strain, and add 1 cupful finely cut pineapple. Put on ice until it begins to harden, then mix in the stiffly-beaten whites of 3 eggs until light. Line a mold with lady-fingers, pour in the mixture, and place on ice until very firm and cold.

Lemon Puffs.

Beat the yolks of 4 eggs until very light, add the stiffly-beaten whites, and then stir in 1 pint milk, add pinch of salt, 3 tablespoonfuls fresh butter melted, and 5 even tablespoonfuls flour that have been wet with a little of the milk from the pint, stir well together and divide batter equally between 8 thick cups. Butter the cups well before pouring in the mixture. Bake in hot oven until brown (generally 25 minutes). Turn out carefully in the dish in which they are to be served, and pour over them the following

LEMON SAUCE.

Put on to boil 1½ cupfuls water with juice of 2 lemons, sweeten to taste, add a few small pieces of cinnamon bark; when boiling stir in 2 heaping teaspoonfuls cornstarch that have been dissolved in a little cold water. Boil a few minutes, then pour over the well-beaten yolks of 2 eggs, stirring all the time. Stir in stiffly-beaten whites of eggs, and pour over and around puffs when cold. Serve cold.

ICE CREAM, FROZEN FRUITS, AND SHERBETS.

Vanilla Ice Cream. No. 1.

Put on 1 quart of rich milk to boil. While boiling, stir 6 eggs with 1 scant cupful sugar until light, stir the boiling milk in, and when mixed put back on the stove in a double boiler, stir until the custard thickens, then remove from the fire and let it get cold. When cold add 1 tablespoonful vanilla and a tiny pinch of salt. Beat 1 pint or 1 quart of rich cream (the more the better) with just enough powdered sugar to sweeten, add one teaspoonful vanilla, beat until it thickens, then add it to the cold custard, and freeze.

This cream is the foundation of any other cream, only use the different flavorings.

Vanilla Ice Cream. No. 2.

Beat 5 whole eggs very light with 1 cupful granulated sugar until all grain is dissolved and mass is a light yellowish color. Whip 1 quart cream until stiff, add to eggs and sugar, then add 1 pint sweet milk, flavor with vanilla to taste, and put in freezer and turn until hard. This is a basis for almost any kind of cream.

Custard Ice Cream.

Beat yolks of 8 eggs very light with 1½ cupfuls sugar. Boil 1½ pints fresh milk, and stir into eggs. Put whole back on fire and let thicken. Let cool, flavor with vanilla and freeze.

TWENTIETH CENTURY COOK BOOK. 235

Neapolitan Ice Cream. No. 1.

Make the ice cream and freeze it same as "Vanilla Ice Cream, No. 1." When frozen, have a form or mold ready. Divide the ice cream into 3 equal parts. Put ⅓ in the bottom of the mold, and the other ⅔ divide in 2 bowls. To 1 bowl add 1 pint canned or ripe strawberries (if canned do not add the juice), mash with the cream and add a few drops of fruit coloring. Mix quickly and put it in the mold on top of the vanilla cream.

To the other bowl add 1 teaspoonful pistache flavoring and enough pistache coloring to make a pretty green. Mix quickly and put in the mold on top of the strawberry layer. Cover the mold with a tight-fitting top and pack in ice and salt for 2 hours. When ready to serve, dip a towel in hot water, wring as dry as possible, and wrap just a moment around the mold before emptying the cream.

Neapolitan Ice Cream. No. 2.

Make plain vanilla ice cream No. 2. When frozen hard put half in a bowl and mix with pistache flavoring, a tiny bit of pistache coloring, and ½ cup ground pistache nuts. Line bottom of mold with this. Then put in a layer of orange or lemon ice, which has already been made and frozen in another freezer. Dissolve beforehand on stove ¼ pound sweet chocolate in a little sweet milk; let it get smooth, remove from fire, cool and add to the remainder of vanilla cream. Mix well and put on top next to orange or lemon ice. Cover mold tightly and pack away as for frozen pudding.

Chocolate Ice Cream. No. 1.

Make same as Vanilla Ice Cream, No. 2, only omitting the 1 pint milk. Dissolve on stove ½ pound sweet chocolate, in 1 cupful sweet milk, rub smooth and thick, let get cold, and add to eggs, just before putting in cream. Flavor with vanilla.

Chocolate Ice Cream. No. 2.

Dissolve 1 pound German sweet chocolate in enough cold sweet milk to cover it. Rub smooth and thick by putting on the stove. Let cool and when cold add to this 1 quart cream, sugar to taste, and vanilla extract. Freeze hard.

Apricot, Peach, Strawberry, Banana or Pineapple Cream. No. 1.

Make a plain vanilla cream, No. 2, omitting the 1 pint milk. If canned fruit is to be used, drain the juice off, and add it to the eggs and cream. Mash the fruit through a sieve, add it to rest of mixture, and freeze the whole. If fresh fruits are used, 1 pint is required. Mash fine, strain and sweeten before adding to the cream. For peach and strawberry a few drops of pink coloring may be added. Bananas must be mashed smooth, but not sweetened. Chop all fruits very fine. For pineapple, the sliced is preferred to the grated. Either canned or fresh can be used.

Apricot, Banana, Pineapple, Strawberry and Peach Ice Cream. No. 2.

Whip 1 quart cream stiff, flavor and sweeten to taste. Mash fruit (1 can or 1 pint fresh fruit) smooth, strain, and mix with whipped cream. Freeze hard.

Banana Ice Cream. No. 3.

Prepare the custard and cream same as for Vanilla Ice Cream, No. 1. Mix together and just before freezing add 6 bananas mashed fine.

Strawberry, peach, pineapple, or apricot ice cream can be prepared same as banana ice cream.

Caramel Ice Cream.

Beat well yolks of 3 eggs. Melt on fire in saucepan 3 cupfuls sugar until liquid and brown, then add 3 cupfuls sweet milk, until whole is smooth and even (a little cold water stirred in liquid sugar first will prevent milk from curdling). When smooth pour over the eggs and mix well. Whip 1 quart cream, and when caramel mixture is cold, add to it. Flavor with vanilla and freeze.

Bisque Glacé.

Make plain vanilla cream No. 2, omitting 1 pint milk. Dissolve 1 cupful stale macaroon crumbs or stale sponge-cake crumbs in 1 cupful sweet milk. Add to other mixture. Flavor either with almond or vanilla extract.

Tutti Frutti Ice Cream.

Beat yolks of 5 eggs very light with 2 cupfuls sugar. Boil 1 pint of milk, stir into eggs and put whole back on stove to thicken. Remove from fire and cool. Whip 1 quart cream, add to custard. Freeze, and when half-frozen stir in ½ lb. crystallized fruit (cherries apricots, pears, pineapple, etc.) cut in small pieces. Freeze again. Then stir in juice of 1 lemon, and wine glass of white wine (sherry preferred). Freeze until hard, and pack away in mold like pudding. Half the quantity can be used.

Burnt Almond Ice Cream.

Make a vanilla ice cream and grind ½ lb. burnt sugared almonds, add to cream and freeze.

Almond Ice Cream.

Blanch 1 pint almonds brown on stove, and pound to a fine paste. Put on to boil 1½ cupfuls sugar and

1 cupful water, until it is ropy, then stir syrup into the well-beaten yolks of 4 eggs. Add 1 quart cream, and the pounded almonds. Put whole on to boil until it begins to thicken, remove from fire, add 1 teaspoonful vanilla extract, and a few drops of almond extract. Freeze until hard.

Orange or Lemon Ice Cream. No. 1.

Make vanilla ice cream omitting vanilla flavoring, and flavor with lemon or orange extract. When half frozen add juice of 2 lemons or 2 oranges and freeze hard. Grate in rind of 1 lemon or orange before freezing.

Lemon or Orange Ice Cream. No. 2.

Grate the rind of either 1 lemon or 1 orange, into 1 quart whipped cream. Add 6 tablespoonfuls of sugar when orange is used and 8 tablespoonfuls when lemon is used. Add 1 teaspoonful either lemon or orange extract. Half freeze the cream, then add the juice of either orange or lemon, and freeze until hard.

Nougat Ice Cream.

Brown 1½ cupfuls sugar, and 1 cupful blanched almonds in a saucepan on stove, and when sugar is dissolved and becomes brown as well as the almonds, pour into a greased platter to cool. When cold, pound and roll very fine. Whip 1 quart cream stiff, sweeten with ½ cupful sugar, and add browned sugar. Freeze hard.

Italian Ice Cream.

Whip 1 quart cream stiff, sweeten cream with 1½ cupfuls sugar and put in freezer. When half frozen add juice and grated peel of 2 lemons, and two tablespoonfuls of brandy. Freeze until hard.

Maraschino Ice Cream.

Stir the yolks of 8 eggs with 1½ cupfuls of sugar until very light, then add 1 cupful boiling water, mix well and put in a double boiler on the stove and stir until thick. Remove from the fire, and when cold add 1 pint cream whipped stiff, add also the stiff beaten whites of the 8 eggs. Mix well, flavor to taste with Maraschino cordial and freeze.

Nesselrode Ice Cream.

Make same as "Maraschino Cream," adding 1 lb. of chestnuts that have been skinned, boiled and mashed fine.

Frozen Peaches. No. 1.

Make a rich custard same as for "Custard Ice Cream," and before freezing add 1 quart soft peaches, peeled, mashed fine and sweetened.

Canned peaches can be prepared same as fresh peaches, only do not sweeten.

Frozen Fruits. No. 1.

All kinds of fruits can be prepared and frozen same as frozen peaches.

Frozen Peaches. No. 2.

Take the contents of 1 or 2 cans of yellow cling peaches, mash and sweeten with sugar, add the juice of 1 or 2 lemons and freeze.

Frozen Fruits. No. 2.

All kinds of canned fruits can be prepared and frozen same as "Frozen Peaches, No. 2."

Apricots are very nice prepared this way.

Frozen Apple Float.

Pare, core and quarter 8 sound apples, put on to boil with very little water, add sugar to taste, a little cinnamon bark and the rind of 1 lemon. Cook until soft, then mash through a fine sieve. Beat the whites of 4 eggs very stiff, then add 4 tablespoonfuls sugar. Mix the apples lightly with the eggs and freeze about 20 minutes like ice cream.

Coffee Mousse.

Beat until very light yolks of 8 eggs with 1½ cupfuls sugar, add 1 cupful hot water, stir on stove until thick, remove from fire and stir until cold, then stir in 1 cupful strong cold coffee, 1 tablespoonful vanilla, a few grains salt and 1½ pints cream beaten stiff, and freeze.

Frozen Egg-Nog.

Boil 1 quart sweet cream in double boiler. Beat yolks of 8 eggs with 1 lb. powdered sugar. Pour hot cream over beaten eggs and sugar, put back in boiler and let thicken. Remove from fire, add ¾ cupful good brandy, then the stiff beaten whites. Set aside to cool, then freeze.

Frozen Milk Punch.

Sweeten 1 quart milk with 1½ cupfuls sugar and grate in ½ nutmeg. When half frozen, stir in 3 cupfuls cream, whipped stiff, and freeze again. Then add 1½ cupfuls rum, ½ cupful brandy, and turn until hard.

Roman Punch.

2 quarts water, juice of 4 lemons, 1 cupful old rum, ½ cupful brandy, rind of the lemons grated, and 1 cupful champagne. Sweeten to taste, and freeze hard. Use more salt on ice, and turn longer, as it is harder

to freeze than ordinary sherbet. A whole pint champagne can be used if desired.

Meringue Glaces.

Prepare the meringue shells according to recipe for same.

Prepare a vanilla ice cream according to any of the recipes given.

Just before serving lay 1 shell on each dessert plate, put a spoonful of ice cream in each shell, and cover the cream with another shell. Serve at once.

Meringue en Surprise.

Prepare the meringue shells by recipe. Also prepare an orange ice cream. Then whip stiff 1 pint cream after flavoring and sweetening it.

Lay 1 meringue shell on each dessert plate, fill the shells with vanilla ice cream; fill just as many shells with the whipped cream, then join the two together, and cover the joints with the balance of the whipped cream.

Strawberry Sherbet.

Mash thoroughly 2 quarts fresh ripe strawberries, then sweeten with 1 quart sugar. When the sugar is dissolved, add 1 quart boiling water and juice of 2 lemons. Mash through a fine sieve or thin cloth, and freeze.

Lemon Water Ice.

Make a syrup of 2½ cupfuls sugar, 1 cupful water and 1 whole lemon cut up. When thick pour into a bowl, add juice of 5 lemons, and 2¼ pints water. Mix well, strain and freeze hard.

Lemon Sherbet. No. 1.

Strain juice 5 lemons, and set aside. Soak hulls in 1 pt. boiling water for 2 minutes, then pour water over 1 pt. sugar, and cook until sugar is melted. Then add lemon juice and freeze. When half frozen, add 2 tablespoonfuls of sweet cream, or beaten whites 2 eggs. Freeze hard.

Lemon Sherbet. No. 2.

Squeeze the juice from 8 large lemons and lay in the rinds, pour 1 quart of boiling water over all. Sweeten quite sweet with granulated sugar and set aside to get cold. When cold, strain and freeze.

Orange Sherbet.

Make same as lemon sherbet, using 6 oranges and 2 lemons.

Orange Water Ice.

Boil ¾ lb. granulated sugar with 1 quart water until it is syrupy. Remove from the fire and let cool. When cold, add the juice of 6 oranges and 2 lemons. Steep the rinds in a little hot water, then add to the syrup as much of the water as required to flavor nicely. Add 2 tablespoonfuls gelatine that has been soaked in ½ cupful cold water 1 hour, and dissolved. Mix all well together, and when cold freeze.

Pineapple Sherbet.

Put 1 can grated pineapple in a bowl, add the juice of 4 lemons, pour 1 quart boiling water over all, sweeten with 1½ cupfuls sugar and set aside to cool. When cold, mash through a fine sieve and freeze.

Tutti Frutti Sherbet.

Make a syrup of 2½ cupfuls sugar, and 1 cupful water, and 1 whole lemon cut up. When thick pour into a bowl and add the juice of 5 lemons. Then add 1 cupful fresh figs chopped in pieces, 1 cupful chopped banana, and 1 can grated pineapple. Mix well, then add 1 pint water and 1 teaspoonful strawberry flavoring. Freeze. (Strawberries in season can be substituted for figs.)

Claret Sherbet.

Make a syrup of 2½ cupfuls sugar, 1 cupful water and 1 whole lemon cut up. When thick and syrupy, pour into a bowl and add the juice of 4 large lemons. Then add 1 pint of claret, and ½ pint water. Freeze a little longer than ordinarily.

Apple Sherbet.

Make a syrup of 2½ cupfuls sugar, 1 cupful water and 1 whole lemon cut up. When thick pour into a bowl and add the juice of 5 lemons. Then add 1 pint of stewed apples mashed fine and sweetened, and 1½ pints water. Freeze, and when half frozen, stir in the beaten whites of 3 eggs. Mix well and freeze hard.

Milk Sherbet.

Put on 2 quarts of milk to boil. While boiling stir in 1½ cupfuls sugar and let it boil a few minutes longer; remove from the fire to cool. When cold, begin to freeze, and when half frozen, stir in the juice of 3 or 4 lemons (dependent on the size) mixed with 1 tablespoonful sugar. Continue to freeze it until like ice cream.

Mint Sherbet.

Soak a handful of mint in a cupful of good whiskey for one hour. Strain this and add 3 pints of strong lemonade; put in an ice cream freezer, and when half frozen, add the whites of two eggs beaten stiff, then freeze again. Requires longer to freeze than ice cream.

Frozen Cream Cheese.

Take 1 pint of cream cheese or curd, mash until perfectly smooth. It is best to mash it through a fine sieve. Add 1 quart rich cream, sweeten quite sweet with sifted powdered sugar, flavor with vanilla. Put in a freezer and freeze like any other ice cream.

Moonshine.

Beat the yolks of 3 eggs to a stiff froth, then add 3 heaping tablespoonfuls sugar, beat for 15 minutes, then add 3 large soft peaches cut in small pieces, add 1 pint thick sweet cream, ½ teaspoonful vanilla, and 2 teaspoonfuls brandy. Freeze like ice cream and serve in thin glasses. For large family use double quantity.

FROZEN PUDDINGS.

Ice must be crushed and mixed with rock salt, the same way as for freezing cream. Pudding mold must have a tight cover. Have a receptacle, sufficiently large (a tin or wooden box will do) to line bottom and sides with a thick layer of mixed salt and ice. Put the mold in the centre, fill with the pudding, cover tightly, then put ice on top and all around. Put a sheet of plain tissue or wrapping paper in top of mold to prevent salt from penetrating. Cover whole with a cloth and stand in cool place until ready to serve. Puddings must stand from 3 to 4 hours. The chemical action of salt and ice is entirely different, than if mold was simply placed on ice in ice-box. If directions are not followed, the result will not be satisfactory. Some puddings are put in molds immediately and packed away ; others frozen in freezer, then put in mold. Only turn them in freezer when expressly stated.

Bisquit' Tortoni.

Mix ½ lb. grated macaroons with 1 yolk of egg, and ½ cupful sugar. Then add 1 pint stiffly-beaten cream, stirring lightly. Flavor with vanilla to taste. Put whole in pudding mold, which has a tight cover. Pack a box or bucket with rock salt and lump ice, place mold on, and cover with ice. Let stand and freeze 4 hours,

Coffee Pudding.

With 1 large cupful of coffee grounds make a cupful of strong black coffee. Strain clear, and put on to boil with 1 cupful sugar. Cook until syrupy. Remove from fire and pour into beaten yolk of 1 egg. Let get cold. Whip stiff 1 pint cream, mix in coffee mixture, place in mold, pack, and let stand 3 hours.

Pudding Imperatrice.

Make 1 pint strong coffee and dissolve in it ¼ lb. sweet chocolate. When cold, add as much sugar as necessary. Blanch and chop 1 cupful almonds, add to coffee. Whip very stiff 1 pint cream, mix in coffee, put in mold, pack in ice and salt, and let stand 4 hours.

Hazel Nut Cream Pudding.

Put 1 pint shelled hazel nuts in a cool oven, heat, then rub between coarse towels to remove skins. Pound the nuts to a paste with white of 1 egg. Make a custard of 3 eggs with 6 tablespoonfuls powdered sugar and 1 cupful milk. When custard is thick, remove from fire and cool. Mix nuts with custard. Whip stiff 1 cupful thick sweet cream, add to custard. Dissolve ½ ounce gelatine in ½ cupful water, and when liquid let it cool, and stir in rest of mixture. (Have gelatine ready before mixing in cream.) Flavor with vanilla. Put in pudding mold, and pack in ice 3 to 4 hours.

Chocolate Cream Pudding.

Dissolve ¼ lb. sweet chocolate on the stove in ½ pint cold milk. When boiling add 2 tablespoonfuls powdered sugar. Beat 1½ pints cream with three tablespoonfuls sugar, very stiff. Let chocolate get ice cold, then divide whipped cream in half, and mix half with chocolate. Put rest on ice to keep cold. Put the mixed chocolate and cream in freezer, and turn until stiff. Have ready a pudding mold, line bottom and sides with this frozen mixture, put remainder of whipped cream in center, cover tightly, and pack away in rock salt and ice 3 hours.

Delightful Pudding.

Make a syrup of 2 cupfuls sugar, 2 cupfuls of water, and while boiling hot stir this into the well-beaten yolks of 5 eggs. Beat smooth, then add 1 pint sweet rich cream. Add 2 ounces each of chopped citron, raisins, candied orange, and lemon peel. Blanch ¼ cupful almonds, pound (not grate) smooth, and add. Put whole on stove, let come to a good boil, then remove and cool. Put in freezer, and when half frozen add a wineglass of brandy and juice of ½ lemon. Freeze hard, then pack in pudding mold, set in ice and salt at least 1 hour, until firm.

Maraschino Cream Pudding.

Cream the yolks of 6 eggs with 4 tablespoonfuls powdered sugar until very light. Add gradually 4 tablespoonfuls maraschino cordial, and stir a few minutes longer. Put in a double boiler on the stove, stir until it comes to a boil, but *do not* let it boil; remove from the fire, set in ice water until cold, then add 1½ pints cream that has been whipped with 3 tablespoonfuls powdered sugar, and 1 teaspoonful vanilla.

Put in a mold and pack in a bucket of rock salt and ice. Let it stand 2½ hours.

Pudding Glacé.

Prepare same as for Maraschino Cream Pudding, only add 6 lady fingers cut in dice, before the cream is packed. Put into a mold and pack in salt and ice for 2½ hours.

Crême de la Crême.

Prepare a vanilla ice cream by one of the recipes, using ½ quantity.

Also prepare a maraschino cream pudding using ½ quantity. Cut ½ lb. crystallized fruit in small pieces. Line a pudding mold thickly on the sides and bottom with the ice cream, then fill up the mold with alternate layers of maraschino pudding and the cut up fruits.

Cover the mold tightly, then pack in salt and ice 2½ hours.

Rum Pudding. (Delicious.)

Beat yolks 2 eggs with ½ cup sugar until light, then add stiffly-beaten whites. Flavor with 1 tablespoonful rum. Whip 1 pint cream very stiff, stir into beaten eggs. Line a melon mold with lady fingers, split in half. Then put a layer of whipped cream over. Chop ½ lb. marron glacé fine and sprinkle some over cream. Put another layer of lady fingers, cream and marrons, and so on until mold is filled. Close tightly and pack in rock salt and ice, from 3 to 4 hours. If desired, whipped cream, flavored with a little rum, can be put around pudding when it is served. It is not necessary, though.

Nesselrode Pudding.

Put on ½ lb. of shelled and skinned chestnuts in cold water, and let them boil until very tender, then press them through a purée sieve.

Beat the yolks of 5 eggs with ½ lb. sugar until light, then add the mashed chestnuts, then stir in 1 pint of sweet cream. Put on to boil in a double boiler, add a few grains of salt, and stir until the mixture begins to boil, then remove at once from fire and set aside to cool.

In a bowl put ¼ lb. crystallized cherries cut in half, ¼ lb. crystallized pineapple cut up, 1 oz. citron cut fine, ¼ cupful stoned raisins and ½ cupful maraschino cordial.

Put the chestnut cream in a freezer, freeze 10 minutes, then add 1 pint cream that has been whipped. stiff with 2 tablespoonfuls powdered sugar, turn until it begins to get stiff, then add the fruits and turn a while longer. Pack in a pudding mold in rock salt and ice 2 hours.

Diplomat Cream.

Whip 1 quart cream very stiff, and add ½ cupful sugar, 1 teaspoonful vanilla, ½ lb. candied fruit chopped fine, ¼ lb. of angelica chopped, ¼ lb. seedless raisins. Put in mold and pack away in salt and ice for 3 hours.

Strawberry Glacé au Crême.

Put 1 quart strawberries in a saucepan on the stove just long enough to heat through, not boil. Press every bit of juice from them by rubbing through a fine sieve.

Boil 1 heaping cupful sugar and 1 cupful water together for 20 minutes, add to the strawberry juice; strain and freeze in an ice cream freezer. Boil 1 cupful sugar with 1½ cupfuls water for 20 minutes.

Beat the yolks of 8 eggs until very light, add the boiled syrup, and put back on the stove, placing the saucepan in another one of boiling water, stir until the mixture is thick, then remove and beat until quite cold; then add 1 cupful of cream whipped stiff and 1 teaspoonful vanilla.

Line the bottom and sides of a tin melon form with the strawberry sherbet when frozen hard, then pour the cream mixture in the center, cover with a piece of white paper, put on the top and pack in salt and ice 2 hours.

Orange Glacés.

Take six sound oranges, and with a sharp knife make an incision around the top of each orange, then remove the tops carefully and with a spoon scoop out the inside of the oranges, being careful not to break the skins. Put the covers on the orange shells, pack them carefully in a pan and set in rock salt and ice for 1 hour.

Prepare an orange sherbet or water ice, and with it fill the orange shells, put on the covers, tie the oranges quickly with ribbon, leaving a bow on top. Pack them again in salt and ice for 1 hour, then serve.

Strawberry Mousse.

Sugar 1 pint of hulled berries with 1 cupful sugar. Let them stand awhile then mash through sieve. Dissolve 2 heaping tablespoonfuls of gelatine in ½ cupful cold water, melt over hot water, then mix with strained berries and set on ice until it begins to thicken. Whip 1 quart sweet, thick cream, until perfectly stiff, drain off all milk or unwhipped cream, mix well with strained berries. If desired, a few drops of pink coloring can be added. Taste, and if not quite sweet add a little more sugar. Some berries are more tart than others. Pour in mold and pack away in salt and ice for 4 hours.

ICING FOR CAKES.

Meringue.

Beat the whites of as many eggs as desired to a very stiff froth, then beat in 2 level tablespoonfuls granulated sugar to each white. Beat until smooth and stiff, and spread at once on the pudding or pie. If desired, a drop or two of lemon juice may be added to flavor.

Raw Icing.

Break into a bowl the whites of 4 eggs, add at once 1 lb. sifted powdered sugar, beat until white and stiff, adding a few drops of lemon juice or cream of tartar to flavor.

Spread over the cake, and set in cool oven to harden.

Boiled Icing.

Boil together 2 cupfuls granulated sugar and 1 cupful water until it threads from the spoon. Beat the whites of 2 eggs stiff, then pour the syrup into it, stirring rapidly; then beat until light and creamy. Flavor with a few drops of lemon or vinegar, or a tiny pinch of cream of tartar. This will ice 1 large cake. Use half quantity for a small one.

Pistache Icing.

Make a boiled icing, when creamy add 1 teaspoonful pistache flavoring, 1 teaspoonful orange flower water, a few drops of almond extract. Mix well, then add ½ cupful chopped pistache nuts. If a smooth icing is preferred, the pistache nuts may be omitted. Color with pistache coloring, a drop at a time, mixing well before adding more, until the desired color is obtained. This is fine for layer cakes, or all nut tarts, omitting pistache nuts when used for the latter.

Cream Icing.

Put on to boil 2 cupfuls granulated sugar, and 1 cupful milk, let boil about 15 minutes, or until it will fall from a spoon in creamy drops. Remove from the fire and beat with a fork or egg whip until it is white and creamy, flavor with a few drops of lemon and spread at once on the cake.

If the icing cooks too long it will get sugary after getting cold. It can be thinned with a little milk, then heated and whipped again.

If the icing does not get thick after beating and getting cold, it shows that it is not cooked enough. It can then be put back on the stove and cooked a little longer, stirring all the time. Remove and beat again same as at first. Pour quickly over the cake. This icing is well worth a trial, and is not as difficult to get right as it seems.

Transparent Icing.

Make a boiled icing of 1 cupful sugar, and 1 cupful water. Let, boil until it begins to get syrupy, then stir into unbeaten white of 1 egg. Beat until it begins to get creamy, add a few drops of lemon juice, and 1 teaspoonful rose water. Spread while warm and thin over cakes. Place cakes in oven or hot sun, for a few minutes to harden. Used principally for angel food and sponge cakes.

Chocolate Icing. No. 1.

Boil 2 cupfuls granulated sugar with 1 cupful water until it threads from the spoon, pour over the stiff beaten whites of 2 eggs, add ¼ lb. grated sweet chocolate, beat until thick and creamy, and spread over cake.

This quantity will ice 1 large cake or 3 layers. Use half quantity for a small cake.

Chocolate Icing. No. 2.

Grate 1 cupful bitter chocolate, put it in a saucepan, and set over boiling water to melt (not boil).

Mix together 1½ cupfuls sugar, raw yolks of 2 eggs, ½ cupful milk and 1 teaspoonful butter, let boil on a hot fire 5 minutes, stirring often, until it begins to thicken. Remove from fire, stir in the grated chocolate, flavor with vanilla, and spread on cake while warm.

Chocolate Glazing.

Grate 2 sticks bitter chocolate, add 5 tablespoonfuls powdered sugar and 3 tablespoonfuls boiling water. Put on the stove, over moderate fire, stir while boiling until smooth, glossy and thick. Spread at once on cake and set aside to harden.

Chocolate Caramel Icing.

Put on to boil 1 pint brown sugar, with ½ cupful milk, ½ lb. sweet chocolate grated, and a small lump of butter. Boil until thick, stirring often. Flavor with vanilla, and spread over cake while warm.

White Caramel Icing.

Put on to boil 2 cupfuls brown sugar, 1 cupful milk and a small lump butter. Boil until it gets as thick as cream, then beat with a fork or egg whip until thick and creamy. Spread quickly on cake.

Marshmallow Icing.

Melt ¼ lb. marshmallows in a saucepan, set in another one of boiling water. Boil 1 cupful sugar, ⅓ cupful water and a tiny pinch of cream of tartar, until it ropes.

Beat the white of 1 egg to a stiff froth, pour gradually over it the syrup, then stir in the melted marshmallows. Beat until it thickens, then spread over the cake. Decorate the top with whole marshmallows.

Golden Icing.

Beat yolk of 1 egg with 8 tablespoonfuls of powdered sugar. Add 1 tablespoonful of boiling water and a teaspoonful vanilla extract. Spread over cake and let harden before cutting. Pretty icing for a silver cake.

LARGE CAKES.

Cake Making.

The mixing of a cake is just as importart as the baking. There are a few rules to be followed if one would be a successful cake maker. If these simple rules are followed one need never have a failure when following a reliable recipe.

In the first place before beginning to mix a cake *all* the ingredients should be weighed or measured and put before you on the table so that nothing will be forgotten. The pans to be used should be well greased with butter, from which all the salt has been cooked out, or lard. If desired, a piece of brown paper can be fitted in the bottom of the cake pan and then greased; but we do not find this necessary unless the pan is very thin. For tarts a "*spring form*" should be used, they can be procured at any store that handles cake pans.

A few necessary implements for good cake making are a pair of scales, a wooden spoon, 2 wire egg whips, one for the yolks and the other for the whites of eggs.

Always use an earthen crock, never use tin to make a cake in.

In winter butter should be set over hot water a few moments to warm, not melt, as it will then cream better. Never let a cake stand after mixing, always bake at once. The oven should always have a moderate heat unless mentioned otherwise,

Flour should always be sifted twice and the sugar also. In measuring the butter always pack the cup, so as to be sure to have the proper quantity. The cup should hold ½ pint.

Fruit Cake. No. 1.

Cream together ¾ lb. butter and ¾ lb. brown sugar, add 2 teaspoonfuls each of cinnamon and allspice, 1 teaspoonful each of mace and cloves, ½ lb. pounded walnuts, 2 cupfuls flour, 1 wineglass brandy and 1 of wine, a little salt, 1 lb. seedless raisins, 1 lb. currants, ½ lb. citron cut fine, ½ lb. dried figs cut fine, ½ cupful flour with ½ teaspoonful cream tartar added, and ½ cupful flour with ½ teaspoonful soda added. Bake immediately 2½ hours. Rub all fruit with flour. And mix just as it is put down.

Fruit Cake. (Fine.) No. 2.

Cream together 1 lb. sugar and ¾ lb. butter, then add the well-beaten yolks of 10 eggs, then the stiffly-beaten whites, then stir in 1 lb. flour, then 1 wineglassful brandy and wine and 1 teaspoonful each of allspice, cloves and cinnamon, ½ teaspoonful mace, a little salt, then add 2 lb. seedless raisins, 2 lbs. currants, ½ lb. citron cut fine, ½ lb. almonds cut fine, and ½ lb. English walnuts cut fine. Add 1 teaspoonful soda with 1 teaspoonful flour, and put in pans and bake at once from 3½ to 4 hours. All fruit must be rubbed with flour before adding. This makes 2 medium sized cakes.

White Fruit Cake. No. 1.

Cream together 1 lb. sugar and 1 lb. butter, add 1 lb. sifted flour, 1 wineglassful brandy or wine, 1 lb.

citron cut fine, 1 lb. blanched almonds cut fine, 1 lb. white crystallized pineapple cut fine, 1 lb. English walnuts cut fine. Roll fruit in flour before adding, add 2 teaspoonfuls baking powder last. Bake slowly.

White Fruit Cake. No. 2.

Cream together 1 lb. pulverized sugar and ¾ lb. butter, add 1 lb. flour, whites of 15 eggs and 2 teaspoonfuls baking powder. Also 1 wineglass wine, 1 large cocoanut grated, 2 lbs. blanched almonds cut fine, 1 lb. citron cut fine, ½ cupful milk. Bake slowly. Roll all fruit in flour before adding.

Cheap White Fruit Cake.

Cream 1 cupful butter with 2 cupfuls of sugar, add 4 eggs, one by one, until whole is light, 3½ cupfuls flour, 1 teaspoonful of soda, 1 cupful sour milk, juice of 1 lemon 1 cupful currants, 1 cupful raisins, 5 cents' worth chopped citron. Bake either in cake pan or long narrow biscuit pan. Must be cut in strips when ready to serve, if latter is used.

Angel Food. No. 1.

If possible place eggs in ice-box several hours to have as cold as possible. Take 10 whites, and add a tiny pinch of salt. Beat whites, and when beginning to get foamy, add 1 level teaspoonful cream tartar. Then beat until bowl can be turned upside down without eggs spilling. Have ready 1¼ cupfuls of granulated sugar, which has been sifted 5 times, and measured after sifted, also 1 level cupful of flour which has also been sifted 5 times, and measured after sifted. The cup should hold 2 gills. A tin cupful with divisions, can be purchased for measuring purposes. Now roll the sifted sugar in gently, folding over and over in the eggs, without stirring, until sugar is all absorbed. Then add flour, folding over in same way, and 1 teaspoonful rosewater or lemon extract. Have ready a tin cake pan, which has never been greased. Put in moderate oven. A pan of water can be set in upper part of oven, until cake has begun to rise. Bake from 35 to 50 minutes. Never remove from pan while hot. Ice when cold, with transparent icing. The angel food pan with removable slides, to loosen the cake without breaking, is very convenient. Turn cake pan upside down, until cool, but do not put in a draught of air. If directions are followed, the cake is very successful, delicate, and inexpensive, and after a little practice, very easy to make.

Angel Food Cake. No. 2.

Beat very stiff the whites of 11 eggs, add gradually 1½ cupfuls granulated sugar that has been sifted six times, then add 1 cupful flour that has been sifted six times, before sifting flour last time add 1 teaspoonful cream of tartar. Add 1 teaspoonful vanilla and bake in angel food pan from 45 to 60 minutes. Do not grease the pans.

Gold Cake. No. 1.

Cream well together 2 cupfuls sugar and 1 cupful butter, add 3½ cupfuls flour, yolks of 8 eggs, beat lightly, a little salt, 1 cupful milk or cream, and 1 teaspoonful baking powder. Flavor with orange juice.

Gold Wedding Cake.

Cream together 1 lb. sugar and ¾ lbs. butter, add yolks of 16 eggs, beat light, 1 lb. flour, 1 cupful milk and 2 teaspoonfuls baking powder. Flavor with vanilla.

Gold Cake. No. 2.

Cream together ¾ cupful butter and 1½ cupfuls sugar, add 3 cupfuls flour, ¾ cupful milk or cream, and yolks of 8 eggs, beat light, flavor to taste and add 1 teaspoonful baking powder.

Silver Cake. No. 1.

Cream together 1 cupful butter and 2 cupfuls powdered sugar, add ¾ cupful sweet milk, 3 cupfuls flour with 1½ teaspoonfuls baking powder, add 8 whites of eggs beaten to stiff froth. Flavor to taste.

Silver Cake. No. 2.

Cream together 1 lb. pulverized sugar and ¾ lb. butter, add ½ cupful milk, whites of 15 eggs beaten stiff, 1 lb. flour and 2 teaspoonfuls baking powder.

Lady Cake.

Cream together 1 lb. pulverized sugar and ¾ lb. butter, add alternately whites of 16 eggs beaten stiff, and ¾ lb. flour and ¼ lb. cornstarch sifted together, 2 teaspoonfuls baking powder. Flavor with rosewater.

Silver Marble Cake.

Cream together 1½ cupfuls sugar with ¾ cupful butter, add 1 cupful milk and stiffly-beaten whites of 8 eggs. Flavor to taste and add 3 cupfuls flour with 1 teaspoonful baking powder.

Take ½ this batter and mix with it 1 cupful grated sweet chocolate, 1 teaspoonful each cinnamon, cloves and allspice.

Alternate in greased cake pan 1 spoonful light and 1 spoonful dark batter until all is used.

Delicate Cake.

Cream together 1 cupful butter and 2 cupfuls sugar, add 1 cupful milk, sitffly-beaten whites of 8 eggs and 3½ cupfuls flour with 1 teaspoonful baking powder. Flavor to taste.

Marble Cake.

White part. Cream 1 cupful butter with 2 cupfuls sugar, add 3 cupfuls sifted flour, ½ cupful milk, 2 teaspoonfuls of baking powder. Beat 7 whites to a stiff froth, and gently stir in.

Dark part. Cream 1 cupful butter with 2 cupfuls brown sugar, 7 yolks beaten in one by one, add 3 cupfuls sifted flour, 2 teaspoonfuls yeast powder, ⅛ lb. grated chocolate, 1 teaspoonful cach cinnamon, cloves, spice, and 1 cupful milk. Grease cake pan, put in layer of dark batter, then white, then dark, then white, and so on until pan is full.

Cup Cake. No. 1.

Cream together 1 cupful sugar and 1 cupful butter, add yolks of 7 eggs well beaten, 1 cupful milk, 4 cupfuls flour, 1 teaspoonful baking powder and stiffly-beaten whites of the eggs. Flavor to taste.

Cup Cake. No. 2.

Cream together 2 cupfuls sugar and 1 scant cupful butter, add 1 cupful milk, 6 eggs beaten separately, 2½ cupfuls flour and 2 teaspoonfuls baking powder. Flavor to taste. Add stiffly-beaten whites last.

1, 2, 3, 4 Cake.

Cream 1 cupful butter with 2 cupfuls sugar, add 1 cupful milk, 3 cupfuls flour and 4 eggs, a little salt and 1 teaspoonful baking powder.

Large Cream Cake.

Cream ½ lb. butter, add ½ lb. sugar, and cream again, then add the yolks of 6 eggs which have previously been well beaten with ½ lb. sugar, then add 1 lb. flour and 1 cupful of sweet cream, 2 level teaspoonfuls baking powder and the stiffly-beaten whites of the eggs.

One Minute Cake.

Cream well 1 cupful butter, then add 1½ cupfuls sugar sifted 3 times, cream again, add yolks of 6 eggs, beaten very light, 2½ cupfuls flour sifted 3 times, 1 teaspoonful baking powder, a pinch of salt and the whites of the 6 eggs beaten very stiff. Bake in a moderate oven.

Lemon Cake.

Cream together until very light 1 cupful butter and 3 cupfuls sugar, add 6 whole eggs each one separately, then add alternately 5 light cupfuls sifted flour, juice of 2 large lemons, rind of 1, and 1 cupful milk. To the last flour add 2 level teaspoonfuls baking powder. Bake in a moderate oven.

Sand Tart.

Cream 1 lb. sweet butter that has no salt in it, add 1 lb. sifted pulverized sugar by tablespoonfuls, stirring all the time, then add yolks of 10 eggs each one separately, then 1 lb. sifted cornstarch by tablespoonfuls, and lastly add gradually the stiffly-beaten whites of the 10 eggs. Flavor with lemon and bake 1 hour. The perfection of this cake depends on the mixing.

Sand Torte.

Cream ½ lb. of sugar with ½ lb. of butter until light. Add one by one 6 whole eggs, beating constantly. Grate in rind of 1 lemon. Sift ¼ lb of cornstarch and ¼ lb. flour with 1 teaspoonful yeast powder, and stir into batter. Flavor with a small wineglass of rum. Bake 1 hour.

Pound Cake.

Cream well together 1 lb. butter and 1 lb. sugar, add the well-beaten yolks of 12 eggs, alternate 1 lb. flour with ½ teaspoonful baking powder, and the stiffly-beaten whites of 12 eggs, add a little salt and flavor to taste. Bake slowly. Baking powder can be omitted, if so, add ½ wineglass brandy to creamed butter and sugar.

Imperial Cake.

Cream very light ½ lb. sugar with ½ lb. butter. Add one by one yolks of 5 eggs, then add ½ lb. almonds, blanched and chopped fine, ⅓ lb. citron cut fine, ½ wineglass brandy, ¼ teaspoonful mace. Mix citron with ½ lb. sifted flour, and 1 teaspoonful baking powder, and stir the whole in eggs. Beat 5 whites very stiff, and stir in lightly. Bake in cake pan. If a very large cake is desired double the quantity of ingredients must be used. Ice with boiled icing.

Sunshine Cake.

Cream for 15 minutes the yolks of 6 eggs with 1 cupful powdered sugar that has been sifted 5 times, grate in the peel of 1 orange and also add the juice; add alternately, 1 cupful flour that has been sifted 5 times and had 1 teaspoonful of baking powder in last sifting, and the stiffly-beaten yolks of 11 eggs. Bake about 1 hour, in angel food pan that has not been greased. Bake in moderate oven.

Brown Coffee Cake.

Cream together 1 cupful butter with 2 cupfuls brown sugar, add 4 eggs beaten separately, 1 cupful molasses, 1 teaspoonful each of cinnamon and cloves, ½ teaspoonful allspice, 4½ cupfuls flour, add 2 level teaspoonfuls soda to last ½ cupful flour, 1 cupful cold coffee, then add 1 cupful seedless raisins, 1 cupful citron cut fine and ½ wine glass whiskey, but the cake can be made without the fruit and whiskey and is very nice.

Sponge Cake. No. 1.

Beat the yolks of 6 eggs very light, add 1 cupful sifted granulated sugar and beat again until very thick, add a pinch of salt, flavor with vanilla, and add alternately 1 cupful flour sifted 3 times and all the stifflybeaten whites except about 2 spoonfuls. Now add 1 kitchenspoonful sifted flour with ½ teaspoonful baking powder in it and the balance of the whites of egg.

Sponge Cake. No. 2.

Beat 8 whole eggs with 1½ cupfuls of sugar half an hour. Add 1½ cupfuls of sifted flour, and flavor with vanilla or rosewater. Bake in cake pan. Moderate oven.

Hot Water Sponge.

Beat 4 eggs very light with 1 cupful granulated sugar, then add 1 cupful sifted flour. Mix well, then stir in ½ cupful boiling hot water, mix, then add 1 cupful flour, with ½ teaspoonful yeast-powder sifted in. Flavor with lemon, and bake in cake pan, until firm and golden brown.

Chocolate Sponge Cake.

Beat 8 whole eggs very light with 1½ cupfuls of sugar. The longer beaten the finer the cake. Grate

⅜ lb. chocolate, add 1 teaspoonful each cloves, spice, cinnamon and yeast powder, 1 cupful sifted flour, and grated rind of 1 lemon. Mix all well together, and stir into the eggs. Flavor with juice of 1 lemon, bake in spring form or cake pan. Moderately warm oven.

Sponge Cake with Matzo Meal.

Beat together until very light, the yolks of 8 eggs and 1½ cupfuls sugar, add a pinch of salt, and grated peel and juice of ½ lemon, then 1 cupful finely-sifted matzo meal, and lastly the stiffly-beaten whites of the 8 eggs. Bake in a moderate oven in spring form or layers.

Nut Sponge Tart.

Beat very light yolks of 4 eggs with 1 cupful sugar, add 1 light cupful flour, a light pinch of salt, stiffly-beaten whites of eggs, and grate in 7 English walnuts and add ½ teaspoonful baking powder.
Bake in form that has tube in center, and when cold fill hole with whipped cream.

Bisquit Törte. (With Potato Flour.)

Beat yolks of 8 eggs very light with 1 cupful sugar. Add 4 tablespoonfuls of potato flour (sifted), juice of 1 lemon, and 8 whites beaten to a froth. Bake in spring form or cake pan.

Spice Cake. No. 1.

Cream together 1½ cupfuls sugar and ¾ cup butter, add ¾ cup grated chocolate, 4 eggs beat separate, 3 cupfuls flour, 1 teaspoonful each of cinnamon, cloves and allspice, and 1½ teaspoonful baking powder.

Spice Cake. (Fine.) No. 2.

Cream together 1 cupful butter and 2 cupfuls sugar. Mix together in another bowl 2 cupfuls sifted flour, 1 cupful grated chocolate, 1 teaspoonful each of cinnamon, cloves and allspice, a little salt, put this mixture in the creamed butter and sugar alternately with 8 eggs not beaten separately. Add 1½ teaspoonfuls baking powder, flavor with lemon and bake.

Almond Tart. No. 1.

Beat until light the yolks of 8 eggs with 1½ cupfuls sifted powdered sugar, add ½ lb. pounded almonds, 2 heaping tablespoonfuls matzo meal, or 1 cupful cracker meal ; whites of 8 eggs beaten very stiff. Flavor with lemon. Bake in a spring form in a moderate oven.

Almond Tart or Mandel Törte. No. 2.

Twelve whole eggs beaten very light with 2 cupfuls granulated sugar. Unless beaten sufficiently, will fall. Add 1½ cupfuls grated bread-crumbs, ½ lb. almonds, grated, teaspoonful brandy, juice and rind of 1 lemon. Mix well. Grease spring form, place a piece of greased paper in bottom of pan, and pour in cake. Moderate oven from 50 to 60 minutes, required for baking. ½ cupful sifted matzo meal can be substituted for the bread crumbs.

Brod Tart.

Beat the yolks of 10 eggs and 2 cupfuls sifted powdered sugar very light, add 1 cupful almonds cut fine, 1 cupful raisins, cut fine, 1 cupful grated chocolate, ¼ cupful citron cut fine ; juice and rind of 1 lemon, a pinch of salt and 2 cupfuls sifted cracker meal ; 1 wineglass brandy, 1 wineglass wine, whites of 10 eggs beaten very stiff, and 1 teaspoonful baking powder. Bake slowly in spring form.

Chocolate Brod Törte.

Beat 12 whole eggs very light with 2 cupfuls of granulated sugar. Then add 1½ cupfuls grated bread crumbs, ½ lb. finely-chopped almonds, ¼ lb. grated chocolate, 1 teaspoonful each cinnamon, cloves and spice. Mix well together. Add juice and rind of 1 lemon, juice of 1 orange and 1 teaspoonful of brandy. Grease spring form, place greased paper in bottom, and put cake in. Bake in moderate oven from 60 to 80 minutes. ½ cupful sifted matzo meal can be substituted for bread crumbs.

Hazel Nut Tart.

Beat yolks of 9 eggs light with 2 cupfuls sugar, add 1 lb. finely-chopped hazel nuts, and stiffly-beaten whites of.9 eggs. Bake in spring form. When cold ice either with pistache icing, or just before serving spread over with stiffly-whipped sweet cream. Cake can be cut in half and put together with jelly.

German Hazel Nut Tart.

Beat together for 20 minutes until *very* light the yolks of 8 eggs with ½ lb. granulated sugar, then add the very stiffly-beaten whites of the eggs, place the bowl in which it has been stirred over a boiler in which water is boiling on the stove, stir continually but slowly until all the batter is well warmed but not too hot, add a small pinch of salt, and ½ lb. grated hazelnuts, add the nuts gradually, mix well and pour into a greased spring form. Bake very slowly. The grated rind of ½ lemon can be added if desired.

Ice with boiled icing. Very fine.

Walnut Tart.

Beat together for 30 minutes the yolks of 12 eggs and 1 lb. sifted powdered sugar, add 1 lb. pounded English walnuts, juice of ½ lemon and the whites of the 12 eggs beaten very stiff, a pinch of salt. Bake slowly in spring form.

Reginten Torte.

Beat 3 yolks of eggs light with ½ cup of sugar, and add ¼ lb. of grated almonds. Grease either small spring form or deep layer pan. Spread bottom with greased paper, and put in cake. Bake and let get cold. Spread with tart jelly or marmalade. Make a meringue of 3 whites beaten stiff, with ¾ cupful granulated sugar, add ¼ lb. of grated almonds, previously blanched. Spread on top of jelly, and brown in oven.

Macaroon Tart.

Beat 8 yolks of eggs light with ¾ lb. granulated sugar. Add ¾ lb. almonds blanched and grated, grated peel of lemon, ½ ounce citron chopped fine, ¼ teaspoonful each cinnamon, cloves, and spice. Beat 2 whites, stir in lightly, and put whole in spring form. Bake until brown.

Chocolate Cake.

6 eggs beaten very light with 1 cupful of sugar, ¼ lb. grated chocolate, ½ cupful cracker meal, ¼ cupful chopped citron, ¼ cupful chopped almonds, and a tablespoonful of brandy.

Rum Tart.

Beat 9 whole eggs with ¾ lb. sugar, until very light— about 30 minutes—then stir in lightly ¼ lb. sifted flour, and ¼ lb. sifted cornstarch. Flavor with vanilla. Bake in cake pan. When perfectly cold, with a very sharp knife, cut cake in half through the center, and spread with apricot jam or marmalade flavored with rum. Put together, then ice the whole. If punch essence is obtainable the jam can be flavored with it.

Chocolate Tart.

Beat together the yolks of 6 eggs and ½ lb. powdered sugar, add ½ lb. grated chocolate, 1 cupful grated bread crumbs, 1 teaspoonful each of cinnamon, cloves and allspice, 1 teaspoonful baking powder, and lastly the stiffly-beaten whites of eggs. Flavor with lemon.

Cherry Cake.

Beat the yolks of 9 eggs with 2 cupfuls sifted powdered sugar, add 2 cupfuls grated stale "lady-fingers," 1 teaspoonful each allspice and cinnamon, ¾ lb. grated almonds, rind and juice of 1 lemon or 1 orange, 1 teaspoonful vanilla, 1 can of white cherries seeded, or 1 quart fresh cherries seeded, then add the stiffly-beaten whites of eggs. Bake in a moderate oven.

Date Cake.

Beat together until very light, the yolks of 8 eggs and 2 cupfuls sugar, add 1 teaspoonful cinnamon, ½ teaspoonful cloves and allspice, ½ lb. dates cut in very small pieces, 1¼ cupfuls grated rye bread, with 1 scant teaspoonful baking powder, a pinch of salt, a few drops of lemon juice, and the whites of the eggs beaten very stiff. Bake in a spring form in a slow oven.

LAYER CAKES.

Marshmallow Cake.

The measuring cup or tumbler should hold 2 gills. The cake should be mixed like an angel food. Beat the whites of 13 eggs very stiff, then add 1½ cupfuls powdered sugar which has been sifted 3 times. Then add 1 cupful flour, sifted 3 times with 1 teaspoonful cream of tartar. Bake in tin layer pans which have never been greased. This makes 2 thick layers. The pans with removable slides are best. Invert the pans until cakes are cold, then remove. Make a thick boiled icing. Spread icing thinly on 1 layer, place on marshmallows which have been stretched out, another thin layer of icing, then put cakes together. Cover the top in same manner, only the last layer of icing should be very thick and not spread too much. This gives an appearance of snowy whiteness. The cake is very nice eaten the second day, but should never be kept longer as it becomes stale and hard.

Cream Cake.

Make same as sponge cake, bake in 2 jelly tins, let them get cold; now take 1 pint of thick sweet cream, flavor with vanilla, add powdered sugar until sweet enough, and whip until it is as thick as ice cream. Blanch and chop fine 1 lb. of almonds, stir into the cream and spread very thickly on bottom layer, put other layer on top and spread the balance of the cream on top and sides. This cake is also nice made as above and leaving out the almonds in the cream.

Banana Cream Cake.

Make same as cream cake, leaving out the almonds in the cream and putting a layer of thinly sliced banana on top of each layer of cream.

Delicate Layer Cake.

Cream together ¾ cupful butter and 1½ cupfuls sugar until very light, add alternately ¾ cupful milk and 3 cupfuls sifted flour, to the last flour add 1 teaspoonful baking powder, flavor with vanilla, add a pinch of salt, and add last the stiffly-beaten whites of 8 eggs. Bake in layers.

Make a cream icing of 2 cupfuls sugar, and 1 cupful milk, and spread between and on top of layers.

Lemon Jelly Cake.

Cream together until very light ¾ cupful butter and 1½ cupfuls sugar, add 3 eggs beaten together until light, a pinch of salt, then alternate ½ cupful milk and 2½ cupfuls sifted flour, add 1 heaping teaspoonful baking powder to the last ½ cupful flour. Bake in 2 deep jelly tins in a moderately hot oven.

FILLING.

Grate the rind of 2 lemons, and use the juice also, add 1 cupful sugar, 1 teaspoonful butter, mix well, stir in 1 cupful boiling water, and set on the stove, stir until the mixture begins to boil, then add 1 tablespoonful cornstarch dissolved in a very little cold water. Stir until thick, then pour over the well-beaten yolks of 2 eggs, put back on the stove and stir for 1 minute. When cold, spread between the cold layers and ice the top and sides of the cake with boiled icing.

Orange Jelly Cake.

Make same as lemon jelly cake, substituting oranges for the lemons in the filling.

Mocha Torte.

Beat yolks 6 eggs with 2 cupfuls of powdered sugar until light, then stir in ½ cupful strong black coffee, 1 tablespoonful grated chocolate, 2 cupfuls sifted flour, 1 teaspoonful yeast-powder, ½ cupful finely-chopped almonds, ½ teaspoonful each allspice, cinnamon, and cloves. Beat whites 6 eggs to a froth, stir in lightly, and bake in two deep layer pans, or 3 thinner pans. When cold put together with coffee filling.

FILLING.

Sweeten and boil 1 cupful milk, and then stir in 1 heaping teaspoonful cornstarch. Break yolks of 3 eggs in a bowl, and beat into this, 1 cupful of strong black coffee. Blanch and chop fine, 10 almonds, and drop in thickened milk. Add coffee and eggs, and stir on stove, until whole is thick. If not quite thick enough, ½ teaspoonful more of dissolved cornstarch can be added. When cold, flavor with vanilla. Put between cakes, and on top. Put a boiled icing over whole.

Mocha Tart.

Beat yolks of 6 eggs with 1 cupful sugar for 20 minutes, add 1½ teaspoonfuls Mocha or coffee essence, 1⅛ cupful flour, ½ teaspoonful baking powder, then stiffly-beaten whites of eggs. Bake in 2 jelly tins.

Beat stiff 1 cupful cream that has been sweetened, and put between layers.

ICING FOR TOP.

1 cupful confectioners' sugar, 1 tablespoonful cold water, 1 tablespoonful Mocha, stir to a cream and spread on top and sides of cake.

White Mountain Cake.

Cream together until very light, 1 cupful butter and 2 cupfuls sugar, add alternately 1 cupful milk and 3½ cupfuls flour; to the last flour add 1 teaspoonful baking powder. Bake in jelly tins in a moderate oven. When cold, make a boiled icing and spread between and on top of the layers; strew a thick layer of freshly-grated cocoanut on top of each layer of icing, being careful to heap the cocoanut on top.

Ice Cream Cake.

Cream together until very light, 1 cupful butter and 2 cupfuls sugar, add alternately 1 cupful milk and 3½ cupfuls flour; to the last flour add 1 teaspoonful baking powder. Bake in jelly tins in a moderately hot oven. When cold ice between and on top of layers with the following:

Beat the whites of 2 eggs stiff, then stir in 1 cupful sifted powdered sugar; when smooth and stiff stir in ¼ lb. almonds that have been blanched and pounded to a paste.

Pineapple Cake.

Cream together ¾ cupful butter and 2 cupfuls sugar until very light, then add 5 eggs, two at a time, beating five minutes between each addition; add alternately 1 cupful milk and 3 cupfuls sifted flour, add 1 level teaspoonful baking powder to the last flour. Bake in 3 layer tins in a moderately hot oven.

When cool put the layers together with boiled icing and on top of each layer of icing spread a layer of grated pineapple, sprinkle powdered sugar over the pineapple.

Jelly Layer Cake.

Cream 1 cupful of butter with 2 cupfuls of sugar, add 5 yolks, beaten in one by one, 1 cupful sweet milk, 3½ cupfuls sifted flour, 2 teaspoonfuls baking powder, and 5 whites beaten to a stiff froth. Mix well, and bake in layer pans. Put together when cold with jelly. Can also be put together with any filling or icing.

Grand Duke Cake.

Cream well together 1 cupful butter and 2 cupfuls sugar, add ¾ cupful milk, 3 cupfuls flour and stiffly-beaten whites of 8 eggs, add 1 teaspoonful baking powder, flavor to taste. Bake in layers and spread with the following

FILLING.

Cut up fine ¼ lb. each of fried figs, citron and almonds, and ½ lb. each of raisins and currants, add the grated rind of 1 orange.

Beat to stiff froth the whites of 2 eggs, add ¾ cupful powdered sugar, beat well and squeeze in the juice of ½ orange. Stir all the fruit into this mixture and spread between and on top of cake.

Walnut Filled Cake.

Beat yolks of 10 eggs with 1¼ cupfuls granulated sugar, add 1 cupful pounded walnuts, 2 cupfuls grated stale lady-fingers, 1 teaspoonful vanilla, ½ teaspoonful baking powder, whites of the eggs beaten stiff. Bake in very slow oven in 2 layers. If desired almonds can be substituted for walnuts.

FILLING.

Boil 1 cupful milk with 1 tablespoonful sugar and ½ teaspoonful butter, when it begins to boil add yolk of 1 egg beaten with 1 teaspoonful cornstarch. Stir on back of stove until it thickens and stir in ½ cupful pounded walnuts. When cool flavor with vanilla. Put between layers and ice top with boiled icing.

Ribbon Cake.

Cream together 1 cupful butter and 2 cupfuls sugar, add 6 eggs well beaten, 1 cupful milk, 4 cupfuls sifted flour and 1½ teaspoonfuls baking powder. Reserve ⅓ the batter and bake the balance in 2 layers.

Add to the batter put aside, ½ cupful raisins, ½ cupful currants, ¼ lb. citron, 2 tablespoonfuls molasses, 1 teaspoonful each of cinnamon, cloves and allspice. Bake in same size layer pan as the other 2 layers. Put the 3 layers together with boiled icing and ice the top. Have the fruit layer in the middle.

Neapolitan Layer Cake.

Cream together 1½ cupfuls sugar, ¾ cupful butter, then add ½ cupful milk, 3 cupfuls sifted flour, 1 teaspoonful baking powder, flavor with vanilla, and lastly add the whites of 8 eggs beaten to a stiff froth. Divide the batter into 3 equal parts. Bake 1 part as it is, in 1 layer pan. To another part add a few drops of fruit coloring to make a nice pink, also add a few drops of strawberry flavoring, and bake in another layer pan the same size as the first one.

To the remaining batter add ½ cupful grated chocolate, and bake in the third layer pan.

When all three layers are baked, put them together with cream icing, then ice the top and sides with the same icing.

Orange Cake.

Cream well together yolks of 6 eggs with 2 cupfuls pulverized sugar, add the juice of 1 large orange and about ½ the peel grated, add ½ cupful cold water and 2 cupfuls flour sifted 4 times with 1 teaspoonful baking powder in, then add stiffly-beaten whites of 3 eggs. Bake in layers and spread between and on top with the following

ICING.

Boil 1½ cupfuls granulated sugar and ¾ cupful

water until it ropes, pour over the stiffly-beaten whites of 2 eggs, beating all the time, add the peel and juice of 1 orange.

Custard Tart.

Cream together until very light, 1 cupful sugar and ½ cupful butter, add 3 eggs beaten separately, 2 cupfuls flour and ½ cupful milk, flavor with vanilla, add 1 teaspoonful baking powder, and a pinch of salt. Bake in layers.

When cold, put together with the following

FILLING.

Put on 2 cupfuls milk to boil. Beat until light the yolks of 3 eggs with 3 tablespoonfuls sugar. When the milk begins to boil, pour it over the eggs and sugar, put back on the stove and stir until thick. While hot pour the custard over 2 tablespoonfuls finely-cut citron. Let the mixture cool, then spread between the layers. Ice the top and sides with the whites of 2 eggs beaten stiff with 1¼ cupfuls powdered sugar, and flavored with a few drops of lemon juice.

Cocoanut Meringue Cake.

Cream together ¾ cupful butter and 2 cupfuls sugar until very light, then add 5 eggs two at a time, beating five minutes between each addition, then add alternately 1 cupful milk and 3 cupfuls sifted flour, add 1 level teaspoonful baking powder with the last flour. Bake in 3 layer tins in a moderately hot oven. When cold, put the layers together with jelly, and ice the top and sides with the following :.

Beat the whites of 5 eggs to a dry froth, then add at one time, 1 cupful sugar and 1 cupful grated cocoanut, stir gently, and spread over cake. Put in oven until a light fawn color.

Chocolate Cream Cake.

Cream together until very light ¾ cupful butter and 1½ cupfuls sugar, add 4 eggs beaten together until light; ¾ cupful milk and 2 cupfuls sifted flour added alternately, then ¼ lb. grated sweet chocolate; add 2 level teaspoonfuls baking powder with a little of the flour that has been reserved. Bake in 3 layers and fill with

FILLING.

Beat 3 whole eggs and 3 good tablespoonfuls sugar until light, stir 1¾ cupfuls boiling milk, put on the stove, and when beginning to boil, stir in 1 good tablespoonful flour rubbed smooth in ¼ cupful cold milk. Stir until thick, then remove from fire, flavor with vanilla and add 4 tablespoonfuls grated almonds. Let it get cold then spread between layers. Ice the top and sides of the cake with boiled icing.

Filled Chocolate Cake.

Cream together 1½ cupfuls dark brown sugar and ¾ cupful butter, add 3 cupfuls sifted flour, 3 eggs well beaten, ¾ cupful milk, and 1 teaspoonful soda dissolved in a little water.

Beat together 1½ cupfuls grated bitter chocolate, 1¼ cupfuls dark brown sugar, ¾ cupful milk, and yolks of 2 eggs. Mix well then put on the stove and boil to a thin custard, stirring contantly.

Pour this custard while hot into the cake batter, add 1 teaspoonful vanilla and mix thoroughly. Bake in 2 or 3 layers and put together and ice on top with boiled icing.

Brown Stone Front.

½ cupful butter creamed with 1 cupful granulated sugar, add 2 whole eggs, ½ cupful warm water with 1 scant teaspoonful soda dissolved in it, then add 2 cupfuls sifted flour and flavor with vanilla. After this is well mixed, mix together 1 cupful bitter chocolate, grated yolk of 1 egg, 1 cupful sugar and ½ cupful warm water. Boil for 2 minutes on a hot fire, stirring all the time; then pour it while hot into the cake batter.

Mix well, then bake in 2 layers, and ice between and on top with the following icing:

CHOCOLATE ICING.

Yolks of 2 eggs, ½ cupful milk, small lump butter, 1½ cupfuls sugar, mix all together and boil 5 minutes, or until it thickens. Remove from fire and add 1 cupful bitter chocolate that has previously been grated and melted over a pan of hot water. Flavor with vanilla, and spread on cake.

Chocolate Layer Cake.

Cream well 1 cupful butter, then add 1½ cupfuls sugar sifted 3 times, mix well, then add yolks of 6 eggs beaten very light, then alternate 2½ cupfuls flour sifted 3 times and the stiffly-beaten whites of the eggs; a little salt, 1 teaspoonful baking powder, flavor with orange flower water and vanilla. Bake in 3 layers, and put together and ice on top with chocolate icing.

Chocolate Nougat Cake.

Cream ½ cupful butter until very smooth and soft, then add gradually 1½ cupfuls granulated sugar sifted 3 times, mix thoroughly. Then add alternately ½ cupful sweet cream or milk, 3 cupfuls of sifted flour, sifted 3 times with 1 teaspoonful baking powder in last sifting, and whites of 5 eggs, with a pinch of salt added, beaten to a stiff froth. Begin with the cream, and add a little of each until all is used up. Flavor with vanilla and bake in 2 thick layers. When cold, spread between and on top with the following

FILLING.

Mix ½ cupful grated bitter chocolate, 1 tablespoonful butter, ½ cupful sugar, and ¼ cupful sweet cream together; put in a boiler, set in another boiler of boiling water, and let cook until thick, or try by dropping a little in ice water, if it forms a soft ball it is done. Stir often. When thick pour in ½ cupful chopped nuts, flavor with vanilla and spread on the cake.

Chocolate Ice Cream Cake.

Cream ½ cupful butter with 1 cupful of sugar, then add 2 whole eggs, ½ cupful milk, 2½ cupfuls flour (sifted after being measured), 2 scant teaspoonfuls of baking powder, flavor with a tablespoonful of whiskey or vanilla. Now take ¼ lb of chocolate, grated, ½ cupful milk, 1 cupful sugar, and the yolk of 1 egg; put in saucepan and boil until mass is thick, then pour immediately into the cake batter. Mix well and bake in 2 or 3 layer pans. Put together either with boiled icing or whipped cream, and ice the top.

Linzer Torte.

Cream 1 lb. butter with 1 lb. sugar until foamy, then add, one by one, 4 whole eggs. Mix well, then stir in ¾ lb. pounded almonds or walnuts, 1 teaspoonful cinnamon, ¼ teaspoonful cloves, 1 lb. flour, 1 teaspoonful baking powder, and a few drops of bitter almond essence. Put in four layer pans and bake in slow oven. Put together with apricot, strawberry, or raspberry jam and pineapple marmalade, each layer having a different preserve. Ice top and sides. If only two layers are desired for home use, half the quantity of ingredients can be used. This is a very fine cake. It is better the second day.

Macaroon Tart.

Beat together until light, the yolks of 6 eggs, whites of 4 eggs, and ¾ lb. powdered sugar, add ¾ lb. pounded almonds, juice of 1 lemon, and 1 tablespoonful cinnamon. Bake in jelly tins.

When baked, spread with jelly, put the layers together and spread the top and sides with icing made of the whites of the other 2 eggs beaten stiff, and 1¼ cupfuls powdered sugar added. Put in the oven and brown lightly.

Brod Torte.

Stir yolks of 8 eggs and 4 whole ones together until very light, add 1 lb. sifted pulverized sugar, and beat again, add ½ lb. grated almonds (not blanched), 1 teaspoonful cinnamon, ½ teaspoonful each of clove and allspice, 2 grated apples, ¼ lb. citron cut fine, 2 scant tablespoonfuls brandy, 1 cupful grated bread crumbs, 2 teaspoonfuls baking powder, and whites of 8 eggs beaten to stiff froth. Bake in 2 deep layer pans. When cold put layers together with whipped cream (that has been sweetened and flavored), and ice the top with cream icing.

Almond Tart.

Beat the yolks of 12 eggs and the whites of 4 together until very light, add 1 lb. of sifted powdered sugar, beat thoroughly, then add 1 lb. grated almonds, (not blanched), and 1 cupful grated bread crumbs, juice and rind of 1 lemon, a tiny bit of salt, and lastly the stiffly-beaten whites of 8 eggs. Bake in 2 thick layers and fill and ice with chocolate or boiled icing.

Cracker Tart.

Cream 1 cupful sugar with 1 tablespoonful butter until light, then add yolks of 6 eggs well beaten.

In another bowl mix 1 cupful grated chocolate, 1 cupful pounded almonds, 1 teaspoonful each of cinnamon, cloves and allspice, 1 cupful cracker meal or ½ cupful matzo meal, and 1 teaspoonful baking powder.

Mix the contents of both bowls together, add the stiffly beaten whites of eggs. Bake in layers and spread jelly between. Ice the top and sides with cream or boiled icing.

Nut Tart.

Cream together ¾ cupful butter and 2 cupfuls sugar until light, add 5 eggs, beat in two at a time, add alternately 1 cupful milk and 3 cupfuls sifted flour, to the last flour add 1 level teaspoonful baking powder. Bake in 3 layers in a moderately hot oven. Spread between the layers the following

FILLING.

Put on to boil 2 cupfuls sugar and 1 cupful water, let boil until it ropes, then pour gradually over the stiffly-beaten whites of 2 eggs, add 1 cupful of hickory nut meats or pecans, a few drops of lemon juice, and spread at once between the layers. Ice the top and sides of the cake with boiled icing.

Strawberry Shortcake.

Cream ¾ cupful butter, add 2 cupfuls sifted sugar, cream again, then add 1 cupful milk, 5 eggs, always beating well between each one, 3 cupfuls flour with 1 level teaspoonful baking powder, a pinch of salt, flavor with vanilla. Bake in 2 layers. When cold put one layer on plate for bottom crust, spread thickly with strawberries that have been well sweetened, put another layer of cake, spread thickly with sweetened berries, and spread thickly over the top of the berries some cream that has been whipped thickly with powdered sugar and flavored with vanilla. Set aside until ready to serve. Serve with thin sweet cream. To be eaten same day it is made.

Strawberry Shortcake with Matzo Meal.

Beat until very light the yolks of 8 eggs and 1½ cupfuls sugar, add rind of ½ lemon, a pinch of salt, 1 cupful sifted matzo meal, and last the stiffly-beaten whites of the eggs. Bake in 2 small square pans in a moderate oven.

When cold, lay 1 cake on a platter, spread thickly with strawberries that have been well sugared. Put the other cake on top. Spread over the top and sides with cream that has been sweetened, flavored and whipped very stiff.

Coffee Cake.

Beat together until very light 1 cupful sugar, and the yolks of 6 eggs, add alternately 1¼ cupfuls sifted flour and the stiffly-beaten whites of the 6 eggs, to the last ¼ cupful flour add ½ teaspoonful baking powder. Put in a biscuit pan, sprinkle over the top ¼ cupful pounded almonds and ¼ cupful powdered sugar that have been mixed together. Bake in a moderately hot oven.

Railroad Cake.

Cream together until light 1 cupful sugar and 2 tablespoonfuls butter, add 3 whole eggs, 1 tablespoonful milk, 1 cupful flour and 1 heaping teaspoonful baking powder. Flavor with essence of lemon. Bake in a long biscuit pan. Serve with any sauce.

Soft Gingerbread. No. 1.

Cream together 1 cupful brown sugar, and ½ cupful butter, add 1 cupful molasses, 1 tablespoonful ground ginger, ½ teaspoonful each ground cinnamon, cloves and allspice, ¼ teaspoonful mace, a pinch of salt, 4 whole eggs, 4 cupfuls flour, 1 cupful sour milk with 1 level teaspoonful soda in it. Bake in a long biscuit pan in a moderately hot oven. Serve with Chand'eau sauce.

Soft Gingerbread. No. 2.

Cream ½ cupful butter with 1 cupful granulated sugar, until light, then break in one by one, the yolks of 4 eggs. Then add 2 cupfuls molasses, 1 tablespoonful of ginger, ½ teaspoonful each cinnamon, allspice, and nutmeg. Stir in 3 cupfuls sifted flour, 1 cup sweet milk, then 1 cupful more of sifted flour with a teaspoonful of baking powder. Pour in flat narrow baking pans. This makes 2 loaves. Half the quantity may be used. When taken from the stove, loosen sides with a knife, turn pan upside down on a board, and put a rag dipped in cold water on bottom as it causes it to steam, and come out easily. Never let cake get cold in pan. If desired for a dessert, can be served with cream or caramel sauce. Have sauce hot, but bread is better cold.

Brown Cake.

Cream 1 cupful butter with 1 cupful sugar. Beat in 5 eggs, one at a time, stirring continually. Add 1 large cupful of molasses, 5 cts. citron, chopped fine, 10 cts. worth almonds, grated, ¼ lb. chocolate grated, ½ teaspoonful spice, 2 teaspoonfuls cinnamon, 1 cupful sour milk, and 5 cupfuls sifted flour with 1 teaspoonful soda sifted in last cup. Mix well, and bake in cake pan, or long, narrow biscuit pan, ice, and cut in squares. Ice with cream icing.

Ribbon Cake.

Cream 1 cupful butter with 2 cupfuls sugar, and beat in, one by one, 6 whole eggs, until whole is light. Add 3½ cupfuls sifted flour, 1 teaspoonful yeast powder, and 1 cupful milk. Divide dough in 3 parts. In one part, grate ⅛ lb. chocolate, and add ¼ teaspoonful each cinnamon, cloves, and spice. Grease narrow, long biscuit pan, spread greased paper on bottom, and put chocolate batter in pan. Then put in plain dough. Color the third part with pink coloring and put on top. Bake in moderately warm oven. When cold, ice with either chocolate or pink icing. Cut in squares when ready to serve. Can also be baked in large cake pan.

Caramel Cake.

Cream 1 cupful butter with 2 cupfuls sugar, add 3 cupfuls sifted flour, ¾ cupful milk, and stiffly-beaten whites of 8 eggs, 2 teaspoonfuls of yeast powder, sifted in with the flour. Bake in narrow, long biscuit pan, or in layers. When cold, spread with caramel icing.

Nut Cake.

Cream 1 cupful butter with 2 cupfuls sugar, until light, add 3 cupfuls sifted flour, 1 teaspoonful baking powder, 1 cupful milk, and 2 cupfuls chopped nuts. Either walnuts, hickory nuts, butternuts, or pecans will do, or even mixed nuts. Beat 5 whites of eggs to a stiff froth, add to batter. Flavor with rose water. Bake in long, narrow biscuit pan or cake pan. When cold, ice, and while icing is moist, cover top with ½ cupful chopped nuts. Cut in squares or diamonds, when ready to serve.

SMALL CAKES.

Butter Cakes.

Cream together ½ lb. butter and 1 cupful sugar, add the yolks of 2 raw eggs, the white of 1, and the yolks of 3 hard-boiled eggs grated; rind and juice of ½ lemon, a few drops of vanilla, 4 cupfuls of flour that has been sifted 4 times. Roll out on a biscuit board. Cut into cakes. Spread the top of each cake with some unbeaten white of egg, then some finely chopped almonds mixed with sugar.
Bake in moderate oven.

Sugar Kringel.

Cream ½ lb. butter with ½ lb. sugar, add the yolks of 6 hard-boiled eggs mashed through a sieve, ½ teaspoonful cinnamon, and grated rind of lemon. Stir well, then add 4 full cups sifted flour. Stand in a cool place for one hour. *Roll in sticks* on board, and shape cakes in different forms, pretzels or round hoops. Sprinkle with sugar and cinnamon, and bake cakes in flat, greased pans.

Short Cakes. (Mürba Kuchen.)

Cream together ½ lb. butter and ¾ cupful sugar, then add the yolks of 4 eggs beaten light, then ½ lb. sifted flour, mix well and add ½ teaspoonful lemon juice and the grated rind of ½ lemon.
Lay on a floured biscuit board and roll out very thin, adding just as little more flour as possible. Cut in fancy shapes and use a feather to spread the tops with some beaten yolks of egg to which has been added a tiny bit of milk. Sprinkle powdered sugar and pounded almonds mixed together, on top of each cake.

Small Sugar Tarts.

Cream 1 lb. sugar with ½ lb. butter until light. Beat in 1 whole egg, ½ wineglass brandy or whiskey, and enough flour to roll out on board. Roll thin, dampen dough with sweet milk, sprinkle plentifully with sugar, cinnamon and handful chopped almonds, cut in diamond or square shapes, and bake in flat greased pans. Should be a day or more old before eating.

Sugar Cakes.

Cream together ¾ lb. butter and 1 lb. sugar, add ½ wineglass brandy and 1¼ lbs. flour, tiny pinch baking powder. Roll out, cut in cakes and bake. The tops can be glazed before baking with the yellow of an egg mixed with a little milk, or a blanched almond can be put in the centre of each cake before baking.

Tea Cakes.

Cream 2 cupfuls sugar with ¾ cupful butter, and ¼ cupful lard (or 1 entire cupful butter if preferred), beat in one by one 5 whole eggs, add a little grated nutmeg, and sift in 7 cupfuls flour, measured unsifted. With the last cupful add 1 teaspoonful of yeast powder. Roll out on board, cut with biscuit cutter, and bake in moderately warm oven.

Cookies.

Cream ½ cupful butter and ½ cupful lard (or all butter if desired), beat well, add one by one 2 whole eggs, 1 cupful sour milk, in which 1 scant teaspoonful of soda has been dissolved, a little grated nutmeg, and 8 cupfuls of sifted flour. Roll out, cut thin, and bake in buttered tins.

Chocolate Cookies.

Beat 4 whites of eggs very stiff, add ½ cupful sugar, 1 oz. chocolate grated, and 2 heaping tablespoonfuls sifted flour. Drop teaspoonful of batter on buttered pans, and bake in moderate oven. Best eaten fresh.

Ginger Snaps. No. 1.

Cream together 1 cupful butter and 1 cupful sugar, add 1 cupful molasses, 1 heaping tablespoonful ground ginger, and add ½ cupful black coffee, in which 2 heaping teaspoonfuls soda have been dissolved, a pinch salt and flour enough to roll out. Roll very thin, cut with biscuit cutter and bake in hot oven.

Ginger Snaps. No. 2.

Melt 1 cupful butter, pour it into 1 pint molasses, add 2 teaspoonfuls of ginger, 1 of cloves, and 1 tablespoonful of soda. Sift in sufficient flour to make a dough that can be rolled out. Cut with a small cutter, and bake in flat greased pans.

Small Lemon Snaps.

Cream 1 lb sugar with ¼ lb. butter, add one by one 3 eggs, stirring briskly, then 1 teaspoonful of ammonia, juice of 1 lemon, then add 1 lb. flour. Flavor with lemon extract. Make a soft dough, but must be rolled out. If too stiff, add a little milk. Roll out thin, cut with small cutter, bake in flat greased pans in a cool oven.

Anise Seed Cakes.

Beat *very light* 3 eggs and 1½ cupfuls sugar, add 2 cupfuls sifted flour and 1 tablespoonful anise seed, a pinch of salt. Drop them by ½ teaspoonfuls in well greased long pans. Let them stand until thoroughly dry, and a crust has formed on top (about 8 or 10 hours). Bake in a slow oven.

Anise Seed Cakes. (*Matzo Meal.*)

Beat very light 3 eggs and 1 cupful sugar, add 1 tablespoonful anise seed and ¾ cupful sifted matzo meal, a little salt. Drop by half teaspoonfuls in buttered pans, and let them dry thoroughly before baking in a slow oven.

Leb Kuchen. No. 1.

Yolks of 7 eggs and whites of 3, beat with 1 cupful brown sugar until light, add 1 cupful molasses, 1 teaspoonful each of cinnamon and salt, ½ teaspoonful allspice, ¼ nutmeg grated, ½ lb. blanched pounded almonds, ½ lb. citron cut fine, ½ lb. grated chocolate, 2½ cupfuls flour, 1½ teaspoonfuls baking powder. Roll the fruit in a little flour before adding.

Spread the dough in long pans with well floured hands, have about 1½ inches thick. Bake in very moderate oven. When baked, cut in squares, and ice on top with icing made of the whites of 3 eggs beaten stiff, and 2 cupfuls powdered sugar added and a little lemon juice. Set in a cool stove or the sun to dry. It is best to let these cakes stand a week before using.

Leb Kuchen. No. 2.

Beat 7 whole eggs with 2 cupfuls of brown sugar, add 2 cupfuls of molasses, 1 teaspoonful each, cinnamon, cloves, spice, and yeast powder, ¼ lb. chopped almonds, 2 ozs. citron chopped fine, and ⅛ lb. grated chocolate. Mix well, then add sufficient flour to roll out, without being stiff. Cut either with a round biscuit cutter, ½ inch thick, or in squares like the bought ones. Bake in flat greased pans, and when cold, ice tops with boiled icing. The cakes are always hard when taken from oven, and must stand in a covered box, at least two days, before being eaten. Will keep two weeks. This quantity makes 100 cakes. For smaller number of cakes halve the ingredients.

Old-Fashioned Leb Kuchen.

Put on 1 quart molasses to boil, when boiling sift in 1½ teaspoonfuls soda, stirring all the time, when the syrup begins to boil up, stir in quickly 2 cupfuls flour, let boil a few minutes, then set aside to cool.

When cool, add 1 cupful pounded almonds, ½ cupful finely-cut citron, 1 cupful brown sugar, 2 teaspoonfuls anise seed, 1 teaspoonful each cloves and allspice, ¼ teaspoonful ginger, a little salt, a few drops lemon juice, 9 cupfuls flour. Roll out on biscuit board ¾ inch thick, cut in shapes, put in greased biscuit pans and let stand over night. Bake in moderate oven. These cakes are better after lying for about two weeks.

Small Spice Cakes.

Beat 6 eggs light with 2 cupfuls of sugar, add ½ lb. almonds, grated, ⅛ lb. chocolate, grated, 1 teaspoonful each cinnamon, cloves, and allspice. Then add 3 cupfuls sifted flour, 1 teaspoonful yeast-powder. Mix well, then flavor with rind and juice of 1 lemon. Spread granulated sugar on wooden board, drop teaspoonful of batter in sugar, roll in small round shape, drop in flat buttered pans, and bake in moderate oven. Better second day than the first.

Chocolate Cakes.

Beat together until light the yolks of 6 eggs, whites of 3 and ½ lb. sugar, add ½ lb. grated chocolate, ½ lb. pounded almonds, 1 teaspoonful cinnamon, ½ teaspoonful each cloves and allspice, rind of ½ lemon, and a few drops lemon juice. Add only enough flour to enable you to roll out, the less flour the better.

Roll out on a large biscuit board, about ½ inch thick.

Beat the whites of 3 eggs very stiff, then stir in 2

cupfuls sifted powdered sugar, add 1 teaspoonful lemon juice.

Spread the icing over the dough, then cut in square cakes. Bake in a moderate oven until light brown.

Cocoanut Cakes.

Mix 1 lb. grated cocoanut and 1 lb. powdered sugar together, then add the stiffly-beaten whites of 3 eggs, mix well, put on the stove and stir while boiling a few minutes.

Beat the white of 1 egg stiff, add 2 tablespoonfuls powdered sugar, pour the boiled mixture into this icing, stirring constantly until cold. Drop on buttered paper and bake slowly.

Cocoanut Drops.

Beat whites of 2 eggs very stiff, add 1 cupful of granulated sugar, 1 tablespoonful of flour, and 2 cupfuls shredded cocoanut. Butter baking pans, cover with greased paper, and bake in moderate oven. Granulated sugar sifted over cakes before baking, makes a nice crust.

Almond Drops.

Beat 2 whites of eggs very stiff, add 1 cupful granulated sugar, beat until dissolved, then ½ lb. of almond cut very fine (not grated). Mix well, line a greased biscuit pan with brown or wrapping paper, and drop by teaspoonfuls. Moderate oven.

Almond Slices or Mondel Schnitten.

Beat 4 eggs with 1½ cupfuls sugar, until light. Add 1 cupful sifted flour, 1½ teaspoonfuls baking powder, 1 teaspoonful each allspice, cloves, and nutmeg, 2 teaspoonfuls of cinnamon, 1 cupful sliced almonds. Mix well, put in flat baking pans, and when cool cut in slices, 3 inches long, 2 inches wide, before removing from the pan.

Chocolate Almond Sticks.

Beat 6 eggs and 2 cupfuls sugar until very light, about 20 minutes, add 1 teaspoonful each cinnamon and cloves, ½ teaspoonful allspice, a pinch of salt, 5 sticks of sweet chocolate grated, 1 lb. of almonds blanched and cut in rather large pieces, flavor with vanilla, add 2 cupfuls sifted flour with 2 scant teaspoonfuls baking powder. Bake in buttered biscuit pans, and when done and cool cut in strips lengthwise.

Half quantity for small family.

Macaroons.

Beat whites of 6 eggs and 1 lb. pulverized sugar together for half hour, then add 1 lb. chopped almonds, a little cinnamon, and rind of lemon. Beat well and drop with teaspoon on buttered paper on tins. Bake slowly.

Kisses or Meringues.

Put the whites of 6 eggs and a tiny pinch of salt in a bowl, with a wire whip begin beating slowly and gradually increase until you have a stiff froth. Have 1 lb. of sifted pulverized sugar ready. Pour it slowly and carefully into the froth, stirring it all the time with a wooden spoon, flavor with a few drops of vanilla or lemon. Lay a piece of white paper over a baking tin. Put the meringues on the paper with a large spoon, forming an egg shape, and leaving a space between each one. Bake in a moderately slow oven, after sprinkling powdered sugar over each one.

Remove from the stove, and let them cool, then turn the papers upside down, moisten well, and let them rest a few minutes, when the meringues can be easily removed. With the fingers press them, each one separately, in the bottom to form an egg shape. Then dry them well in a warm place.

Pecan Kisses.

Put the whites of 5 eggs in a large flat dish, add 10 heaping tablespoonfuls granulated sugar. Beat with an egg whip until perfectly stiff; then flavor with a few drops of vanilla; stir in 5 ounces of pecan meats, broken in small pieces, and when well mixed, drop by teaspoonfuls on writing paper, laid in a pan. Do not grease the paper on pans. Bake in a moderate oven until dry and a *very* light brown.

Little Indians.

Beat for 30 minutes 10 eggs with 2 cupfuls sugar that has been sifted five times, add 2 tablespoonfuls whiskey, and 2½ cupfuls flour sifted five times, a pinch of salt.

Bake in deep muffin rings. When cold, cut the tops off carefully, take out the insides, then fill with sweetened and flavored whipped cream. Put back the tops, and ice with chocolate icing.

Half quantity for small family.

Minute Cakes.

Cream 1 cupful butter, then add 1½ cupfuls sugar sifted 3 times, cream again, add yolks of 6 eggs beaten very light, a pinch of salt, flavor with orange flower water, alternate the whites of the 6 eggs beaten very stiff and 2½ cupfuls flour sifted three times. 1 teaspoonful baking powder. Bake in plain muffin rings in moderately hot oven. When cold, ice with boiled icing flavored with extract of lemon.

Small Pineapple Cakes.

Beat 5 eggs and 1½ cupfuls sugar 20 minutes, then stir in 2 tablespoonfuls milk, 2 cupfuls sifted flour with 1 scant teaspoonful baking powder in it, flavor with vanilla and add pinch of salt. Bake in muffin rings, and when cold make an incision in the top of each and put in some grated pineapple and cover over with following

ICING.

Two cupfuls powdered sugar with ½ cupful cold water, boil until it ropes, then pour over stiffly-beaten whites of 2 eggs. beat well until smooth and glossy and spread over cakes.

Small Sponge Cakes.

Make same as for pineapple cakes, only leave out the pineapple. Ice with the same icing.

Small Ice Cream Cakes.

Cream together until very light 1 cupful butter and 2 cupfuls sugar, then add 1 cupful cornstarch dissolved in 1 cupful sweet milk, a pinch of salt, flavor with vanilla, add 3 cupfuls sifted flour with 1 teaspoonful baking powder; lastly add the stiffly-beaten whites of 6 eggs. Pour into a greased biscuit pan and bake in a moderate oven. When *cold* cut in diamond shapes, and ice all over except the bottom with the following

ICING.

Boil 2 cupfuls sugar and 1 cupful water until it begins to rope, then pour into the stiffly-beaten whites of 2 eggs, continue beating until it thickens a little, flavor with ¼ teaspoonful lemon extract.

Jelly Roll. No. 1.

Beat 6 whole eggs very light, then add ½ lb. granulated sugar, place bowl on back of stove in a warm but not hot place, and beat well for 15 minutes; add ½ teaspoonful vanilla or lemon flavoring. Sift ½ lb. of flour and stir in slowly, rolling flour over and over in eggs, but *do not beat* any more. Butter large flat biscuit pans, put a paper in bottom, pour in batter ⅓ inch thick (no thicker, or it will not roll). Spread evenly with a knife. Bake in quick oven, remove when the top is not quite brown, spread jelly on while cake is still in pan and hot, and begin to roll by peeling off paper and rolling up as quickly as you loosen it from the pan. If too hot, use a napkin. Wrap in a napkin, roll tightly up and let stand until cold. Cut in slices crosswise.

Jelly Roll. No. 2.

Cream ½ lb. of butter with ½ lb. sugar for 30 minutes, add 6 whole eggs, beating in one by one, then ½ teaspoonful of lemon or vanilla flavoring, then ½ lb. sifted flour, stirring flour in gently and not beating any more. Prepare pans same as in above recipe, and bake and arrange same way.

Lady Fingers.

Beat 6 whole eggs very light, add ½ lb. granulated sugar, place bowl on back of stove in warm but not hot place, and beat briskly for 15 minutes. Add ½ teaspoonful vanilla extract. Sift in ½ lb. of flour, *stirring* gently *but not* beating. Remove from stove, have molds ready, put batter in, sift a little powdered sugar on top, and bake in quick oven. Do not let brown. If molds are not convenient, butter a flat pan, place a piece of wrapping paper over, drop batter in shape of a finger, about ½ inch wide (as they spread), sprinkle with powdered sugar and bake. Remove immediately from pan.

COFFEE CAKES. KUCHEN.

Coffee Cake—Kuchen.

Soak ½ cake compressed yeast in ½ cupful lukewarm milk; when dissolved put in a bowl, or round agate pan, and stir in 1 heaping cupful sifted flour, 1 teaspoonful sugar and ¼ teaspoonful salt, mix thoroughly, and put in a warm place (not hot) to rise, from 1 to 2 hours.

When *well* risen, cream *well* together 1 cupful sugar and ¾ cupful butter, then add 3 eggs, 5 cupfuls sifted flour, 1 cupful milk and 1 teaspoonful salt, mix together until light, then stir in the risen yeast, and with a spoon work well for 10 minutes, and set aside to rise again, 5 or 6 hours, or all night. Dough should not be very stiff. When well risen it can be used for cinnamon cake, pies or pocket books. This recipe makes 1 large cinnamon cake, 3 pies, and about 1 dozen pocket books.

Cinnamon Cake.

Take enough of the " Coffee Cake Dough " to cover a biscuit pan 1 inch thick, or thicker if desired, flour the hand and spread the dough in the greased pan with it, and put aside in a warm place to rise. When *well* risen, beat the yolk of 1 egg with 2 tablespoonfuls milk, wet the top of the cake with it, strew *thickly* with granulated sugar and cinnamon mixed together (some pounded almonds can be added if desired), drop bits of butter all over the top, put in a moderate oven and bake until a nice even brown.

Cheese Pie.

Take a handful of "Coffee Cake Dough," put it on a well-floured board and mix with it just enough flour to enable you to roll it out nicely. Line a greased *deep* pie plate with the dough, set aside a short while to rise, then fill with the following:

Cream 1½ cupfuls cream or Dutch cheese until perfectly smooth and there are no lumps in it (it is best to run it through a patent potato masher before creaming it), add a pinch of salt, 1 good tablespoonful sifted flour, and 2 tablespoonfuls cream (not milk), mix well together. In another bowl, beat the yolks of 3 eggs and 3 good tablespoonfuls sugar until light, add 1 tablespoonful fresh butter, and mix well. Pour the contents of the cheese bowl into the eggs, mix well together, add ½ teaspoonful vanilla essence, then the stiffly-beaten whites of the eggs, and when well mixed, pour into the pie. Sprinkle sugar and cinnamon on top and bake in a moderate oven. This makes 1 deep pie.

Apple Pie. No. 1.

Take a small handful of the "Coffee Cake Dough," lay on a well-floured board, and mix just enough flour with it to enable you to roll out nicely. Line a greased pie plate with it, and set aside for a few minutes to rise. When risen, cut 5 small apples or 4 large ones in quarters, then in half again. Lay the apples lengthwise on the pie in a circle, and fill up all the empty spaces with small pieces of apple. Sprinkle thickly with sugar, then sprinkle cinnamon over, and drop bits of butter all over the top. Beat up 1 egg with ¼ cupful milk, pour over the pie and bake in a moderate oven. Care must be taken to have the apples well done.

This makes 1 pie.

Apple Pie. No. 2.

Put in a saucepan ½ cupful sugar and ¼ cupful water, let it boil a few minutes, then lay in 5 large apples or 6 small ones (which have previously been peeled, cored and quartered), cover with a lid, and stew a little while until very tender, but not soft.

Line a greased pie plate with some of the "Coffee Cake Dough," let it rise some, then fill the crust with the cooked apples; sprinkle with sugar and cinnamon, and bits of butter, and bake in a moderately hot stove until the crust is brown.

Fresh Strawberry Pie. No. 1.

Line a greased pie plate with some of the "Coffee Cake Dough," same as for the other pies. Set aside a few minutes to rise. Pick and wash ¾ of a quart of fresh strawberries, drain them well. Lay them on the risen pie-crust, sprinkle heavily with sugar, sprinkle a little ground cinnamon over, and put bits of butter all over the top. Put in a moderately hot oven, and bake until done.

Fresh Strawberry Pie. No. 2.

Take a small handful of the "Coffee Cake Dough," lay it on a well-floured board, add just enough flour with it to enable you to roll it out nicely; line a greased pie plate with the dough, and set aside to rise for a short while.

Wash and stem ¾ of a quart of ripe strawberries, cut them in half if large, pour 2 tablespoonfuls sugar over, and set aside for half an hour. Beat the yolks of 2 eggs and 2 heaping teaspoonfuls sugar until very light, stir in 1 tablespoonful milk, then add the sugared berries; when well mixed, pour into the pie plate and bake a light brown in a moderate oven. When light brown, spread over it a meringue made of the whites of 2 eggs beaten to a stiff froth and 4 tablespoonfuls

granulated sugar added. Put in oven again and brown nicely. Very nice.
This makes 1 pie.

Canned Strawberry Pie.

Prepare the dough and line a greased pie plate with it, the same as for the other pies.

Take 1 pint can of strawberries, drain every bit of liquor from them, and proceed same as for the Fresh Strawberry Pie No. 2, only do not add sugar to the "berries" as they are already sweetened.
This makes one pie.

Huckleberry Pie. No. 1.

Take a handful of "Coffee Cake Dough," roll out and line a greased pie plate with it, and set aside a few minutes to rise. Pick, clean and wash well 1 pint of huckleberries, drain and lay them thickly on the risen crust, sprinkle thickly with sugar, and lightly with cinnamon, then put bits of butter over the top and bake in a moderately hot oven until done.

Huckleberry Pie. No. 2.

Take a handful of "Coffee Cake Dough," roll out and line a greased pie plate with it, and set aside a few minutes to rise. Clean, pick and wash well 1 pint of huckleberries and drain them.

Beat until light, the yolks of 2 eggs with 4 heaping tablespoonfuls sugar, add 1 good tablespoonful milk, then stir in the drained huckleberries, and pour all on the pie crust. Bake until light brown in a moderately quick oven, then spread over the top a meringue made of the stiffly-beaten whites of the 2 eggs with 4 tablespoonfuls sugar added. Brown nicely.

Canned Peach Pie.

Line a greased pie plate with some of the "Coffee Cake Dough" same as for the other pies, and let it rise a few minutes. Take 1 small can of peaches, or ¾ of a large can, drain all the liquor from it. Lay the halves of peaches thickly and closely over the pie crust, sprinkle thickly with sugar, lightly with cinnamon, and lay bits of butter over the top. Bake in a moderately hot oven until brown. The liquor from the can of peaches will make a nice glass of jelly, if it is strained and an equal quantity of sugar added, and cooked together until thick.

Yellow peaches make the best pies.

Fresh Peach Pie.

Make same as "Canned Peach Pie," substituting freestone peaches, and breaking them in halves after they are peeled.

Onion Pie.

Line a pie plate with "Coffee Cake Dough" and let it rise a few minutes.

Put on the fire a skillet with a tightly-fitting top, put in 2 tablespoonfuls butter; when hot lay in 5 medium-sized onions, or 3 large ones cut in round slices, add about 1 cupful water, cover tightly, and let the onions steam until tender and all the water is cooked out, then brown a nice yellowish color.

Remove from the fire, cream the onions until very soft and creamy, add 1 tablespoonful flour.

Beat the yolks of 3 eggs and 3 tablespoonfuls sugar until light, add 1 tablespoonful butter, cream again, add the onions and flour, a good pinch of salt, and a good tablespoonful cream, lastly add the stiffly-beaten whites of the eggs. Put on the crust, sprinkle sugar and cinnamon over and bake in a moderately hot oven.

Fresh Prune Cake (*Kuchen*).

Line a greased biscuit pan with some of the "Coffee Cake Dough." Roll the dough thin, and let it come up on the sides of the pan, then set aside to rise. When risen, cut the prunes in halves (they must be the fresh ones, not dried), lay in rows thickly and close together all over the bottom of the pan, do not leave any space between the prunes. Sprinkle very thickly with sugar, lightly with cinnamon, and lay bits of fresh butter all over the top. Bake until done in a moderately hot oven. Very nice.

Pocket Books.

Take as much of the "Coffee Cake Dough" as you desire, lay it on a well-floured biscuit board, and mix just enough more flour with it to enable you to roll it out without sticking to the board. Roll out about ¼ inch thick and cut the dough in squares about as long as your finger.

Beat the yolk of 1 egg and 2 tablespoonfuls milk together; wet each square well with the mixture, lay one raisin in the centre (after the seed has been removed from it), sprinkle thickly with sugar and cinnamon mixed together, then put a small dab of butter on top. Catch the four corners of each square together, so that the inside is protected. Lay the pocket books, not too closely together, in a greased pan, and set aside to rise. When well risen bake in a moderately hot oven until baked and browned nicely.

Dampfnudeln.

Take as much of the "Coffee Cake Dough" as required, lay it on a floured biscuit board, and add just enough flour to it to enable you to keep it from sticking to the hands (be careful not to make the dough too stiff). Mould the dough into small biscuits, lay them on a flowered board or dish, and set aside until nicely risen.

When risen, cover the bottom of a deep, round iron skillet with rendered butter, put it on top of the stove, let it get hot, then lay in some of the dumplings (being careful not to crowd them as they spread), pour a cupful of cold water or milk in immediately, put a close-fitting lid on the skillet and let the dumplings cook on one side until brown; you can tell that they are frying when you hear that the water has cooked out. When brown on one side, remove the lid and brown on the other side. Proceed in like manner until all the dumplings are cooked.

Serve with caramel sauce.

Bunt Kuchen.

Dissolve ½ cake compressed yeast in ½ cupful lukewarm milk, add 1 teaspoonful sugar, a pinch of salt, and just enough flour to make a batter that will drop easily from the spoon, but not run.

Put aside in a warm place to rise. When well risen, cream together until light, ½ cupful of butter, and 1 cupful sugar, add 3 eggs beat in separately, a good pinch salt, ½ cupful milk, and 3 cupfuls sifted flour. Add the risen yeast, beat in very well, flavor with a little lemon or vanilla. Pour into a cake pan, half full, set in a warm place to rise; when the pan is nearly full, place in a moderate oven and bake until a nice brown.

YEAST, BREAD, BISCUITS, MUFFINS, WAFFLES, HOT CAKES, ROLLS, DOUGHNUTS, ETC.

Bread Making.

There are three important points to be observed in bread making, they are: good flour, good fresh yeast, and patience to work it well.

Try the yeast always, by setting to rise in a cup of lukewarm water or milk. If it fails to rise after a certain time, do not attempt to make bread of it, as it will surely fail. Bread should never be cut while very hot. Stand the loaves on end, so that the air can circulate freely all around.

In using soda in biscuits, muffins, etc., the teaspoon should be scant or heaping, according to the sourness of the milk.

It is very necessary to have rendered butter at hand, for greasing pans, frying doughnuts, etc.

Rendered Butter.

Procure as much country or Western butter as desired, you may get 20 or 30 lbs. of it when it is cheap during the summer, for if it is put in jars and well covered, it will keep for six months or longer.

Put the butter in a porcelain-lined kettle, being careful not to put in too much at one time or it will boil over. Boil slowly for several hours, until it becomes quite clear. Do not stir it, but from time to time skim it. When perfectly clear, and all the salt has settled at the bottom, the butter is done. Set aside a few minutes, then strain into stone jars through a fine sieve, and when cold tie up tightly with paper and cloth. Keep in a cool, dry place.

Buttermilk Yeast.

Soak 1 large yeast cake in 1 cupful *warm* water, not hot; when dissolved, mix with 1 pint pearl meal, 1 cupful buttermilk, 1 teaspoonful salt and 2 teaspoonfuls sugar. Set aside to rise. When well risen, mix in enough dry corn meal to work out in cakes. Use as little meal as possible. Put the cakes aside to dry, when they will be ready for use. Keep in a tightly-covered box in a cool, dry place.

Potato Yeast.

Put on to boil 8 good-sized Irish potatoes, when done mash them thoroughly in the water in which they have been boiled, let cool, then stir in 1 teaspoonful sugar and one of salt, also stir in 1 large yeast cake that has been dissolved in lukewarm water, and thicken, not stiff, with corn-meal; cover and set aside till morning or until it rises very light, then stir in enough meal to make very stiff and make into cakes. Let the cakes get thoroughly dry, then put in a tightly-covered box for future use.

Vienna Bread.

Dissolve 1 cake compressed yeast in 1½ tablespoonfuls cold water. Mix ½ pint milk and ½ pint water together, heat to a temperature of 75 degrees, add 1 teaspoonful salt, then pour in the dissolved yeast; add flour gradually until the dough can be kneaded for 5 minutes without sticking to the hands or bowl.

Grease a bowl, lay in the dough and grease the top of the dough. Cover with a towel, and keep in a place of 75 degrees temperature. Let stand 3 hours counting from the time the first flour was added. It should then be twice the size it was when put in the bowl.

Mould into loaves, put in Vienna pans, let rise 1 hour, till risen twice its size, then bake in a very hot oven.

White Mountain Bread.

Dissolve ½ cake compressed yeast in 1 cupful lukewarm water and milk mixed, add 2 tablespoonfuls sugar and 1 of salt and let it dissolve. Take 1 pint sifted flour and stir the yeast into it after it is dissolved, have the batter the consistency of waffle batter, more warm water can be added if necessary. Mix well and put aside in a warm place (not hot) to rise, usually 1 or 2 hours.

Now take 1½ quarts sifted flour, add 1 tablespoonful salt, 1 good tablespoonful butter and same quantity lard, mix together and pour in the risen yeast, mix well and set aside to rise all night, say 6 or 7 hours. When *well* risen, pour the dough out on a well-floured biscuit board, knead well for 10 or 15 minutes, and break in 3 equal pieces; braid together like a hair braid, put in a bread pan, cover with another pan and let rise again. Then keep cover over the pan, set in the oven and bake, not too fast. When almost done, remove the cover and brown nicely.

Rye Bread.

Sift 1½ pints rye flour, 1½ pints wheat flour and 2 teaspoonfuls salt in a bowl. Soak ½ cake compressed, or 1 cake of any other kind of yeast in 1 pint lukewarm water. When the yeast is dissolved, pour it into the flour and make into a dough. Lay it on a biscuit board, and knead until smooth and elastic, put it back in a bowl, cover with a towel, and set aside over night to rise. Next morning, lay the dough on a biscuit board again, and knead well. Make into a loaf, put into a pan, and when well risen, moisten the top with a little cold water, and bake in a moderate oven.

Water Bread.

To 1 pint of water add 1 teaspoonful sugar, 1 teaspoonful salt, 2 teaspoonfuls butter, and 1 cake compressed yeast that has been dissolved in a little warm water. Sift in enough flour to make a dough stiff enough to work. Put on a biscuit board, and work until smooth and elastic, and air blisters come on the surface. Return to the bowl, cover with a cloth and lid, and put in a warm place to rise. Let rise to twice its bulk, work again on the board, shape into a loaf or loaves, put into a well-greased pan, and put aside to rise again until light; then bake in a moderately quick oven. Use only best flour.

Boston Brown Bread.

Sift 1 cupful rye or graham flour; 1 cupful white flour, 2 cupfuls Indian meal, mix and add 1 cupful molasses, 2 scant teaspoonfuls soda, ½ teaspoonful salt, 1 cupful sour milk and 1½ to 2½ cupfuls water. Mix well and steam for 3 hours, then dry inside the oven ½ hour.

Brown bread should be eaten warm, what is left over can be steamed again or toasted.

Graham Bread.

Put in a bowl 3 cupfuls sifted graham flour, 1 cupful sifted white flour, 1½ teaspoonfuls salt, 2 heaping teaspoonfuls baking powder. Mix all together with a spoon, then make a hole in the center, pour in 1 kitchenspoonful molasses, and 1¾ cupfuls cold water. Stir together until well mixed, then pour into a well-greased, narrow bread pan (if the pan is too wide the loaf will be flat). Bake at once in a moderate oven 1¼ hours. Remove from pan when baked, and wrap in a damp towel until cold.

Corn Bread.

Put 1½ cupfuls sour milk in a bowl, stir in 2 eggs, ½ teaspoonful salt and ½ teaspoonful soda, mix well together, then sift in 1 pint pearl meal, when well mixed, pour in 2 tablespoonfuls melted butter while hot, mix well, and pour in a hot buttered pan and bake. For a large family use double quantity.

Excelsior Egg Bread.

Sift 2 cupfuls pearl corn meal in a bowl, scald it with ¾ cupfuls boiling water, stir well, then add 1 cupful sour milk or buttermilk, and when well mixed, stir in the well-beaten yolks of 3 eggs, 1 teaspoonful salt. Pour in 1 heaping tablespoonful of butter melted and hot, stir well into the batter; then add a scant ½ teaspoonful soda dissolved in 1 teaspoonful warm water, and when mixed in, add lastly the stiffly-beaten whites of the 3 eggs. Bake in a hot greased pan in a hot oven.

Egg Bread with Sweet Milk.

Beat the yolks of 3 eggs very light, add 2 cupfuls sweet milk, then sift in 3 cupfuls of pearl meal, add a large pinch salt, 1 tablespoonful butter and 1 of lard melted, and poured in while hot; then sift in 2 teaspoonfuls baking powder, and lastly add the stiffly-beaten whites of eggs.

Pour in a hot buttered pan and bake in a quick oven. Only use sweet milk when clabber or buttermilk cannot be had.

Sally Lunn.

Sift 1 pint flour, ½ teaspoonful salt and 2 teaspoonfuls baking powder together. Beat yolks 2 eggs, add 1 cupful milk, and ¼ cupful melted butter. Then add sifted flour and baking powder. Mix quickly and add the beaten whites of 2 eggs. Fill greased muffin-pans two-thirds full, and bake 15 minutes in a very hot oven. This makes 8 muffins. If desired, 2 tablespoonfuls of sugar can be added to the flour, ½ cupful butter, and ½ cupful milk be used instead of above quantity. Can also be baked in flat biscuit pan, but will take longer to bake.

Auflauf.

Boil 1 pint milk, and when boiling stir in quickly 1 cupful of sifted flour, and work smooth, until all lumps are out, and it is the consistency of soft mashed potatoes. Stir all the while over fire. When smooth remove from stove, and while yet warm, break in one by one, yolks 6 eggs, a pinch salt, then the beaten whites of 6 eggs. Bake in well-buttered hot square pans, in very hot oven, from 15 to 20 minutes. Serve as soon as done, with jelly or preserves. If batter is not thick enough a little more flour must be added to the milk.

Yeast Powder Biscuits.

Sift together 5 cupfuls flour, 1 teaspoonful salt and 2 heaping teaspoonfuls baking powder; add ½ cupful fresh butter and ½ cupful lard, mix with the flour; add 1 good cupful sweet milk, mix with a knife and handle as little as possible. Roll on floured board ½ inch thick, cut with biscuit cutter and bake in quick oven. ¾ cupful butter can be used instead of half butter and half lard, but the biscuits will not be so good.

Soda Biscuits.

Sift 5 cups flour with ½ teaspoonful soda in it, make a hole in the center, put in it ½ cupful lard and ½ cupful fresh butter, add a good pinch salt, pour in 1 cupful and a little over of sour milk. Mix with a knife working as little as possible. When well mixed roll out 1 inch thick on a well floured board, cut with a biscuit cutter or baking powder can top, put in pans and bake in a quick oven. Dough should be rather soft, and the less it is handled the better the biscuits will be. ¾ of a cupful of butter can be used instead of half butter and half lard, but the biscuits will not be as fine.

Beat Biscuits No. 1.

Sift 1 quart flour on biscuit board, add 1 tablespoonful sugar, 1 teaspoonful salt, soda about the size of small hazel nut, and 1 tablespoonful lard. Mix well, then add ½ cupful ice cold water mixed with ½ cupful cold sweet milk. Work well, then beat with a rolling pin until dough is smooth and satiny, and the surface blisters. Roll out ½ inch thick and cut with a small cutter. Bake in flat, ungreased pans. The success depends upon amount of beating. A machine biscuit beater can be purchased, and saves much labor.

Beat Biscuits. No. 2.

Sift 1 quart flour, add 1 teaspoonful salt, 1 tablespoonful lard, and 1 cupful ice cold water. Mix well, then add soda, size of small hazel nut. Work well, beat and bake same as above recipe.

Muffins with Soda.

Beat 3 eggs until very light, then add 1 pint sour milk and 4 cupfuls sifted flour alternately; beat thoroughly, add a good pinch of salt and ½ cupful fresh butter melted; mix well, then sift in 1 teaspoonful soda, and after giving it several hard beats, pour into hot buttered muffin rings and bake in a moderately hot oven.

Muffins.

Stir 1 pint sweet milk into 1 quart of sifted flour, add pinch salt, and 1 tablespoonful melted butter (half lard and half butter can be used). Beat 3 yolks light, add to batter, mix well, then stir in 1½ teaspoonfuls yeast-powder. Last, add stiffly-beaten whites 3 eggs. Bake in hot greased muffin pans, with quick oven. Half the quantity can be used.

Sweet Muffins. No. 1.

Cream together ½ cupful fresh butter and ½ cupful sugar until light; then add 2 eggs, 3 cupfuls sifted flour, 1 cupful sweet milk, and a good pinch salt. To the last half cupful of flour add 1 heaping teaspoonful baking powder. Mix well together; put in hot buttered muffin rings and bake in a moderately hot oven about 20 minutes.

Sweet Muffins. No. 2.

Cream a kitchenspoonful of butter with 4 tablespoonfuls of sugar. Stir in, one by one, 4 yolks of eggs, then add 3 cupfuls flour, 3 teaspoonfuls yeast powder, and last, beaten whites of 4 eggs. Grease muffin rings and bake in quick oven.

Cornmeal Muffins.

Scald 1 pint cornmeal with 1 cupful hot water, then add ½ teaspoonful salt, 1 cupful sour milk or buttermilk, and 2 well-beaten eggs. Then if batter is stiff, add as much of 1 extra cupful of sour milk as is required (all of it may not be needed). Then melt ½ tablespoonful fresh butter, stir in batter, and last, 1 teaspoonful soda dissolved in lukewarm water. Fill hot greased muffin rings ¾ full, and bake in a hot oven 20 to 30 minutes.

Graham Muffins. No. 1.

Cream 2 tablespoonfuls of sugar with ½ tablespoonful of butter, then add 2 well-beaten eggs, 1 saltspoonful salt and 1 quart graham flour. Add about 2 cupfuls of sweet milk, then as much more as is necessary to make a good batter. Sometimes 2 cupfuls are sufficient, again it takes more. Bake in greased muffin rings (small ones best), in a moderate oven.

Graham Muffins. No. 2.

Beat 3 eggs until very light, stir in 1 pint sweet milk, then sift in 3 cupfuls graham flour, mix well, add 1 teaspoonful salt and 1 tablespoonful sugar, lastly 1 heaping teaspoonful baking powder, mix thoroughly, and bake in hot, well-greased muffin rings. This makes 18 muffins.

Popovers.

Beat 3 eggs till light, add ½ teaspoonful of salt, and 2 cupfuls milk. Then add 2 cupfuls of sifted flour, stir until smooth, then strain. Have gem or muffin pans hot and greased. Fill quickly with mixture, bake in a quick oven, and serve immediately.

Waffles.

To 3 cupfuls sifted flour take 2 cupfuls sour milk, mix well, add ½ teaspoonful of salt, and yolks 2 eggs. Dissolve 1½ teaspoonfuls of soda in a little cold sour milk, mix in batter, then mix in stiffly-beaten whites 3 eggs, then add 1 heaping tablespoonful butter, melted and hot. Have waffle irons hot and greased, and cook over quick fire.

Butter Waffles.

Sift 1 pint flour, 1 good handful pearl meal, and 2 teaspoonfuls salt, together; add 1 pint buttermilk or sour milk (buttermilk is best), mix and add 2 whole eggs and 1 teaspoonful soda; stir well, then add 1 cupful rendered butter and lard mixed (half and half) that has been melted, and if batter is not thin enough, add a little more buttermilk or sour milk. Fry in very hot waffle irons, the irons need only be greased the first time.

German Waffles.

Cream together for half an hour ½ lb. fresh butter and ½ lb. sugar, then add 8 eggs, each one separately, then 8 heaping tablespoonfuls sifted flour, stir well and add 1 cupful sweet cream, pinch of salt. Fry in well-greased waffle irons well heated, but not too hot.

French Waffles.

Cream ½ cupful sweet butter with ½ cupful powdered sugar. Break in one by one, yolks of 4 eggs, mix well, then add 1 teaspoonful brandy, grated peel of a lemon, ¼ teaspoonful mace. Make a sponge of ½ small cake compressed yeast dissolved in 1 cupful lukewarm milk and mixed with ½ lb. flour, mix and beat the whole until it bubbles, then let rise three hours. Bake in greased hot waffle irons, inside the stove; sprinkle with powdered sugar and serve hot.

Cornmeal Cakes. No. 1.

Sift ½ pint cornmeal, ½ cupful of flour, ½ teaspoonful salt. Add to this 2 cupfuls sour milk, 2 whole eggs beaten very light, 1 tablespoonful syrup, 1 teaspoonful soda, dissolved first in a little sour milk. Grease frying pan, have very hot, and brown cakes first on one side, then the other. Eat with preserves or syrup.

Cornmeal Cakes. No. 2.

Sift 2 cupfuls cornmeal and ½ cupful flour together in a bowl, stir in 2 cupfuls sweet milk, and when well mixed, add 2 eggs, 1 tablespoonful syrup, 1 teaspoonful salt, and 1 heaping teaspoonful baking powder. Beat well and fry in cakes on a hot griddle. Brown on both sides. Eat with syrup or preserves.

Flour Cakes.

Sift 2 cupfuls flour in a bowl, add ½ teaspoonful salt, stir in 1 cupful sweet milk, and 1 tablespoonful sugar or syrup, then add the well-beaten yolks of 2 eggs and the whites beaten to a stiff froth. Add 1 heaping teaspoonful baking powder, mix well and fry in cakes on a hot greased griddle. Serve with syrup or preserves.

Sour milk always makes the lightest cakes, but when it cannot be had, sweet milk will answer every purpose.

Flour, Buttermilk Batter Cakes.

Pour 1 pint buttermilk in a bowl, add 3 cupfuls sifted flour, mix until smooth, and set aside over night to rise. When well risen, add 1 teaspoonful salt, 2 well-beaten eggs, and 1 teaspoonful soda dissolved in a little warm water. Fry on a hot, well-greased griddle. Brown on both sides.

Flannel Cakes.

Beat 2 eggs until light, then stir in 1 pint sour milk or buttermilk. Sift in ½ teaspoonful salt and 1½ pints flour. Mix well. Dissolve 1 teaspoonful soda in 1 tablespoonful warm water and mix thoroughly with batter. Bake in small round cakes on a hot, well-greased griddle. Brown on both sides.

Flannel Cakes With Yeast.

Soak ¼ cake compressed yeast in ¼ cupful lukewarm water, when dissolved, stir in a good half cupful sifted flour, mix well, and set aside to rise. When well risen, about 1 to 1½ hours, add 3 eggs, mix well, stir in 1 pint sweet milk, then sift in 4½ cupfuls sifted flour, beat for 5 minutes, add 1 heaping teaspoonful salt, 1 tablespoonful sugar, and when well mixed set aside to rise, 4 or 5 hours, then stir in 1 tablespoonful syrup and fry on a hot griddle. Brown on both sides. Serve with syrup or jelly.

White Mountain Flannel Cakes.

Mix 2 eggs with 1 cupful molasses and 2 cupfuls sweet milk, add 1 lb. flour sifted with 1 heaping teaspoonful baking powder in it, a good pinch salt. Mix together and add enough milk to make a thin running dough. Fry on a hot griddle.

Old-Fashioned Buckwheat Cakes.

Dissolve ½ cake of any good yeast in 2 cupfuls luke-warm milk and water mixed. Sift 3 cupfuls buckwheat in a bowl, and stir in the dissolved yeast; mix well and set aside to rise, 6 or 8 hours, or all night. When *well* risen, put in 1 tablespoonful molasses, 1 teaspoonful salt and 2 eggs, mix all well together, and fry by spoonfuls on a hot greased griddle. Brown on both sides.

Buckwheat Cakes With Buttermilk.

Sift 3 cupfuls buckwheat flour (not self-rising) in a bowl, mix well with 2½ cupfuls buttermilk, and set aside over night to rise. Next morning add 1 tablespoonful syrup, 2 eggs, 1 teaspoonful salt and 1 teaspoonful soda dissolved in a little warm water. Fry in cakes on a hot greased griddle. Brown on both sides. If the cakes are too thick, before frying add a little sweet milk.

Self-Rising Buckweat Cakes.

Sift 3 cupfuls self-rising buckweat flour in a bowl, stir in 2 heaping cupfuls sweet milk, mix well, then add 2 eggs, salt to taste, 1 tablespoonful syrup and a tiny pinch of soda. Mix well and fry in cakes on a hot greased griddle. Brown on both sides. Eat with maple syrup.

Snip Noodles, Fried.

Sift 1 pint flour with 3 teaspoonfuls baking powder and 1 teaspoonful salt in it, make into a dough by adding enough sweet milk to make soft as biscuit dough. Break off small pieces and roll between the hands in the shape of croquettes.

Now put ½ cupful rendered butter in a skillet that has a top to it; when the butter is hot, lay in the pieces of dough (do not put too many in at one time), throw in ½ cupful cold water, put on the cover and let cook until the water is cooked out and noodles are brown on one side. Remove the cover and brown on the other side.

Snip Noodles, Boiled.

Make same as "fried snip noodles," and after rolling into croquette shape, drop into boiling salt water for 15 or 20 minutes. They will come to the top of the water and be very light when done. Usually fry half of them and boil the other half. When boiled, just before sending to the table, pour over them the following

CREAM SAUCE.

Scald 1 cupful sweet cream, and when it comes to a boil, pour over the well-beaten yolks of 2 eggs; add pinch of salt, and stir briskly in 1 tablespoonful vinegar. Mix quickly or the cream will curdle.

Capital City Rolls.

Boil 1 small Irish potato until done. Soak 1 yeast cake in ¼ cupful lukewarm water. Drain the water off the potato, mash until soft and creamy, then add 1 teaspoonful salt and 1 tablespoonful sugar. Mix well, then add 1 cupful cold water and 1 good pint flour. Stir in the dissolved yeast cake, beat well and set aside to rise. When it bubbles, add 1 quart flour, and 2 heaping teaspoonfuls lard, or butter and lard mixed, mix, then pour on a biscuit board and knead for 10 minutes; then put back in a bowl, rub the top with a little butter to keep from getting crusty, and let rise again. When well risen, make into rolls, put in pans, and when risen again, bake at once.

Vienna Rolls.

Sift 1 quart flour 3 times. Add 1 teaspoonful salt, a tablespoonful of butter, 2 teaspoonfuls baking powder, and 3 cupfuls milk. Mix well and roll out on board ½ inch thick. Cut with biscuit cutter, moisten tops with milk, fold over, moisten again with milk and put in pan. Do not let rolls touch each other. Bake in hot oven.

Parker House Rolls.

Measure 1 quart of flour, sift, then add 1 tablespoonful sugar, pinch salt, and 2 tablespoonfuls lard. Scald 1 cupful milk, then remove from fire, and when cold mix in with flour. Dissolve ½ cake compressed yeast in ½ cupful milk and mix in batter. Work up on board until light, then set aside over night to rise. In the morning, work together, roll out, cut with round cutter, butter the top, fold over and place rolls in biscuit pan, so far apart that they will not touch. Let rise again, then bake until brown. If for supper, mix in the morning and cut out in the afternoon.

Rolls.

Scald 1 pint milk, add 1 teaspoonful of salt, 1 tablespoonful sugar, 1 tablespoonful butter, and let it cool. Dissolve ½ cake compressed yeast in a little lukewarm milk, and stir in the other milk. Then add enough bread flour to make it stiff enough to work. Put on board and work till smooth. Put in a bowl in warm place, and let rise until twice its bulk. If desired for breakfast, can be worked up at night, and let rise until morning. Shape into small rolls and place in a large flat pan, close together, to prevent spreading. Let rise again. Then bake.

Rolls or Turnovers.

Dissolve ¾ of one piece compressed yeast in 1 cupful lukewarm milk. Make a soft batter of 1½ cupfuls sifted flour, the dissolved yeast, and 1 teaspoonful sugar and a pinch of salt, mix well and set aside to rise.

When *well* risen, cream together ½ cupful butter and 1 cupful sugar until light, add 2 eggs well beaten, then add the risen yeast, 1 teaspoonful salt, and work in gradually 5 good cupfuls sifted flour, work until the dough leaves the sides of the bowl, and set aside to rise again. After it is *well* risen, five or six hours, roll lightly on a well-floured board to 1 inch thickness, cut with a biscuit cutter, rub the top of each one with melted butter, fold over once and put in pans and let rise once more, about 1 or 2 hours, then bake in a moderate oven. When half baked, glaze with a little egg and milk.

Doughnuts.

Make the dough same as for "Turnovers," and when *well* risen, roll out on a floured board to ½ inch thickness, cut with a biscuit cutter and with a small tin top cut a round piece out of the center of each one, or the centers can be cut out with a knife,

Lay on floured dishes and let rise; when well risen drop them in a deep skillet half full of boiling hot butter, and fry a nice brown. The hot butter should be dipped over them with a spoon while frying. Sprinkle with powdered sugar and serve. Do not put too many in the kettle at one time.

Filled Doughnuts.

Make the dough same as for "Turnovers," and when *well* risen, roll out on a floured board to the thickness of ¼ inch, cut half of it with a biscuit cutter, and the other half with a smaller top or cup. Now beat the yolk of 1 egg and glaze around the edges of the larger pieces with it, put a bit of jelly or jam in the center, cover with one of the smaller pieces and press the edges of the small piece down against the egg so that it will stick. Proceed in this way until all the dough is used. Lay on floured dishes to rise, and when well risen, about 2 hours, drop them in a deep kettle of hot butter, small side down, cover with a lid, and when brown on one side, remove the cover and brown on the other. Sprinkle with powdered sugar and serve. These are best eaten fresh. Do not put too many in the kettle at one time.

Puffs (Purim).

Make the dough same as for "Turnovers," and when *well* risen, roll out on a floured board ½ inch thick, cut in triangles, lay on floured dishes or board to rise. When well risen, drop in a deep kettle of boiling butter, and with a spoon baste with the butter until brown; remove with a perforated skimmer and sprinkle with powdered sugar.

Doughnuts.

Cream together ½ cupful butter and 1 cupful sugar. When light, add 1 egg, then ½ cupful milk, a pinch of salt, flavor with vanilla, work in 5 cupfuls flour, until it makes a soft dough. Roll out ½ inch thick on a floured board, cut with a large biscuit cutter, then with a small top or cup, cut out the center of each piece, leaving a ring about 1 inch wide. Fry in a kettle half full of boiling hot butter or lard. Dust with powdered sugar.

TOAST, PANCAKES, FRITTERS, WAFERS, DUMPLINGS, ETC.

Buttered Toast.

Slice even slices of bakers' bread, not too thin, put in a biscuit pan on the top rack of a very hot oven, brown nicely on one side, then turn and brown on the other, spread with fresh butter, and a little powdered sugar, if desired, and serve at once. Or put the slices on a long fork, hold before a red coal fire, without flame, toast on both sides and proceed as above.

Milk or Cream Toast.

Toast as many slices of stale light bread as desired a light brown. Heat milk or cream allowing ½ cupful for each slice, add small lump butter. When just at the boiling point, pour over bread which has been placed in dish, sprinkle with sugar and cinnamon, cover, and serve immediately. Nice for invalids.

French Toast.

Dip slices of stale bread in milk, just to moisten and remove immediately. Beat some eggs very light, dip moistened bread in egg, then fry in a pot filled with boiling fat. Brown on one side, then the other, take up with a skimmer, to allow the grease to drain off, place on hot platter and sprinkle with sugar and cinnamon. Serve hot.

Egg Pancakes.

Beat the yolks of 6 eggs until *very* light, add 2 teaspoonfuls cornstarch, and when well beaten, stir in the stiffly-beaten whites of eggs. Fry at once, by large spoonfuls, on a hot greased griddle. Brown on both sides. Sprinkle with powdered sugar and lemon.

Pancakes must be made and fried only when ready to be served, as they fall from standing.

Use half quantity for small family.

German Pancakes. No. 1.

Beat the yolks of 8 eggs until *very* light, then add 1 cupful milk and stir in 1½ cupfuls sifted flour, ¼ teaspoonful baking powder, a good pinch of salt, and lastly, just before frying, add the stiffly-beaten whites of eggs and mix well together.

Put on fire an iron skillet with a close-fitting top; heat in it 2 tablespoonfuls rendered butter; when very hot, pour in enough of the batter to cover the bottom of the skillet, cover at once with the top, and when the pancake is brown on one side, remove the top and let it brown on the other side. Take it up with a perforated skimmer, lay on a plate and sprinkle with powdered sugar and some lemon juice. Serve at once. Use half quantity for small family.

Pancakes must only be made and fried when ready to be eaten, as they fall from standing.

German Pancakes. No. 2.

Beat 4 whole eggs very light, then add 4 tablespoonfuls sifted flour, 4 tablespoonfuls of milk or cream, and a pinch of salt. Have hot skillet ready, grease with a little fresh butter, and pour batter in. Put it in a hot oven, and serve as soon as done. This makes a pancake for 2 people.

Bread Pancakes.

Soak 4 slices of stale bread in sour milk over night. When ready to use, mash whole smooth and fine. Beat 4 eggs very light, mix with bread, add pinch salt,

2 teaspoonfuls soda dissolved in a little hot water, and 4 tablespoonfuls of flour which have been sifted several times. Grease frying pan with fresh butter, and brown cakes first on one side, then the other. To be eaten hot with either jelly or syrup.

Potato Pancakes. No. 1.

Peel, wash, and dry thoroughly, 3 large Irish potatoes, or 6 small ones. Grate them in a bowl, add 4 eggs and 1 teaspoonful salt. Mix well, fry by spoonfuls on a hot griddle. Brown on both sides. Serve at once. The potatoes must only be grated when ready to serve, as they turn black from standing.

Potato Pancakes. No. 2.

Grate 6 large Irish potatoes, and drain off water. Peel 4 apples, cut in small thin slices, and add to potatoes. Season with salt to taste. Then add a kitchenspoonful of flour, and three well-beaten eggs. Grease skillet, drop cakes in, and brown first on one side, then the other. Eat as soon as cooked, with preserves or syrup.

Plain Wafers.

Rub 2 cupfuls sifted flour, ½ teaspoonful salt and ½ cupful fresh butter thoroughly together, add enough cold water to make a rather stiff dough, but which can be easily rolled. Work as little as possible. Break into small pieces, roll very thin, put one piece at a time in a hot greased wafer iron. Press the iron and cut off all superfluous dough. Brown nicely on both sides.

Sweet Wafers.

Cream together until light ½ cupful sugar with 1 heaping tablespoonful fresh butter, add 3 eggs, 2 cupfuls sifted flour, a pinch of salt and 2 tablespoonfuls sweet cream. Mix well together and drop 1 teaspoonful of batter in very hot wafer irons, press tightly together, and with a knife scrape off all rough edges, bake quickly until light brown on both sides. Remove from the wafer iron, and roll together loosely in the shape of a cigar. Must be done quickly or it will break. Sprinkle with powdered sugar.

Crullers.

Cream 2 tablespoonfuls of butter with ½ cupful of sugar, then beat in, one at a time, 2 whole eggs. Mix well, then add ½ cupful milk, 1½ teaspoonfuls of yeast-powder, and sufficient flour to make a soft batter to roll out. (Try 3 cupfuls and then add as much more flour as necessary.) Last add ½ teaspoonful cinnamon. Roll ½ inch thick, cut in strips 1 inch wide, 3 inches long and fry in hot fat.

Queen Fritters.

Put in deep skillet on the fire 2 cupfuls water, and 1 cupful fresh butter; when it comes to a boil, stir in 2 cupfuls sifted flour, and continue stirring until the dough leaves the side of the skillet clean. Remove from the fire, and when cool, break in 9 eggs one by one, stirring all the time. Add a little salt. Mix all well, then drop pieces about the size of a walnut into a plenty of boiling hot lard or butter and fry a light brown. Eat with caramel sauce.
Half this quantity is sufficient for small family.

Matrimonies.

Sift 3 cupfuls flour in a bowl, pour in 2 scant cupfuls sour milk, beat very thoroughly, add 1 teaspoonful salt, the well-beaten yolks of 3 eggs, mix well, then add the stiffly-beaten whites of the eggs, and 1 level teaspoonful soda sifted with 1 teaspoonful flour. Mix well and fry at once in very hot butter or lard. Baste

the grease over them with a spoon until they are nicely browned.
Serve with chand 'eau sauce or preserves.

Bell Fritters.

Stir 3 eggs until very light, then stir in 1 cupful sweet milk, then sift in 3 cupfuls sifted flour, beat for 10 minutes, then add 1 heaping teaspoonful baking powder, and fry by spoonfuls in hot butter or lard. Serve with chand 'eau sauce or preserves.

Banana Fritters.

Make same as "Bell Fritters," and add 3 bananas, cut in thin round slices. Serve with chand 'eau sauce.

Apple Fritters.

Make same as "Bell Fritters," and add 3 sound apples, peeled, cored, and sliced in thin round slices. In frying take up 1 slice of apple and some batter in the spoon for each fritter. Serve with syrup or preserves.

Lemon Fritters.

Beat yolks 5 eggs with ½ cupful sugar, grated peel of lemon, grated nutmeg, pinch cinnamon, and pinch of salt. Stir in ½ cupful sweet cream or milk, 1 teaspoonful yeast powder and sufficient flour to roll batter out. Cut in small cakes, fry in hot fat. Serve with lemon sauce.

Delmonico Fritters.

Boil ¼ lb. of butter, with 1 pt. milk, then stir in ½ lb. of flour, until it does not stick to the pot. Let cool, then stir in one by one yolks 7 eggs, and a pinch salt. Beat whites to a froth, mix well and fry by spoonfuls in boiling fat. Serve with wine sauce, or preserves.

Chrimsel.

Sift 1 cupful matzo meal in a bowl, stir into it 1 cupful boiling soup stock or wine. When mixed, add 1 tablespoonful chopped almonds, 1 teaspoonful sugar, a pinch of salt and the yolks of 4 eggs well beaten; then add the stiffly-beaten whites of the 4 eggs and fry by tablespoonfuls in boiling hot butter or goose grease. Sprinkle with powdered sugar and serve with Wine Sauce.

Fried Apples.

Core and slice thin as many nice sound apples as required. Drop the pieces into boiling butter for a few minutes; brown on both sides, remove to a platter with a perforated skimmer, sprinkle powdered sugar over, and serve. Nice for breakfast.

Fried Bananas.

Peel nice sound bananas, slice them in half lengthwise, drop the halves in some nice hot butter and brown quickly on both sides. Remove to a dish with a perforated skimmer and sift powered sugar over them. Serve at once.

French Puffs (Windbeutel) to Serve with Vegetables.

Boil 1 cupful water with 1 heaping tablespoonful butter, 1 teaspoonful salt, and 1 tablespoonful sugar. Add sufficient flour to make a smooth paste, and cook until whole mass looks like mashed potatoes. Remove from fire, and when cool break in, one by one, 4 whole eggs, stirring briskly as each egg is added. Fill skillet with fat, and when boiling drop batter in by spoonfuls. Baste while frying. Remove with skimmer, and place in dish around carrots, asparagus, or beans.

Baked Apple Dumplings.

Sift ½ lb. flour on a biscuit board, make a hole in the center and lay in ¼ lb. fresh butter and a good pinch salt, mix all together slightly, then pour ½ cupful water in the center and make into a dough. Put the dough on ice until you prepare the apples for filling.

Pare and core 4 small apples, cut them in quarters, then slice through lengthwise again.

Or, pare and core 9 very small apples. Divide the dough into 9 equal sized pieces, and roll out each piece on a floured biscuit board, to the thickness of ¼ inch. Arrange 4 slices of apple, or 1 whole small apple in the center of each piece of dough (if the whole one is used, fill the cavity with a little apple jelly). Sprinkle sugar and cinnamon over the apples, and catch the rims of the pieces firmly together so that the apples are entirely enclosed. Lay the dumplings in a biscuit pan, put ½ teaspoonful butter on top of each one, divide 1½ cupfuls sugar over them, sprinkle with cinnamon and pour enough water in the pan to cover the dumplings half way.

Sprinkle 1 tablespoonful sifted flour in the water. Bake in a moderate oven until done, about 45 minutes. Baste often. Serve with the same sauce poured over them.

Baked Apple Roll.

Prepare and bake same as "Baked Apple Dumplings," only the cut up apples must always be used. Roll the dough out ¼ inch thick on a biscuit board; lay the cut up apples on the dough, and after seasoning roll over and over until the apples are entirely enclosed, pinch the ends together, put in the pan and proceed same as for dumplings.

Boiled Apple Dumplings.

Sift ½ lb. flour, 1 heaping teaspoonful baking powder and ½ teaspoonful salt on a biscuit board, make a hole in the center, lay in 2 tablespoonfuls butter, and rub the flour and butter together between the hands until thoroughly mixed. Pour in a scant half cupful of sweet milk and make into a dough. Break into 8 equal sized pieces, roll out ¼ inch thick. In the center of each piece lay 1 whole very small apple, peeled and cored, or 4 pieces of cut apple. Catch the ends of the dough together, until the apples are entirely enclosed. Tie each dumpling in a piece of thin cloth, leaving space to rise. Boil in boiling salt water 1 hour. Serve with " hard sauce."

Boiled Apple Roll.

Make same as " Boiled Apple Dumplings," use only apples, peeled, cored, quartered and cut in half lengthwise again. Roll the dough out on the biscuit board, spread the apples over it, and roll until the apples are entirely enclosed. Boil in salt water one hour and a quarter. Serve with " hard sauce."

EGGS.

Boiled Eggs.

Be sure and have fresh eggs. Put them in a saucepan of boiling water, being careful not to crack them. If you only wish the whites set, boil 2 minutes; if the yolks are to be set, boil 3 minutes; if hard, boil 10 minutes.

Fried Eggs.

Break the eggs in hot lard or butter; while frying, sprinkle with salt and pepper. Turn them over if desired.

Fried Eggs with Ham.

Cut thin slices of ham, fry in spider with hot fat, remove to a hot platter, and over each piece of ham lay one or two eggs fried as in the above recipe.

Eggs with Sausage.

Boil 1 large sausage until tender. Cut in thin round slices, lay in a fryer with 1 spoonful hot butter, cook 3 minutes; then pour over it 6 eggs previously beaten together in a bowl. Brown lightly on one side, sprinkle salt and pepper over, then fold up like an omelet and serve at once.

Shirred Eggs.

Get ready as many small earthen dishes as required, allowing one for each person. Break into each dish 2 eggs, being careful not to break the yolks. Place in a hot oven and bake until set. Take out of the stove, sprinkle salt, pepper and bits of butter over and serve.

Poached Eggs.

Fill a deep saucepan half full of water, add a good pinch of salt. When the water boils, and not till then, break in as many eggs as desired. Be very careful to keep the eggs whole and drop each one on the spot where the water bubbles. Poach 3 minutes, lift carefully with a skimmer, lay on buttered toast, sprinkle with salt and pepper, drop a small piece of butter on each egg and serve at once.

Scrambled Eggs. No. 1.

Break into a bowl as many eggs as required, add salt and pepper. Have some very hot butter in your frying pan on the stove; pour in the eggs, stir constantly until set, not stiff, and serve on a hot platter at once.

Scrambled Eggs. No. 2.

Into a clean frying pan pour a cupful of sweet cream or milk; when hot, pour in a dozen eggs previously beaten in a bowl. Stir constantly until set or like a thick batter. Season with salt and pepper and serve at once.

Scrambled Eggs with Brains.

Scald brains with hot water, clean and skim, and boil a few minutes in fresh water. Melt a little butter in skillet, put in brains, chopped finely, and stir well until dry and done. Add 1 teaspoonful chopped parsley, pinch salt, and eggs well-beaten. Stir with a fork until eggs are evenly cooked, put on hot platter, and serve immediately.

Deviled Eggs.

Boil your eggs until perfectly hard, then put in cold water; shell and cut the eggs in half crosswise; remove the yolks and mash up smooth, and season with pepper, salt, a little butter and enough cream to moisten. Stuff the whites with this mixture. Serve cold. Or place in a hot oven a few minutes and bake.

Fried Eggs and Oysters.

Place oysters in a pan with butter, salt and pepper, and cook in oven until beards of oysters begin to curl. Fry eggs in skillet on top of stove, leaving the yellows whole. Toast bread, and butter it while hot. Place 4 oysters on every piece of toast, place fried egg over oysters, sprinkle egg with pinch of salt and pepper, and serve immediately.

Eggs à la Champignon.

Put 2 tablespoonfuls butter in saucepan; when hot add 1 tablespoonful minced mushrooms, season with salt and pepper, add 5 eggs well beaten, stir constantly until set, and serve hot on toast. Can be prepared in chafing dish.

Egg Vermicelli.

Boil hard 3 eggs. Separate the yolks from the whites and chop the whites.

Toast 5 slices of bread, cut half of it in squares and half of it in triangles and butter while hot.

Heat 1 teaspoonful butter in a saucepan, stir in 1 heaping teaspoonful flour until smooth, season with salt and pepper. Add 1 cupful hot milk and stir until thick; then add the chopped whites and pour over the squares of toast. Rub the yolks through a strainer, sprinkle over the mixture, and garnish the dish with a border of toast triangles and parsley.

Escalloped Eggs. No. 1.

Boil hard 6 eggs. Cut whites in thin slices and mash yolks fine. Mix yolks and whites and put in a baking dish. Melt in a saucepan on stove, 2 tablespoonfuls butter, add 1 tablespoonful flour, stir till smooth, then add 1 pint milk, pinch salt and pepper. Boil till thick, and pour over eggs. Mix 1 cupful bread crumbs with 1 tablespoonful butter, sprinkle over dish, and bake 15 minutes in a hot oven.

Escalloped Eggs. No. 2.

Boil hard 12 eggs, slice when cold. Put in a pudding dish alternate layers of sliced eggs, bread crumbs and small lumps of butter, salt and pepper until dish is filled; pour over this 1 cupful sweet cream and brown in stove.

Plain Omelet.

Beat separately the whites and yolks 3 eggs, add pinch salt to whites before beating, and when stiff stir lightly in yolks. Have hot skillet greased well with fresh butter, pour omelet in, and shake, to spread evenly. Put cover on top. When omelet is light brown at bottom, roll over in folds, put on hot plate, and serve immediately.

Ham Omelet.

Beat yolks 3 eggs, add 1 tablespoonful very finely-chopped ham, 1 teaspoonful finely-chopped parsley, pinch salt and pepper. Then stir in lightly the beaten whites 3 eggs. Bake in same way as above recipe.

Cheese Omelet.

Prepare same way as ham omelet, substituting 1 tablespoonful grated cheese for ham, and omitting pepper.

Oyster Omelet.

Scald 1 dozen oysters in their own liquor, season with salt and pepper. Make an omelet by recipe given for plain omelet. When nearly done, drain the oysters from the liquor, lay them in the centre of the omelet and fold up and serve.

Sweet Omelet.

Beat separately the yolks and whites of 6 eggs, add a pinch of salt and 1 teaspoonful brandy. Fry quickly in a spider and spread with any kind of preserved fruit and roll up like any other omelet.

Rum Omelet.

Make same as sweet omelet, when dished up, pour over it 1 spoonful rum, ignite, and send to the table.

Omelette au Rum.

Beat 6 yolks of eggs well, add 2 tablespoonfuls of cream, 2 tablespoonfuls of flour, pinch salt, pinch yeast powder, then stir in stiffly-beaten whites 6 eggs. Butter skillet well, pour in, cover, and when nearly done, remove cover and put in oven for a few seconds. Roll and place on heated platter. Sprinkle with finely sifted powdered sugar, pour a wineglass of rum over whole, light with paper and serve immediately. Double the quantity can be used for a larger omelet.

Banana Omelet.

Prepare in same way as above, adding 1 tablespoonful of sliced banana to the yolks before stirring in whites. When done, sprinkle with powdered sugar, and serve immediately, without rum.

Omelet Souflé.

Beat until very light, about 15 minutes, the yolks of 5 eggs with 4 ounces powdered sugar, add ½ teaspoonful vanilla.

Beat the whites of 12 eggs to a very stiff froth, add to it the beaten yolks and sugar; mix lightly together. Now lift this mixture lightly with a large flat spoon or skimmer to a long deep platter or dish. Pile as high as possible to make it dome shape. Place at once in a moderate oven and bake for 15 miuutes. Sprinkle with powdered sugar and serve at once.

Crab Omelet.

If fresh crabs are to be used, boil, then clean them and pick out the meat of 1 dozen crabs. Canned crabs will answer as well. Drain off the liquor, and mash until smooth.

Beat yolks of 6 eggs, add the crabs, pinch of salt, pepper and cayenne pepper, also juice of ¼ onion. Then add the stiffly-beaten whites of eggs. Shape and fry in hot lard. Serve at once. Garnish with thin slices of lemon and sprigs of parsley.

BREAKFAST DISHES.

Farina.

Put on to boil 1½ cupfuls milk and ½ cupful water, when boiling, stir in gradually 2 good tablespoonfuls farina, and continue stirring until thick as pap, add a good pinch of salt. Serve at once with cream or hot milk. If desired, a little sugar can be added.

Fried Farina.

Make the farina same as in foregoing recipe. When done, pour into a flat platter and let it stand until cold and stiff. Then cut into square pieces, dip each piece in beaten egg and fry in very hot butter. Serve hot.

Oatmeal Pap.

Stir 2 heaping tablespoonfuls well-cooked oatmeal into 2 cupfuls cold milk. When mixed, put on to boil, adding a tiny pinch of salt, and a little sugar. Continue to boil, stirring occasionally until the milk is as thick as sweet cream, then strain and mash as much as possible through a fine sieve. Nice for invalids and infants.

Rice Pap.

Stir 4 heaping tablespoonfuls freshly boiled rice into 2 cupfuls cold milk, add a pinch of salt, if the rice has not already been salted, add also a pinch of sugar. Put on the fire and stir occasionally until the milk is as thick as thick cream, then strain and mash as much as possible through a fine sieve. Nice for invalids and infants.

Flour Pap.

Boil 1 cupful sweet milk. Dissolve 2 heaping tablespoonfuls of flour in a very little cold milk until a creamy paste, and stir into the hot milk. Stir until it has thickened well, sprinkle sugar and a little cinnamon on top and serve immediately. This will serve two portions.

Cornstarch Pap.

Put on three cupfuls milk to boil in a double boiler. Dissolve three heaping tablespoonfuls cornstarch in a little cold milk. When the milk begins to boil, stir in the dissolved cornstarch, add a pinch of salt, 1 teaspoonful sugar or more if desired, push to the back of the stove and boil slowly for 10 minutes, stirring often. Serve at once with powdered sugar and cinnamon sprinkled over.

Arrowroot.

Put on 1 cupful milk to boil. Dissolve one heaping teaspoonful arrowroot in a very little cold milk, add sugar and salt to taste. When the milk begins to boil stir in the dissolved arrowroot, and remove from fire as soon as thick, which only takes a few seconds. Serve at once. For family use, use two or three times this quantity.

Boiled Hominy.

Wash and pick over as much hominy as required. Put in a saucepan, add a good pinch of salt, cover well with water, cover with a lid, put on the stove, and let it begin to boil, then move to the back of the stove and let boil and steam slowly for about 30 minutes. If necessary, add a little more water while cooking. After the hominy is cooked, add 1 cupful milk and let it soak and steam in.

Fried Hominy.

Pour the boiled hominy in a platter and let it get perfectly cold and stiff; then slice in squares. Dip in some beaten egg and fry in boiling hot butter or fat.

Flake Oatmeal.

Put 1 cupful oat flakes on to boil with 1 pint of cold water and a pinch of salt. Stir frequently to prevent burning, and when oatmeal has absorbed all water, it is ready to serve. A tablespoonful of fresh butter stirred in oatmeal while still in saucepan, improves it. Serve with sugar and cream. Plain oatmeal takes longer to cook and needs more water.

Big Hominy.

Put a pint of big hominy in a large vessel with a great deal of cold water, and 1 teaspoonful of salt. If the grain is desired for breakfast, must be cooked the day previous for 5 or 6 hours. The next morning, heat before serving. If for dinner, can be put on in the morning. Drain, dry and serve plain if it is to be eaten with cream and sugar. Otherwise, drain dry and stir in 1 tablespoonful of fresh butter.

SUPPER OR LUNCHEON DISHES.

Salmon Cakes. No. 1.

In a fryer on a hot stove put 1 tablespoonful butter, when melted and hot, add half a small onion cut fine, when light brown, add ½ can tomatoes, brown lightly. Empty 1 can of salmon in a bowl, mash with a spoon, add three whole eggs, 1 kitchen spoonful sifted flour, salt, pepper and parsley to taste. Mix the tomatoes with the salmon, and drop by spoonfuls in very hot butter. Brown on both sides.

Fish Cakes.

Prepare same as salmon cakes, substituting any cold boiled fish for the salmon.

Salmon Cakes. No. 2.

Drain a 2 lb. can of salmon, remove bones, and mash fine. Add 2 whole beaten eggs, 1 tablespoonful flour, pinch salt and pepper, a little grated onion. Mix well. 1 tablespoonful of chopped parsley can also be added. Make in croquettes, and brown in hot skillet with very little hot grease. Turn first on one side then the other. Too much fat makes them greasy. To be eaten either with Hollandaise sauce, or preserves.

Pressed Chicken.

Boil the day previous a hen, until meat is tender and liquor is boiled down to a large cupful. Strain liquor, and set aside in ice box over night. Chop chicken fine, removing all skin, bones, fat and gristle.

In the morning, skim grease off liquor, heat and season with salt, pepper, juice of ¼ lemon, and 1 teaspoonful Worcestershire sauce. Mix in chicken, put in mold, put a heavy weight on meat, set on ice, until jellied. Turn out on platter, and serve with slices of lemon.

Chicken Aspic.

Boil a large hen until tender, and liquor is boiled down to 3 cupfuls. Cut meat in dice and set aside. Dissolve ½ box gelatine, add to chicken liquor, season with juice ½ lemon, salt, pepper, and 1 teaspoonful Worcestershire sauce. Mix all with chicken, add a few slices of lemon. Put in a mold, and set on ice, until jellied and ready to serve.

Meat Aspic.

Take 3 beef shank bones, those nearest the foot are best, and put on to cook in a large kettleful of cold water. Boil all day slowly, until the meat drops from the bones. If it cooks down too low, add a little more water. Strain, and set aside in ice-box over night to jelly. In the morning skim off all grease, and set aside. Take 2 lbs. round steak, cut in very small pieces, salt and pepper it, then fry in a skillet until very brown, stirring constantly to prevent burning. Pour meat jelly in a sauce pan, add browned meat, scraping skillet well. Make a small spice-bag of several bay leaves, a few whole spice, whole black peppers, and some cloves with the tops removed, also one or two red peppers. Drop this bag into the pan. Cook until the meat is very tender, cooking the jelly down to about half the quantity. It may take about 6 hours. Season with salt, making much saltier than the taste would demand as it loses in hardening. Pour into a mold, first removing spice-bag. Let harden, turn out, and cut in slices. In winter will keep for several days. Is nice for supper or evening entertainments. In summer, it is best to keep on ice until ready to serve.

Meat Soufflé.

Chop 1 cupful of cold meat, chicken, or game, very fine. Melt in a saucepan 1 teaspoonful of butter, add 1 heaping teaspoonful of flour, pinch of salt and pepper, and 1 cupful milk. Stir well until it has thickened and is smooth, then add a little chopped parsley, and a few drops of onion juice. Beat yolks of 2 eggs well, add to sauce, stirring carefully, then add meat. Beat whites of 2 eggs to a stiff froth, add to meat. Put in a buttered dish, bake 20 minutes, and serve immediately.

Cold Meat Croquettes.

Chop cold cooked meat very fine, and measure 2 cupfuls. Beat 2 whole eggs very light, stir into chopped meat, add salt, black pepper, a tiny pinch of cayenne, 3 tablespoonfuls grated bread crumbs, 1 tablespoonful of fresh butter, and a little grated onion juice. Make into shape of croquettes, and if a little soft, add more grated bread crumbs. Dip in beaten egg, then in bread crumbs, then fry in hot fat. Serve either with tomato, or egg sauce. Different kinds of meats left from meals may be mixed and chopped fine. Cold veal makes the best croquettes.

Brain Croquettes.

Scald brain, and clean. Cut in small pieces. Put 2 tablespoonfuls of butter in saucepan on stove, cut up a little onion, and let brown, add 1 slice of bread, which has been soaked in cold water and squeezed dry, cayenne pepper, salt, and a little chopped parsley. Mix well, then add brain, stirring constantly. Take from stove, add 1 well-beaten egg, and ½ cupful milk, mix well and set aside until cold. When cold form into croquette shape, dip in egg, then in grated bread crumbs, and fry brown in hot fat,

Cold Meat Stew.

Cold veal, lamb, or mutton is best for this. If possible, a little meat gravy, or strained soup stock should be saved over. Cut the meat in strips of 2 by 3 inches. Brown ¼ onion in 1 tablespoonful of beef drippings or butter, then brown 1 tablespoonful of flour. Add the bones of the meat and 2 cupfuls of stock, or 2 cupfuls hot water. Let come to a boil, drop the meat in, and cook up. Taste, and if necessary, add salt and black pepper. Season with a little Worcestershire sauce, a tiny pinch of cayenne, and if convenient, chopped parsley or celery. This tastes the same as if fresh. One-half can tomatoes, and a teaspoonful of tomato catsup, can be added, if desired.

Veal Croquettes.

2 lbs. lean veal, 1 sprig parsley, 1 small onion, 1 bay leaf, 4 cloves. Simmer the veal with the onion, parsley, bay leaf, and cloves. When very tender, drain, chop fine, and to every pint of chopped meat, add 1 cupful cream sauce.

CREAM SAUCE.

Heat 1 cupful milk in double boiler. Melt in pan, 1 tablespoonful butter, 2 tablespoonfuls flour, 1 teaspoonful salt, ¼ teaspoonful grated nutmeg, and a few grains of cayenne. When smooth add the hot milk, beating all the time, until thick. Then add teaspoonful onion juice, then 1 tablespoonful chopped parsley. Mix this well with meat, and let cool. When cold shape into cone-shaped croquettes. Beat 1 egg with 2 tablespoonfuls milk. Roll each croquette in finely grated bread crumbs, then in egg, then in bread crumbs. Fry in boiling fat 1 minute. Put on platter and garnish with parsley.

Chicken Souflé.

In a saucepan put 1 tablespoonful butter, when soft add 1 tablespoonful flour, rub smooth, then add 1 pint milk, stir well and when boiling, season with salt and pepper and add ½ cupful grated bread crumbs, boil 2 minutes, then add some finely chopped parsley and 2 cupfuls finely chopped chicken (which has previously been boiled and chopped), add yolks of 3 eggs well beaten. Then add 1 wineglass sherry or Madeira wine and the stiffly-beaten whites of eggs. Pour into a buttered pudding or chafing dish and bake in oven half an hour.

Individual Oyster Loaves.

Allow 1 loaf individual French baker's bread about 5 inches long for each person. Fry oysters, allowing 3 to each loaf. Heat the loaves, cut off the tops, scoop out some of the inside and butter the loaves while hot. Put 3 oysters inside of each loaf, also 1 olive, 1 small pickle, put back the top, and serve hot. Nice for late suppers.

Broiled Sardines on Toast.

Open 2 cans of imported sardines, remove from can and put on a platter to drain off oil. Toast slices of stale bread, cut in triangles or squares, removing crust, and butter while hot. Dip each sardine in bread crumbs, put on a broiler, and broil over clear coal fire, first on one side then the other. Lay the broiled sardines, 2 on each piece of toast, put a slice of lemon on top, and serve immediately.

Mock Duck.

Season a round steak, with salt, pepper and ginger. Make a bread dressing, same as for fowls, lay over steak. Sew up in shape of filet. Put in roasting pan inside stove, with a little water. Put a few slices of bacon on top. Baste often, and cook until it is well done. Serve with parsley. Slice same as you would filet.

Smoked Tongue.

Secure a fat, tender smoked tongue. Put in a boiler, cover with cold water, and boil steadily until done, test by sticking a fork in it. When done, remove from fire, and while warm pull off the outer skin, cut off the root and set away to cool. When cold cut in very thin slices, lay on a platter, and garnish with sprigs of parsley.

Pickled Tongue.

Secure a nice, tender beef tongue from a butcher, wash thoroughly, cut off the root, and with a mixture of salt, pepper, ginger, saltpetre, and a little garlic, rub thoroughly all over, make a few incisions in the thick skin so that the seasonings will penetrate well. Lay it in a crock, cover with a clean piece of cloth, and weight down with pieces of stone. Put in a cool place for 3 or 4 days or a week, depending on the weather. Turn occasionally. When thoroughly seasoned put in a boiler, cover well with cold water, and boil until tender. Cut in thin slices when cold, and garnish with sprigs of parsley. Or serve hot before slicing, with green peas.

Pickled Meat.

Secure as large a piece of nice brisket as desired, have plenty hard fat on it. Wash and dry well, then rub all over with some powdered saltpetre. Then in a bowl mix salt, ground pepper, ground ginger, a little garlic, and a tiny bit of sugar. Rub the meat on all sides with the mixture, and stick it with a fork so that the seasoning will penetrate well. Lay the seasoned meat in a flat bowl, add 2 bay leaves, 3 cloves, and a tablespoonful whole pepper; cover with a clean, damp cloth, put pieces of clean stone on top, and put aside in a cool place from 4 days to 1 week; time is dependent on the size of the meat and the weather; if it is cold it will keep longer than when warm. Turn the meat occasionally, and when well pickled, put on in cold water and let boil until tender.

Cheese Souflé.

Melt a piece of butter the size of an egg in a saucepan on the stove, stir in 1 tablespoonful flour, when smooth, add gradually 1 pint milk, and stir until thick. Drop in the yolks of 5 eggs one at a time, until thoroughly mixed, remove from fire and let cool.

Beat the whites of 5 eggs stiff and stir in the cold mixture, then add 5 tablespoonfuls grated Parmesan or American cheese. Bake in individual shells or entree dishes in a hot oven. Bake 10 minutes. Serve at once.

Cheese Cream Pudding.

Take 2 cupfuls cottage cheese which has dripped the previous night and mash smooth and fine. Add 1 heaping tablespoonful of flour, yolks 6 eggs, ¼ cupful granulated sugar, juice of 1 lemon and a pinch of salt. Add 1 cupful cream and 1 cupful milk. Beat 6 whites stiff, mix well, pour in baking dish and bake in very hot oven. If possible use 1 pt. cream instead of half milk and cream. If cheese is very stiff, must be thinned with a little more milk, to get it smooth and even. Can be eaten hot or cold.

Pressed Cheese.

Get a curd press, the heart shaped ones are prettiest. Pour clabber in and set aside in a cool place until all whey is pressed out, and cheese is firm. Turn out on dish, and sprinkle with sugar and cinnamon, and rich sweet cream.

Cottage Cheese.

Take clabber, and pour into a bag of cheese cloth. Let drip over night, or about 6 hours if put up in the morning, until all whey is out. Mash fine and smooth, with a little cream, salt, and black pepper. Put 2 or 3 tablespoonfuls of thick cream on top. Boiled potatoes with their jackets on, can be served with it.

Eggs à la Hausman.

Chop some cooked ham or tongue very fine, add a few bread crumbs, some chopped parsley and a little melted butter. Season with salt and white pepper, moisten with milk and put in individual shells well buttered. Break 1 fresh egg over each shell carefully, so as to keep it whole. Put shells in a pan, place in moderate oven and bake until the whites are set.

Eggs au Parmesan.

Toast enough bread to cover the bottom of a pudding pan or chafing dish. Sprinkle a layer of Parmesan cheese over toast. Now break 1 whole egg over each piece of toast, being careful to keep each egg whole. Sprinkle another layer of cheese over the eggs, drop small bits of butter, salt and pepper over all. Pour over the whole about 2 tablespoonfuls sweet cream. Set in stove until the eggs are firm.

Sweetbreads à la Créole.

Scald and clean the sweetbreads, then boil them until tender, with salt, pepper and chopped parsley added; when almost done add 1 teaspoonful butter and enough flour to thicken the gravy. In another saucepan put 1 can tomatoes, add 1 teaspoonful sugar, 1 teaspoonful vinegar, a little salt and pepper, cook 15 minutes and strain.

Have ready some very small pieces of fried bread.

On a hot platter pour the sweetbreads, then over it pour the tomatoes. Lay on the croutons. Serve at once.

Veal Salad.

Cut cold veal in half-inch pieces, season with 2 tablespoonfuls vinegar, pinch of salt and pepper. Make a dressing of yolks of 3 hard-boiled eggs, mashed smooth, add gradually 2 tablespoonfuls butter, melted, or cold chicken or turkey grease, stir until smooth and thick; then add 1 teaspoonful prepared mustard, large pinch salt and pepper, 1 teaspoonful sugar, 1 teaspoonful each mustard and celery seed, and 5 tablespoonfuls white vinegar. Mix the dressing well with the veal, and serve with or without lettuce leaves.

Liver with Tomato Sauce.

Fry liver in slices, 3 inches long, 2 inches wide. Remove from skillet, put in hot platter, and keep in hot place until ready for it. Brown an onion in remainder of fat, also 1 tablespoonful of flour, add ½ can of tomatoes, pinch salt, sugar, cayenne and black pepper. Mix well, strain, add a little chopped parsley, and pour over fried liver.

Welsh Rarebit.

Toast bread without crusts, butter and keep hot, until ready for use. Melt in a double boiler 1 tablespoonful of butter, add ½ lb. American cheese shaved fine, stir until smooth, add pinch of dry mustard, salt, and cayenne pepper. Stir well, then add ½ cupful ale or beer. Stir well, then pour while hot on toast, and serve immediately. Is best prepared at the table on a chafing dish, and served immediately. A yolk of 1 egg can be stirred in while cooking if desired, but care must be taken that it does not curdle.

Cheese Fondu.

Put in a bowl ½ cupful grated dry bread crumbs, mixed with 1 tablespoonful of fresh butter. Heat 1 cupful sweet milk, and scald bread crumbs. Add one by one, the yolks of 3 eggs. Then add ¼ lb. grated cheese, then stiffly-beaten whites of 3 eggs. Add a pinch of salt, white pepper, and a tiny bit of cayenne. Pour in a baking dish, sprinkle top with bread crumbs, bake in a hot oven 20 minutes, and serve immediately. This makes a dish for 6 persons. For more, the quantity must be doubled. Can also be prepared on a chafing dish instead of baked in oven.

Leaf Puffs.

Cream 1 cupful butter until soft, add 2 cupfuls sifted flour, mix well, and add just enough sweet cream to make a nice dough, not too soft. Roll thin, cut in long strips or squares, bake in long pans in a moderately hot oven. When light brown, draw to the door of the oven, sprinkle with powdered sugar and let stand a few moments longer in the oven.

Snowballs.

Put 2¼ cupfuls sifted flour on a biscuit board, make a hole in the centre of the heap, put in the cavity a piece of fresh butter as large as a guinea egg, 1 teaspoonful sugar, a pinch of salt, 1 teaspoonful white wine or lemon juice (wine preferred), and break in 3 eggs. Work the whole together with a spoon until the flour is incorporated with the other ingredients, and you have a dough easily handled. Break the dough in pieces about the size of a walnut; roll each piece out separately just as thin as possible without tearing (the thinner the better), make 3 lengthwise slashes in the centre of each piece of dough after rolling out.
Heat a large deep skillet about half full with boiling

hot butter, drop in the snowballs, not more than 2 or 3 at one time, brown quickly on one side, then on the other, turn carefully with a perforated skimmer as they are easily broken. Remove to a platter, sprinkle with powdered sugar and cinnamon and a few drops of lemon juice.

Noodle Puffs.

Sift 1 cupful flour on a biscuit board, make a hole in the center of the flour, break in the yolks of 4 eggs, and a pinch of salt; gradually work in the flour until the dough is stiff but can be easily handled. Roll out somewhat thin, cut in strips 4 inches long by 1 wide.

Have a skillet half full of boiling hot butter, drop in the strips a few at a time, baste with the hot grease until brown on both sides. Remove to a platter, sprinkle generously with powdered sugar and serve.

BEVERAGES.

How to Roast Coffee.

Put the coffee in an agate or tin baking pan, if you have no family coffee-roaster. Put in a moderately hot oven to get a dark golden brown, not black; toss the coffee frequently with a wooden spoon, and when done, drop in a small lump of butter, and stir until the coffee is glazed. Put in an earthen jar and cover tightly.

How to make Coffee.

To each cupful, use 2 heaping tablespoonfuls coffee, ground neither too coarse nor too fine, and it must be freshly ground. Mixed Java and Mocha is best with a little Maracaibo. Put the ground coffee in a thin flannel bag inside the filter of a French coffee-pot; pour 1 teaspoonful cold water over the grounds, then set the pot on the stove to heat thoroughly, then pour as much *boiling* water over the grounds as required, not forgetting to allow 2 heaping tablespoonfuls coffee to each cupful water; let the coffee drip through the bag, then pour over the grounds twice more, being careful to keep the pot on the back of the stove, as the coffee will not be fit for use if it boils after pouring the water over it. Serve at once.

Iced Coffee.

Make coffee in the morning, having it a little stronger than usual. Sweeten to taste, and serve with cracked ice. If desired, a spoonful of whipped cream can be added to each glass.

Chocolate.

Put on to boil 1 cupful water and 3 cupfuls milk. Dissolve 8 heaping teaspoonfuls grated sweet chocolate (the best, of course) in very little cold milk. When the milk and water begin to boil, stir in the dissolved chocolate, and stir occasionally while boiling for 20 minutes, sweeten to taste. Pour over the well-beaten yolks of two eggs. Serve at once, with a spoonful of sweetened whipped cream on top of each cup.

Cocoa.

Use 1 heaping teaspoonful of cocoa to each cup, and dissolve it in very little cold milk. Let the quantity of milk required come to a boil, stir in the dissolved cocoa, and stir occasionally while boiling 15 minutes. Sweeten to taste.

Tea.

An earthenware or copper teapot is best. Have the water boiling, allow 1 teaspoonful of tea to every cup of hot water, pour boiling water into teapot, let stand 1 minute, and pour off immediately and serve. Tea made in this way is very stimulating, but if allowed to stand longer, with the leaves, becomes poisonous.

Iced Tea.

Make plain tea, and keep in an earthen or china vessel on ice until ready to prepare. Just before serving add lemons and sugar to taste. Put a spoonful of cracked ice in each glass and serve.

Russian Tea.

Make as in above recipe and pour the tea into an earthen vessel to cool. Sweeten to taste. When cold, pour into thin glasses, put a tablespoonful of sherbet into each glass, and serve.

Lemonade.

To every glass allow ½ lemon. Squeeze out juice, strain, and put in glass. Add ½ glass of water. Sweeten to taste, and fill up remainder of glass with cracked ice. A slice of fresh pineapple can be added, or a few fresh strawberries in season.

Apollinaris Lemonade.

Make same as plain lemonade, using apollinaris water, instead of plain. Always serve with slice of lemon, and slice of pineapple.

Champagne Punch.

To every quart bottle of champagne allow 1 pt. of white wine, and 2 cupfuls water. Sweeten to taste, add the juice of 2 oranges, the juice of 2 lemons, ½ pt. of sliced pineapple, and a few sliced oranges. Put in punch bowl, add a big lump of ice, and serve as desired.

Claret Punch.

To every glass of punch allow ½ lemon. Put strained juice in glass, put ¼ glass of crushed ice, 1½ tablespoonfuls of sugar, ¼ glass of claret, and fill up remainder of glass with water. Serve with a slice of lemon or orange. If punch is to be made in large quantities, allow the same proportions, for as many glasses as needed. Sliced pineapple, sliced lemon, sliced orange, and candied or maraschino cherries are added. Do not crush the ice, but put a large lump in punch bowl, pour in punch, and serve as desired.

Milk Punch.

Fill a large glass ⅔ full of sweet milk, add 1 large tablespoonful of sugar, a wineglass of brandy, or whiskey, or less if desired, and the remainder of the glass with crushed ice. Pour into the tin shaker, and shake until it is foamy. Grate a little nutmeg on top, and serve at once.

Glee Wine or Hot Claret Punch.

To 1 qt. bottle of claret, allow 2 lemons, 1 cupful hot water, sugar to taste, and ½ teaspoonful each whole cloves, spice, and 1 stick cinnamon. Put whole on to boil, let begin to thicken and serve hot.

Claret Cup.

Squeeze into a glass pitcher the strained juice of 1½ lemons, add 2 tablespoonfuls powdered sugar, 1 tablespoonful red curacoa; then pour in 3 cupfuls claret, and 1 cupful apollinaris water. Mix thoroughly, add a few slices of orange, or pineapple, or both.

Cut the rinds from 2 cucumbers without breaking them, hang them on the inside of the pitcher from the top; drop in a good-sized lump of ice, and serve at once in thin glasses.

Sauterne Cup.

Take equal parts of sauterne and apollinaris water, and put in a pitcher, allowing six lumps of sugar to every quart. Add a long paring of cucumber rind and a few slices of pineapple. Put the pitcher in a bucket of cracked ice and salt, or fill a towel with cracked ice and salt, and wrap around the pitcher. Do not put ice *in* the mixture. Just before serving throw in some sprigs of mint.

Mint Julep.

Put a teaspoonful of sugar, a few sprigs of mint, and a teaspoonful of water in a glass, mix well, and crush the mint as much as possible. Fill the glass with crushed or shaved ice, add 1 tablespoonful of brandy, 1 teaspoonful of Jamaica rum, 2 sprigs of mint, and add more sugar on top. Stir gently and serve with straws.

Egg-Nog.

Separate the whites and yolks of the eggs. To every yolk add 1 tablespoonful of sugar, and beat until *very* light. Beat whites to a stiff froth. It takes 1 egg to every glass of egg-nog. Add 2 tablespoonfuls brandy or rum, then ⅛ cupful milk or cream to each glass, and lastly the whites of the eggs. Pour in glass, put a spoonful of whipped cream over, and grate nutmeg on top.

Egg-Flip. No. 1.

Beat the yolk of 1 egg and 1 teaspoonful sugar in a glass until light and foamy, then stir in 1 tablespoonful sherry wine or brandy. Beat the white of the egg to a stiff froth, and stir it in with the egg and wine. Serve at once. This is very strengthening for invalids, and is good for hoarseness.

Egg-Flip. No. 2.

Separate the yolk and white of 1 egg. Add sufficient sugar to the yolk, to make it stiff, beat white stiff, add to the yolk. Stir in ½ tablespoonful of brandy, ½ tablespoonful of rum, put in a glass, and fill up with hot milk. Grate nutmeg on top and serve immediately. Fine for colds.

Tom and Jerry.

Prepare same as Egg-Flip No. 2, only using hot water instead of hot milk.

Geranium Cordial.

Have ready a 1 quart glass jar or bottle with big mouth that can be tightly corked. Fill half full with rose-geranium leaves that have been thoroughly washed and had the stems removed. Fill the jar with finest whiskey or brandy, cork tightly and put aside in a dark closet for 6 weeks.

After 6 weeks, strain through a fine sieve. Put on the stove 1 cupful sugar and ¾ cupful water, let boil until it begins to rope, pour over the strained whiskey stirring all the time. Strain again, bottle and cork tightly, do not need to seal. The cordial can then be used in 2 weeks and keeps any length of time.

Blackberry Cordial.

Wash the blackberries well, put in a porcelain kettle on the back of the stove, let them *heat* all through, stirring often but *do not boil*. Do not add any water. Strain through a cheese cloth bag, being careful to get every bit of the substance, leaving only the seeds in the bag. Measure the juice, and to every quart add 1 pint sugar; put on the stove, drop in some whole cinnamon, spice and cloves tied in a thin rag. Boil until the syrup is thick, about 20 minutes, when done set aside to cool. When cold, add 1 pint brandy to every quart of syrup. Bottle and seal tightly.

Cherry Bounce. No. 1.

The little wild cherry is excellent for this purpose, as the stone kernels contain alcohol. Wash carefully, sugar plentifully, and add whole spice, cloves (with the heads removed) and stick cinnamon. Fewer cloves than the other spices. Get good whiskey and allow ⅓ as much cherries as whiskey. To a quart bottle allow scant ½ pint sugared cherries to 1½ pints of whiskey. Bottle and seal. Let stand at least 2 months. Open, shake bottle well and taste, and if necessary add more sugar. Seal again, and let stand another month. Is not good under three months and the older it gets the finer it becomes.

Cherry Bounce. No. 2.

Secure nice sound large cherries. Have ready a large mouthed bottle. Put in a thick layer of cherries, then a layer of cut loaf sugar, then some cloves with the heads removed and some whole spice and cinnamon, continue this same way until the bottle is almost full, then pour fine whiskey over all until the bottle is full. Put in a dark closet for six or eight weeks. The longer it stands the better it will be.

Raspberry Vinegar.

6 quarts berries, put in a stone jar and pour 1 scant quart white vinegar over them. Let it stand 3 or 4 days and stir every day. Then strain through a flannel bag and boil, allowing 1 pint of sugar to every pint juice, skim and boil until like a syrup. Bottle and seal when cold.

Raspberry Syrup.

To every 3 pints berries, use 1 lb. sugar and ½ pint water. Put water on with sugar and let it boil until it forms a syrup, when clear put in the berries, and stir with a silver spoon (do not mash). After boiling a few minutes strain through a flannel bag and seal in bottles when cold.

Maraschino Glacé.

Fill a punch glass half full with finely-shaved ice, then put in 2 tablespoonfuls maraschino cherries and their liquor. Serve at once.

Strawberry Glacé.

Mash 1 quart strawberries with a pounder, add the juice of 2 lemons and 1 quart cold water, let stand 3 hours, then strain and add 1 lb. sugar, stirring until the sugar is dissolved well, then put on ice for another hour. Have a thin glass half full of finely shaved or crushed ice, then fill with the strawberry syrup.

Champagne Punch. No. 1. 3 Gals.

1 quart French brandy, 1 quart St. Croix rum, 2 lbs. loaf sugar (dissolved in water), the juice of ½ doz. oranges (strained), the juice of ½ doz. lemons, ¾ quart strong black tea (strained and cold), 6 quarts of Champagne.

Flavoring, a small whiskey glass of chartreuse and Maraschino. ½ hour before serving add 1 lb. ice.

Claret Punch. 5 Gals.

3 gals. claret, ¾ gal. black tea (strained), the juice of 2½ doz. lemons (strained), the juice of 1 doz. oranges (strained), ½ gal. rye whiskey, 2½ lbs. granulated sugar (dissolved in warm water). 1. Flavoring, use 1 can pineapple and 1 bottle Maraschino cherries ; or flavoring No. 2. ½ oz. tincture of cloves, ½ oz. cinnamon.

CANDIES.

Molasses Candy.

One quart molasses, 1 tablespoonful brown sugar, butter size of an egg, ½ teaspoonful soda.

Boil the molasses, sugar, and butter together for a while, then add the soda dissolved in a little cold water. Test by dropping a little in iced water. When done it will easily form a ball.

Pour into buttered dishes, and when cool pull until light. A little flour put on the hands will make it pull easily.

Cream Candy.

Put on to boil 2 heaping cupfuls sugar, ¼ cupful white vinegar, and ¾ cupful water, add a pinch of soda, or cream tartar. Boil without stirring until it will form a ball in iced water. Flavor with lemon or rosewater. Pour into buttered dishes, and when cool, pull same as molasses candy.

Peanut Nougat.

Get as many parched peanuts as desired, usually 1 or 2 quarts. Shell the nuts, and remove the skins, then roll the nuts with a roller on a marble slab, until they are as fine as possible. Measure the nuts, and for every cupful of nuts, take 2 cupfuls granulated sugar. Put the sugar in an agate boiler without a drop of water, let melt very carefully, and when thoroughly melted and brown, not burnt, remove from the stove, stir in the nuts at once, pour on a marble slab, and roll very quickly with a roller until thin as a wafer, then cut in strips.

Plarines.

1 lb. dark brown sugar, 1 lb. pecans weighed before shelling.

Put on the sugar with just enough water to dissolve it ; let boil, stirring constantly until you can form a ball between your fingers, then add a good pinch of soda ; after mixing the soda well into the candy, add the nuts. When it begins to turn back to sugar, remove from the fire, and drop into cakes on a greased marble slab.

Fondant, or French Creams.

To every lb. of sugar allow ½ pt. water (granulated sugar No. 1. is best) and 1 teaspoonful of glucose. Glucose is preferable to cream tartar and can be purchased of almost any confectioner by the ½ pint. If it is not obtainable, use ¼ teaspoonful of cream tartar. Boil until when dropped in cold water it will make a soft ball that can be rolled between the fingers. Remove immediately, as it will sugar if cooked too long. Pour in a flat china platter (ungreased), or best of all, on a marble slab, and let stand until it begins to cool. Take a wooden paddle and begin to work, always moving paddle in one way. Drop a few drops of essence of vanilla on it. Work steadily until it becomes creamy, and finally hard and white. This is the foundation for any cream or French candy. Will keep a week. If too hard to mold well, put fondant in kettle, place kettle in boiling water, and let melt.

Walnut Creams.

Take a small piece of fondant, while pliable, but not too soft, place a half walnut on either side and put aside to stand for a day. A variety can be made by dividing a piece of fondant in 3 parts, coloring one green and adding a few drops of pistache flavoring. To the other part add a few drops of strawberry coloring, and flavoring. Fix walnuts in same manner.

Coffee Creams.

Melt fondant in double kettle or in saucepan over kettle of hot water. Flavor and color with coffee extract. Take ½ walnut, dip in melted fondant, roll until it is thickly covered, and place on waxed paper to harden.

Pistache Creams.

Melt fondant in double boiler, color and flavor with pistache. Take a candied cherry, roll in melted fondant, and put on waxed paper until the next day.

Date Creams.

Remove seeds from dates, roll a piece of fondant oblong, half the size of a finger, place in date, and set aside until next day.

Fruit Roll.

Take a piece of fondant, roll out 1 inch thick. Chop up figs, dates, and nuts, work in fondant, and roll out again. Roll together in shape of jelly roll. Let stand until firm, then cut in thin slices crosswise. Is made much finer if candied fruits are used.

Strawberry Creams.

Place fondant in kettle, put kettle in hot water and set on stove. Add a few drops of strawberry flavoring, and a tiny bit of pink coloring. Have strawberries ready, carefully selected ones with stems on. Catch by the stem, roll in melted fondant, set on dish to harden, and serve same day as prepared or strawberries will spoil. Can be colored and flavored with pistache. These are nice served as bon-bons for teas and luncheons.

Cherry Creams.

Prepare same way as Strawberry Creams, cut away part of the stem of the cherry.

Chocolate Creams.

Prepare fondant the day before. Sprinkle wooden board lightly with cornstarch, roll a small piece of fondant out thin, cut off a piece, and shape into cones, or little balls like the confectioners' drops. Set aside over night to harden. Next day grate ¼ lb. Baker's chocolate, put in a sauce pan, and place over a kettle of boiling water. Let melt but do not add water to it. Add 2 or 3 drops of glycerine, and a few drops of vanilla flavoring. Take a needle or hat pin, stick through creams, roll in melted chocolate, put on waxed paper, and let stand until next day.

Peppermint Creams.

While fondant is soft, add a few drops of oil or essence of peppermint, and drop with a teaspoon on buttered paper. Let stand until next day. If fondant is firmer mold pieces in shape of a quarter dollar. Chocolate can be melted, and prepared in same way as for chocolate cream drops. Dip creams in and let dry.

French Cream Candy. (Uncooked.)

Break into a bowl the white of 1 egg, add to it an equal amount of water, after measuring in a tablespoon, and stir in confectioners' sugar until you have the mixture stiff enough to mould into balls with the fingers. Flavor with a few drops of vanilla. This candy will only keep fresh a few days.

Walnut Creams.

Make some uncooked French cream. Mould it with the fingers into neat round balls, about the size of a walnut. Crack a pound of walnuts, being careful not to break the meat.

Take one of the cream balls, place half a nut on either side of it, pressing them firmly into the cream. When all are done, stand aside for a few hours to set.

Coffee Walnut Creams.

Make same as Walnuts Creams, only using strong coffee instead of water in mixing the sugar.

Chocolate Caramels.

Boil ¼ lb. grated chocolate, 1 cupful cream, 1 cupful New Orleans molasses, butter the size of an egg, 1 cupful of brown sugar, and a few drops of vanilla extract. Boil until it makes a little ball in cold water, but not too soft. Pour in shallow greased tins, allow to cool, then mark off into blocks. Is best the second day.

Cream Caramels.

Boil 3 cupfuls of sugar with 1 teaspoonful vanilla extract, and 1 cupful sweet cream. When it begins to boil add ¼ teaspoonful cream tartar, and fresh butter size of an egg. When it makes a soft ball in ice cold water, remove immediately, pour in flat buttered pans, and do not stir until cold. Cut and block. If cooked too long, will sugar. Must be watched carefully, and stirred while cooking, but not after it is done.

Taffy Buttercups.

2 cupfuls white sugar, 1 cupful syrup, and ½ cupful butter. Put on in an agate boiler, and boil, not too fast, stirring occasionally until it candies. Test by dropping a little on a cold marble, if it will pull when

cold, it is done. Remove from the fire, flavor with vanilla, pour on a buttered marble or platter, and when *cool*, pull like molasses candy until cold, then stretch and cut with a sharp scissors in blocks, 1 inch square.

Glacé for Candies.

Boil 1 lb. sugar with ½ pt. of water, until it ropes, then add ½ cupful vinegar (1 gill), and boil until it hardens. Dip fruit in, orange slices, or nuts, and put aside on a buttered platter to set. Green grapes with the stems on are nice glacéd. The orange slices and glacé grapes are used for teas and luncheons.

PRESERVES.

Strawberry Preserves. No. 1.

Pick and wash the berries well, then weigh them.
To every pound of berries use 1 pound sugar.
Put the sugar on a hot fire with just enough water to dampen it well. Let cook until it forms a syrup, then drop in the berries carefully. Cook until the berries are done, but not to pieces; they should be whole, and generally require about 20 minutes to cook them.
Remove the berries with a perforated skimmer and put them in jars. Continue cooking the syrup until thick, then pour over the berries, and seal tightly. The less of this preserves cooked at one time, the brighter it will be.
If there is too much syrup to fill the jars, strain it, and cook a little longer. It will make nice jelly.

Strawberry Preserves. No. 2.

Pick strawberries, weigh, then wash carefully. Put berries in bottom of preserving kettle. Weigh sugar, allowing lb. for lb. and put over berries in kettle. Put whole over a slow fire, cook the berries done, remove with a skimmer, and put in glass jars, nearly ¾ full. Let syrup cook down thick, pour over berries in jar, filling up to the brim, put brandied paper on top, screw on top of jars, and seal immediately. Be careful to discard all spoiled berries and fruit will keep any length of time.

Blackberry Preserves.

Prepare the same as Strawberry No. 2.

Seedless Blackberry Jam.

Get 1 peck ripe blackberries, wash and pick them well, put in an agate kettle on the back of the stove without water, stir often from the bottom with a wooden spoon until thoroughly heated all through, but do not boil.

Remove the berries from the stove, and with a pounder mash them thoroughly; then mash them through a very fine sieve, being careful to get all the pulp and leave only the seeds. Sometimes it is necessary to put them through a thin cheesecloth bag. Measure the juice, and to 1 quart juice, add 1 pint sugar, put on the stove and boil slowly until thick, then put in jars and close tightly.

Blackberry Jam.

Weigh blackberries, wash carefully, put in preserving kettle, and mash as much as possible. Put over slow fire and let cook about 20 minutes, stirring berries. Weigh sugar, allowing ¾ lb. of sugar to every pound of fruit. Heat sugar in oven, stirring constantly to prevent burning or melting, drop in with berries, mix well, and let cook until thick. Pour into glass jars, cover with brandied paper and seal while hot.

Plum Preserves. No. 1.

Secure large plums that are three-quarters ripe. Wash and stem, then weigh them. Use 1 lb. sugar to every pound plums.

Put the sugar in a porcelain-lined kettle, put in enough water to cover sugar, add a small, thin bag of spices (cinnamon, cloves and allspice). When the sugar begins to get syrupy lay the plums in carefully, let them cook about 15 minutes, remove to a platter carefully with a perforated skimmer. Continue cooking the syrup until it begins to thicken. Put the plums back, cook a while longer until syrup is thick, then put in jars and seal tightly.

Plum Preserves. No. 2.

Weigh plums, wash and stem, drain dry, and prick plums with fork, to prevent bursting. Plums should not be too ripe as they burst, or too green, or they shrivel. Weigh sugar, allowing 1 lb. to every pound of fruit. Put sugar in kettle and for every 5 lbs. of sugar, allow 1 pint boiling water. Let syrup come to a good boil, skim carefully, and add plums. Do not put all in at one time, as it is impossible to cook them evenly. When plums are done, which should be in a very short time, remove with skimmer and put in glass jars ¾ full. Let syrup cook thick, pour over fruit up to the brim of jar, put brandied paper over and seal.

Fig Preserves.

Secure the figs with stems on, just before they are ripe. Pour water over them, and dry each one carefully and separately with a piece of thin soft cloth. Weigh the figs and to each lb. of figs use ¾ lb. sugar.

Put the sugar on the stove in an agate kettle with barely enough water to cover it. To 1 pk. figs add to the syrup, 2 lemons cut in slices, and 8 pieces of whole white ginger. Let the sugar boil until it begins to get syrupy, then lay in the figs, boil until the figs can be pierced with a straw. Remove them to a platter with a perforated skimmer, and put them in the sun. Continue cooking the syrup until it begins to get thick, put the figs back, and cook until the figs are clear and the syrup thick. Put in jars and seal tightly.

Peach Preserves.

Select yellow freestone peaches of the best quality. Pare and stone them, breaking them in half. Weigh them and throw them in cold water to keep from discoloring.

Use 1 lb. sugar for every lb. of fruit. Put the sugar in an agate kettle with just enough water to cover it, add a handful of the peach kernels, and a small bag of spices. Boil the sugar until syrupy, skimming off all the scum, then add the peaches. Boil steadily, not too fast, until they are tender and clear, then with a perforated skimmer put them in jars. Continue boiling the syrup until clear and thick, then pour it over the fruit, and seal.

Peach Butter.

Secure ripe freestone peaches, yellow ones are best, peel and stone them. To every lb. of fruit use ¾ lb. sugar. Put the sugar over the fruit in an agate kettle, add a handful of peach kernels and a small bag of spices, pour enough water over to cover the fruit about half way, boil very slowly, stirring very often, should cook 5 or 6 hours.

Pear Preserves.

Proceed same as for peach preserves. Pare, core and either halve or quarter them, dependent on the size of the fruit. The pears should cook longer than peaches because they are tougher.

Sun them while the syrup is continuing to cook, and drop them back in the syrnp just before taking it up, and let them boil up once or twice.

Crab Apple Preserves.

Select small, yellow, sound apples with the stems on.

Allow 1 lb. sugar for every pound fruit. Boil the sugar with just enough water to cover it, add a small thin bag of spices. As soon as the syrup begins to boil put in the apples, and boil until they can be pierced by a straw; take them up with a perforated skimmer, and put in the sun on platters. Continue cooking the syrup until it begins to thicken, then put the apples back, and boil 15 or 20 minutes longer, until clear and thick. Seal at once.

Citron or Watermelon Rind Preserves.

Cut the rind of the melon in small fancy shapes, squares and triangles. Peel off the green outer skin and all inside pulp which is the least bit soft. Put in an earthen jar, and cover with a strong brine. Let stand 2 days. Wash in cold water the third day, and let stand in a solution of alum water until evening. Wash again and soak over night in cold, fresh water. The next morning weigh, and to every pound of fruit allow 1 lb. of sugar. Put sugar in preserving kettle, and to every 4 lbs. of sugar add 1 pint water. Let boil until thick and clear, and then drop in rind. Add a handful of white ginger. Boil until melon rind can be cut easily with a knife. If syrup is not sufficiently thick, sun the rind until syrup has thickened. Do not let cook until sticky. Fill jars, allow plenty of syrup to each jar, and seal while hot. If properly made will keep for 2 or 3 years. If citron for cakes is not convenient, this can be substituted by draining off syrup, wiping dry, and cutting in small pieces.

Canteloupe Preserves.

Secure thick rind melons, cut in halves, discard the seeds and all soft inner part, pare thinly and slice in pieces as long as your finger and 3 inches broad. Soak in brine over night, next morning wash and soak in fresh water 2 hours. Weigh the fruit and use 1 lb. sugar to 1 lb. fruit. Put on the sugar in a kettle with just enough water to cover. Let boil until syrupy, add a few pieces of whole white ginger. Drop in the fruit, boil until tender, then remove, and sun until syrup has boiled thick, drop in the melon again, boil up once or twice, then bottle and seal hot.

Watermelon rind can be preserved in the same way.

Quince Preserves.

Pare, quarter and core the quinces, saving the skins and cores. Put the quinces on to boil in preserving kettle, with just enough clear water to cover them, and cook until tender, but do not break. Take quinces out, lay on dishes to cool, keeping each piece separate. Put skins and cores in the water the quinces were boiled in, and boil 20 minutes longer. Strain through a jelly bag, and to each pint of juice allow 1 lb. sugar. Put on to boil, let cook until half done, then put in the fruit and boil 15 minutes longer. Take fruit out, fill jars ⅔ full, and if syrup is not quite thick enough, cook longer, then pour while hot over fruit in jars and seal. It is best to put only a few of the quinces in the syrup at a time. Cook until done, then put more in, and so on.

Ripe Tomato Preserves.

7 lbs. tomatoes peeled, 7 lbs. sugar; let it stand over night in a jar.

Next morning drain off the syrup, boil in an agate kettle until clear, skim well, drop in the tomatoes, boil 20 minutes longer. Remove the tomatoes with a perforated skimmer; continue boiling the syrup until thick, add the strained juice of 3 lemons, boil slowly, and stir often. Put in jars, and do not seal till cold.

JELLIES.

Put fruit on with sufficient water to cover it, and let boil, until soft and mushy. Watery fruits, such as grapes, plums, and blackberries, require less water. Pour while hot in cheese-cloth bags, and let drip at least six hours. Can be dripped over night if weather is not too warm. To every pint of juice allow 1 pint of sugar. It is best to cook only 1 pint at a time, as the fruit jellies better and is clearer, and cooks much more rapidly. Heat the sugar in oven, but do not let melt. Put juice on to boil, then drop heated sugar into juice, let begin to thicken, and when juice thickens on the end of spoon, strain and pour into glasses.

Apple Jelly.

Use tart, juicy apples, not too ripe, cut them in quarters without peeling or coring, throw the pieces in cold water immediately to keep from turning brown. Put on with enough water to just cover. Be sure and use either an agate or porcelain-lined kettle. Let boil until the apples are soft. Pour apples and all into a cheese cloth bag and let juice drip through without squeezing, but be sure and get all substance, then drip through a flannel bag to get clear.

Use 2 glasses of juice to 2 glasses sugar, always boil a small quantity at a time, it will be clearer and lighter. Boil on a quick fire until it drops from the spoon, then pour *at once* into glasses. Let stand until cold, then dip a piece of writing paper in whiskey and lay on top of jelly, and seal tightly with the covers, or paper fastened down with the white of an egg or mucilage.

Crab Apple Jelly.

Wash the fruit, cut in halves without coring or peeling, cover about half way with water, then cook and prepare same as Apple Jelly.

Strawberry Jelly. No. 1.

Put the strawberries in an agate boiler, set on the stove, and stir until thoroughly heated all through, but do not boil, remove from the fire, and mash through a very fine sieve, then strain through a thin cheese cloth bag. Measure 1 cupful juice to 1 cupful sugar, and cook same as Apple Jelly.

Strawberry Jelly. No. 2.

Put on the strawberries with a very little water, cook until the berries are soft, then pour into a flannel bag, and let the juice drip. Use same quantity of sugar as berries. Cook only 1 or 2 glasses at a time.

Peach Jelly.

Use peaches not too ripe, cut them up without peeling and add a few of the peach kernels. Boil until the peaches are soft, then proceed same as for Apple Jelly. A few drops of lemon juice may be added if desired, when the sugar is added.

Wild Plum Jelly.

Wash the plums and cover with water in an agate kettle. Boil until plums are done and burst open, then proceed same as for Apple Jelly. Nice to serve with meats or fowls.

Plum Jelly.

Cook same as Wild Plum Jelly.

Grape Jelly.

Wash the grapes thoroughly and pick them from the stems. Put on in an agate kettle with barely enough water to cover them. Cook until the grapes are soft, then proceed same as for Apple Jelly.

Currant Jelly.

Select fresh, sound currants not too ripe. Pick and wash well, and place them in an agate kettle on the stove, stir often from the bottom with a wooden spoon. When they are thoroughly scalded, not boiled, pour into a clean bucket and mash them thoroughly with a pounder. Strain through a flannel jelly bag, measure the juice and use the same quantity of sugar. By boiling only 2 or 3 glasses at one time, the jelly will be brighter. Boil on a hot fire until it drops from a spoon, then pour into jelly glasses.

Currant and Raspberry Jelly.

Use equal parts of currants and raspberries. Wash and pick them, and proceed same as for Currant Jelly.

Calf's Foot Jelly.

Secure 4 well-cleaned young calf feet, wash and then put on in a large agate boiler or preserving kettle, pour a gallon of water over, add a pinch of salt, and boil slowly on the back of the stove until the feet are so well done that they almost fall to pieces, and the water is reduced to about 1½ quarts, or less. This will require 4 or 5 hours. Remove from the fire, strain through a fine sieve, and put in the ice box in a bowl to jelly. Next morning, put the jelly in an agate boiler on the stove, when it begins to boil, add the stiff beaten whites of 5 eggs, also the crushed shells. Boil until perfectly clear, then strain through a flannel bag like jelly (do not squeeze), add sugar and sherry wine to taste, put in jars or glasses, and keep in a cold place to congeal. Excellent for the sick.

CANNING.

Canned Peaches.

Select firm sound peaches, the yellow freestone are best. Peel the peaches and divide in halves, removing the stone. Measure the peaches after peeled and stoned. Then weigh for each quart of peaches ½ lb. of sugar and place in kettle over the fire, with enough water to cover. When the sugar and water boil until syrupy, add the peaches and allow to boil until they can be pierced with a fork, no longer. Always use a silver fork.

Heat air-tight jars in hot water and fill with the peaches and syrup to *overflowing*, screw on tops and put aside to cool gradually. When cold see that tops are tight, and put away in a cool, dark place.

Canned Pears.

Pare the fruit and leave the stems on, if large cut in half. Prepare same as Canned Peaches. The pears will take a little longer to become tender, but be careful not to boil until soft. When done, fill the jars to overflowing. Seal quickly and tightly, and keep in a cool, dark place. Examine often to see if the tops are air-tight.

Canned Pineapple.

Pare and core the fruit, and cut in round slices. Prepare same as Canned Pears.

Huckleberries.

Are canned same as peaches, using only ¼ lb. sugar for every quart berries. The berries must be carefully picked over, discarding all the stems, and imperfect ones, and washing carefully.

Fill the jars to overflowing, seal quickly, and set in a cool, dark place.

Strawberries.

Prepare same as peaches, using ½ lb. sugar for every quart berries.

If the berries are exposed to the light after canning, they will lose their bright color.

Green Gages.

Wash carefully, and prick with a needle to prevent bursting.

To every quart of gages use ¾ lb. sugar. Prepare same as the peaches, letting the gages boil only 5 minutes slowly. Fill the jars to overflowing, and seal tightly and quickly. Keep in a dark, cool place.

Blue Plums.

Prepare same as green gages, using the same quantity of sugar.

PICKLES AND CATSUP.

Pickles.

Pickles should never be put up in vessels of copper, iron or tin. Use only earthenware or glass.

Use only the best white wine vinegar, and always keep in a dark, cool place. Examine at frequent intervals.

When cooking them always use agate or porcelain-lined kettles, as acid will not affect them.

In putting up pickles in brine, always weight the contents of the jars with heavy stones. Cover with a clean cloth, which must be removed and washed every second day.

Sweet Pickles.

To 8 lbs. of fruit, take 5 lbs. sugar, 3 pints vinegar, 2 tablespoonfuls each whole spice and cloves, remove the heads from the cloves. Boil to a syrup, and pour over the fruit three mornings in succession, heat the syrup every morning before pouring over the fruit. The fourth morning, drop the fruit in the hot syrup and boil about 10 minutes. The fruit must of course be peeled or have the skins rubbed off before being put in the jars the first morning.

Sweet Pickled Peaches.

Peel large clingstone peaches.

To 9 lbs. peaches take 4½ lbs. granulated sugar. Put on the sugar with 3 cupfuls water, add three pints best vinegar, 2 tablespoonfuls whole cloves, with heads removed, and some pieces cinnamon bark. When it boils 15 minutes, lay in the peaches, boil until tender enough to pierce with a straw (no longer), remove peaches with a perforated skimmer, put in jars and continue cooking syrup until somewhat thick, pour over the peaches and when cold seal tightly. Before cooking, the peaches should be dropped in boiling strong soda water and the fur rubbed off.

Pickled Figs.

Wash the figs carefully, using only those that are perfectly sound, have stems on, and just *before* they are ripe. Wipe each one separately with a dry cloth, then proceed same as for Pickled Peaches.

Pickled Pears.

Peel pears, cut in half, core. If small, may be left whole. Weigh fruit and add ½ as much sugar as you have pears. To 10 lbs. of fruit allow 5 lbs. of sugar. Add 1½ qts. of vinegar. To every 5 lbs. of sugar allow 2 cupfuls water. Put sugar, water and vinegar, whole cinnamon, cloves, and spice on to boil, drop in pears, boil until tender, remove, and put pears in jars. Boil syrup twenty to thirty minutes longer, pour over pears and seal.

Watermelon Rind Pickle.

Pare the rind of the watermelon, and remove all the red meat, cut in small square pieces, and soak in salt water over night. Next morning, soak in fresh water for 2 hours.

Put on enough vinegar to fill the jars, add 1 cupful sugar to 1 quart vinegar, add also a few cloves, with heads removed, a few allspice and a little cinnamon. Tie the spices in a thin piece of cloth. Let the syrup come to a boil, then add the watermelon, boil until the pieces can be pierced with a straw and the syrup is clear. If necessary, remove the melon to the jar and continue cooking the syrup. Cover closely and keep in a cool place.

Piccalilli.

1 large head sound white cabbage, ½ pk. green tomatoes, ½ pk. green peppers, 1 doz. large cucumbers, peeled, 3 bunches white celery, ½ doz. large white onions. Chop up all together until fine. Sprinkle with salt, let stand 2 hours, then drain and squeeze out. Add ½ lb. white mustard seed. Pour vinegar over to cover, add 1 cupful brown sugar, put on fire, let come to a boil, then put in jars for three weeks.

Chow Chow.

Small peck green tomatoes, same quantity green peppers, same of beans, same of white onions, ½ doz. cucumbers, 2 large heads of cauliflower (or 2 of solid white cabbage if can't get cauliflower), cut all vegetables in small pieces, add 125 tiny cucumbers (not cut).

Put all in an earthen jar, cover with strong salt water for 24 hours. Then pour off the salt water. Boil together 15 cts. worth dry mustard, 5 cts. worth tumeric (from drug store), 3 tablespoonfuls flour, ½ cupful sugar, and enough vinegar to cover vegetables. Boil together well, then pour over vegetables in jar and put away for several weeks.

Mustard Pickles. No. 1.

Get large, yellow cucumbers. Peel with a silver knife (steel will discolor), halve and quarter lengthwise, and scrape out all seeds. Sprinkle thoroughly with salt, and put in a bag over night to drain. Next day wipe each piece, and pack away in jars, adding mustard seed plentifully, a few bay leaves, white whole pepper, and a few cloves with the tops removed. Put a little dill in each jar. Boil sufficient white wine vinegar to cover pickles, and add a pinch of alum. If vinegar is too sour, can be diluted with water. Pour hot vinegar over pickles, and seal jars. In two days, drain off vinegar, boil again, and pour over pickles. Let stand two days more, and do this the third time. Seal until ready for use.

Mustard Pickles. No. 2.

Use only large yellow cucumbers. Peel with a silver knife, halve, then quarter lengthwise, and scrape out all seeds and soft part. Salt thoroughly and leave in brine over night. Next morning wipe each piece with a dry cloth and lay in a stone jar.

Place over the fire enough white wine vinegar to cover the pickles. To ½ gallon add 1 cupful mustard seed, 1 tablespoonful celery seed, 2 or 3 pods red pepper, and ½ cupful brown sugar. When this reaches boiling point, pour it over the cucumbers and cover closely until ready for use. They can be eaten 10 days after preparing.

Cucumber Salad.

Peel cucumbers and slice ¼ inch thick. Salt well and leave over night.

Peel, slice, and salt onions, in the proportion of 1 quart of onions to 1 peck of cucumbers, and leave these also over night. The next day drain the brine from each and mix.

Place over the fire white vinegar, 3 pints to the peck, with a generous handful of mustard seed, 1 tablespoonful of celery seed, 2 or 3 bay leaves, a dozen spice and cloves from which the heads have been taken, 1 cupful of sugar, and 3 pods of red pepper. Heat all together, and when boiling, drop in the cucumbers and onions and allow them to boil up once or twice. Then fill air-tight jars, which have been previously heated, screw on tops and put away where they will cool *gradually*. When cold, see that the tops are tight. Examine occasionally for a month, and if signs of fermentation appear, re-boil and put in fresh jars.

Pepper Mangoes.

Rub thoroughly free of dust and grit ½ peck of bell peppers. Cut off small ends about 1 inch deep, and with a sharp knife, carefully cut out seeds and cells. Sprinkle well with salt and leave over night. This amount of peppers will require 2 large heads of hard cabbage, 1 quart of cucumbers, 2 quarts of onions. Cut the cabbage fine as for slaw, slice the onions, peel and chop the cucumbers, and salt each separately, to remain over night as the peppers. The next day press the cabbage, the onions and the cucumbers free of brine, and mix them together with a generous handful of mustard seed, a tablespoonful of celery seed, a tablespoonful of black pepper, and the seeds of two pepper pods. Shake the peppers and ends free of salt, fill with this mixture, and tie together with cord. Pack in layers in a stone jar and pour over enough hot vinegar to cover. Cover jar closely, and allow to stand for a week, when they will be ready for use.

Mangoes.

During the summer keep a five gallon keg handy. Make a brine strong enough to float an egg, then throw in it whenever convenient such vegetables as small sound onions, cucumbers, small sound heads of white cabbage, young mangoes, or small green musk-melons (cut a slit in them and remove seeds), cauliflower, and green peppers.

When ready to make the pickles, take from the keg the quantity desired. Soak in fresh water over night. Next morning, cut the mangoes in half, chop up the other vegetables, add a good quantity of mustard seed, less of celery seed, the seeds of 2 pepper pods. Put enough white wine vinegar on the fire to fill the jars, add just enough sugar to remove the sharp taste of the vinegar, add a few spice and cloves. Fill the mangoes with the chopped vegetables and seeds, tie them securely and lay in stone jars. Cover with the heated vinegar, tie up securely and put aside for a month.

Pepper Hash.

Take equal parts of green bell peppers, discarding seeds, and white cabbage, chop very fine, and put in a kettle on stove. Add enough vinegar and water to cover it, allowing 1 pint of water to every pint of vinegar. Let come to a good boil, remove from fire, and drain off all liquor. Throw away this liquor, put pickle back in kettle, with sufficient strong vinegar to cover it, sugar and salt to taste, mustard and celery seed. Let come to a boil, and if not hot enough, add a few seeds of the bell pepper. Bottle while hot.

Tomato Catsup.

Cut up 1 peck ripe tomatoes, and 4 large onions, boil until soft, and mash through a sieve, then add 2 tablespoonfuls each of salt and pepper, 1 teaspoonful of cayenne pepper, 1 teaspoonful mace, and 2 tablespoonfuls ground mustard. Boil 3 hours or less, slowly, stirring very often, until thickened, then add 2 pints vinegar and 1 cupful brown sugar, and boil 1 hour longer, stirring well. Bottle and seal while hot.

Cucumber Catsup.

Take 2 dozen fresh cucumbers, peel, and soak in salt water about 2 hours. Cut in half, scrape out seeds with a silver knife, and grate cucumbers. Also grate 2 large onions. Drain off cucumber water, measure it, and for every cupful of water drained off, add 1 cupful of vinegar to the grated cucumber. Discard the water. Season with pepper and salt. Taste, and if too sour, add a little cucumber water. Bottle, and put away in a cool place. Is not cooked at all. Very nice served with meat, or fish.

Chili Sauce.

Pare 24 large ripe tomatoes and chop with 6 green peppers, 4 large onions, add ½ cupful sugar, 1 tablespoonful salt, 1 teaspoonful each white mustard seed, allspice and cloves, 4 cupfuls vinegar. Boil 2 hours or until thick, then seal in bottles.

Salt Water or Dill Pickles.

Use none but perfectly sound cucumbers, have them as near one size as possible, the medium-sized ones are best. Lay the cucumbers in cold water for 4 or 5 hours, then drain them, and put them in an earthen or stone jar; first a layer of cucumbers, then a few pieces of " dill " or fennel, a little cayenne or black or whole peppers, a handful of salt, then another layer of cucumbers, and so on until the jar is full; on top of all, put a layer of fresh grape leaves, fill the jar with water, adding 1 cupful vinegar to every gallon jar of pickles, put clean stones on top of leaves to keep the pickles under the brine. Taste the brine, and if not strong enough add more salt. Cover with a cloth. Examine the pickles about once a week, and remove the scum that rises.

It will take from one week to 10 days for these pickles to be good.

How to Keep Fresh Okra all Winter.

Get as much tender okra as desired. Pack it in stone jars. Make a brine strong enough to float an egg, and pour it over the okra, being careful to have it well covered. Put stones on top to keep the okra from rising. Cover and tie with a clean cloth, and keep in a dry, cool place.

When ready to use the okra, soak it over night in fresh water, and it will be equal to any freshly bought.

BRANDIED FRUITS.

Melange. No. 1.

This French brandied fruit requires no cooking, is very easily made, and will keep any length of time.

Secure a round earthen crock or vessel, not too high, and with a close fitting top to it.

Begin by putting in 1 lb. granulated sugar and 1 pint alcohol. Then add any desired fruit, always adding ¾ lb. sugar for every lb. fruit.

Cherries, peaches, pears, pineapples and plums can be used. I prefer the pineapples and peaches. The large fruit must be cut in pieces. Berries can be added, but I do not like them in it. The fruit need not be all put in at one time, but can be added whenever convenient, always adding the required quantity of sugar the same time. Cover the jar with the top, tie thick brown paper over, then a clean cloth. The surplus juice can be cooked thick and used for pudding sauces.

Melange. No. 2.

Take 1 lb. of rock candy and 1 qt. of alcohol, put in stone jar. Every lb. of fresh fruit that is added must be sugared well. Pineapple is best, and peaches are very fine. As much more fruit may be added, each in season, as desired. Strawberries and raspberries are the only berries that should be added, but no more alcohol. The fruits make their own juice. Keep in a cool, dark place, well covered.

Brandied Peaches.

Weigh fruit, and to every lb. of peaches allow 1 lb. sugar. Make a strong solution of soda water, boil and drop peaches in, remove immediately, and wipe with a towel. This removes all fur, and leaves the skin smooth and glossy. Put sugar on to boil, with just sufficient water to dissolve it, and a bag of whole spice, cinnamon, and cloves. Let syrup boil clear, drop in part of peaches, let boil 20 minutes, then put fruit out to sun. Drop in remainder of peaches. After fruit is removed, let boil down thick. Remove and let cool, then add 1 pt. brandy to every 3 lbs. of sugar. Stir well, put peaches in jar, and cover well with syrup. Seal and stand in a cool place.

Brandied Figs.

Wash the figs in clear water, then prepare same as Brandied Peaches.

Brandied Pears.

Prepare same as Brandied Peaches, only cook the pears a little longer than the peaches as they are tougher.

FOODS FOR INVALIDS UNDER MEDICAL DIRECTION.

Barley Water.

Put 2 teaspoonfuls of washed pearl barley in a saucepan with a pint of water; boil slowly down to ⅔ of a pt. Strain.

Oatmeal or Cracked Wheat Water.

Add from 1 to 3 tablespoonfuls of well-cooked oatmeal or cracked wheat porridge to 1 pint of water; heat almost to boiling point, with constant stirring, until a smooth mixture is obtained. Strain.

Lime Water.

Take a piece of unslacked lime as large as a walnut, drop it into two quarts of pure water contained in an earthen vessel, stir thoroughly, allow to settle, and use only from the top, replacing the water and stirring as consumed.

Raw Beef Juice.

Take 1 lb. of thick, lean sirloin of beef, heat quickly on both sides in a broiler over a quick fire, cut into cubes ¼ inch thick, place in a lemon squeezer or a meat-press and squeeze out juice. Remove the fat, if any, that rises to the surface, after cooling. *Never actually cook the meat.*

If wanted to serve hot, squeeze the blood in a cup set in hot water, and serve at once.

Beef Broth.

Mince 1 lb. of lean beef, put it with its juice into an earthen vessel containing 1 pt. of water at 85° F., and let stand 1 hour. Strain through thick bag, squeezing all juice from meat. Place this juice in pan over the fire, and while stirring briskly, slowly heat just to the boiling point. Remove at once, and season with salt.

Chicken Broth.

A small chicken or half of a large one, thoroughly cleaned and with all the skin and fat removed, to be chopped, bones and all, into small pieces; put them with a little salt into a saucepan, and add a quart of boiling water. Cover closely, and simmer over a slow fire for 2 hours. Remove, but let stand covered for an hour. Then strain through a sieve.

Veal Broth.

Mince ½ to 1 lb. of lean veal, and pour on it 1 pt. cold water. Let stand for 3 hours, then slowly heat to boiling. Boil for 2 minutes, strain through a fine sieve, and season with salt.

Mutton Broth.

Add 1 lb. of loin of mutton to 3 pts. of water. Boil gently until very tender, adding a little salt. Strain, and when cold, skim off all fat. Warm, when ready to serve.

Barley Jelly.

Put 2 tablespoonfuls of washed pearl barley into a quart saucepan with 1½ pts. of water; boil slowly down to 1 pt.; strain, and set aside until liquid forms into a jelly.

Flour Ball for Pap.

Take 1 lb. good wheat flour (unbolted is best), tie it up very tightly in a strong pudding bag, place in a saucepan of water, and boil constantly for 10 hours; when cold, remove cloth, cut away soft outer covering of dough, and, as required, reduce the hard-baked interior to powder by grating. When using, rub the required quantity of powder, with 1 tablespoonful of milk, into a smooth paste; add a second tablespoonful of milk, rubbing until a creamy mixture is obtained; finally add this, with constant stirring, to total quantity of liquid for the meal.

Whey.

Heat 1 pt. milk to a point that can be agreeably borne by the mouth; add, with gentle stirring, 2 teaspoonfuls of Fairchild's essence of pepsin; let stand until firm coagulation takes place, beat with a fork until the curd is finely divided, strain.

Junket.

Treat 1 pt. of milk as if for whey without breaking. Serve the curd with sugar, nutmeg and cream.

Rice and Milk Pudding.

Take 2 tablespoonfuls of rice, 1 tablespoonful of cornstarch, and 2 pts. of milk, boil in a double kettle until each grain of the rice becomes saturated and the whole is creamy in color. Sweeten, if desired, when ready to serve.

Stewed Prunes with Senna.

Infusion of senna. Make a small ball of senna leaves and steep in boiling water, like tea.

Wash ½ pound prunes, carefully, and if hard, soak one hour or more in cold water, before boiling.

Put in a porcelain or granite kettle with enough boiling infusion of senna to cover; cover the kettle closely, and boil 10 to 15 minutes until prunes are swollen and tender, add 1 tablespoonful sugar and boil 15 minutes longer. Flavor with a little lemon.

OBESITY LIST.

Stout people should not eat liver, oysters, and clams; apples, arrowroot, barley, beets, beans, white bread, crackers, cake, chocolate, carrots, grapes, gravies, honey, macaroni, oatmeal, peas, parsnips, rhubarb, rice, rice pudding, sago, sugar, soups thickened with rice, flour, barley, or tapioca; cider, champagne, sweet wines, malt liquors, or sparkling wines.

May eat: All other meats, game, fish, except the above. All poultry except ducks and geese. Asparagus, almonds, artichokes, butter, gluten bread, toasted bread, cheese, cauliflower, chicory, small quantities of cream, celery, cucumbers, dandelions, eggs, lettuce, mushrooms, young onions, radishes, spinach, sprouts, squash, string beans, strawberries, raspberries, truffles, turnips, tomatoes and water cress. May drink all spirits, tea and coffee.

FACTS WORTH KNOWING.

Salt thrown on a coal fire when broiling steak, will prevent blazing from the dripping fat.

Salt puts out a fire in the chimney.

Salt put on ink when freshly spilled on a carpet will help in removing the spot.

Salt used in sweeping carpets keeps out moths.

Vinegar will brighten copper.

Kerosene will remove rust from bolts and bars.

Ammonia cleanses hair brushes.

Ammonia in dish water brightens silver.

Ammonia in water keeps flannels soft.

To remove iron rust stains from linen, cover the stains with salts of lemon, moisten with cold water, and expose to strong sunlight. When dry moisten again. A few applications will remove the stains without injury to delicate fabrics.

To clean marble, use 2 parts washing-soda, 1 part ground pumice-stone, and 1 part finely pulverized chalk, mix to a smooth paste with water. Rub well over the marble, and wash off with soap and water.

To remove white spots from polished furniture, take ½ oz. *each* of raw linseed oil and spirits of turpentine, mixed with 40 drops of spirits of ammonia. Apply with a soft cloth. A gentle rubbing will remove stains in a few minutes, and gives a fine polish to any hard wood.

For silver polish use a few drops of ammonia mixed with common whiting, and sufficient water added to make a paste the consistency of cream. Bottle, and keep tightly corked. Drop a little of this mixture on the polishing cloth, rub the silver lightly, and rinse in warm water.

To remove paint and putty use same mixture as above, letting whiting almost dry on glass before polishing.

For freshly-spilled ink, apply two or three applications of fresh sweet milk, changing milk with each application, then rinse in warm soap suds, then in clear warm water.

To preserve fish in very hot weather, cover with a little vinegar. Often improves flavor of fish even in cold weather, and makes flesh firm.

To kill cockroaches, take equal parts of pulverized camphor and carbolic acid, bottle, and use mixture to paint the cracks and holes where the insects nest.

Plaster of Paris mixed with flour and sugar, and sprinkled around, will also kill roaches.

To preserve apples through the winter, select sound ones, and cover with shelled corn. Does not injure the corn.

Old brass can be brightened by scrubbing with strong ammonia, then rinse in clear water.

Yellow stains from sewing machine oil on *white* goods, can be removed by rubbing the spot with ammonia before washing with soap.

Equal parts of ammonia and turpentine will remove paint from clothing even if hard and dry. Saturate as often as necessary, then wash out in soap suds.

To remove rust from finely-polished steel without injury to the surface, mix 10 parts putty powder, 8 parts ammonia, and 25 of alcohol, then rub article with soft blotting paper.

THE END.

www.ingramcontent.com/pod-product-compliance
Lightning Source LLC
Chambersburg PA
CBHW032024220426
43664CB00006B/359